CAERPHILLY COUNTY BOROUGH

D0227246

EMISSARIES
OF SATAN

Tynnwyd o'r stoc
Withdrawn

ABOUT THE AUTHOR:

Born in Winchester, Hampshire, in1948, **Christopher Berry-Dee** is a direct descendant of Dr John Dee, Court Astrologer to Queen Elizabeth I. He served as a Royal Marines 'Green Beret' Commando, and is the former founder and Director of The Criminology Research Institute (CRI), as well as the former publisher and Editor-in-Chief of *The Criminologist* – the world's oldest and most respected journal on matters concerning law enforcement, penology, forensic psychiatry/psychology, penal reform, the judiciary, and all criminology subjects.

Christopher has interviewed and interrogated over thirty of the world's most notorious serial killers and mass murderers, and has appeared on TV as a consultant on serial homicide. He was co-producer/interviewer for the acclaimed twelve-part documentary series *The Serial Killers*, and has consulted on the cases of Fred and Rose West, Ian Brady and Myra Hindley, and Dr Harold Shipman in the TwoFour-produced TV series *Born to Kill*.

Notable book successes include: *Monster* – the book that formatted the movie about the US serial killer, Aileen 'Lee' Carol Wuornos; *Dad Help Me Please* – concerning the tragic case of Derek Bentley, who was hanged for a murder he did not commit (subsequently detailed in the film *Let Him Have It* starring Christopher Ecclestone); and *Talking With Serial Killers* – his 2003 bestselling true-crime book, and its successor volume, *Talking With Serial Killers 2*. His most recent book is *Love of Blood*, the first full-length examination of the British serial killer Joanne Dennehy, who was sentenced to a full-life prison sentence in 2014.

EMISSARIES OF SATAN

Serial Killers Under the Microscope

CHRISTOPHER BERRY-DEE

JOHN BLAKE

CAERPHILLY COUNTY BOROUGH COUNCIL	
3 8030 08264 0700	
Askews & Holts	17-Feb-2015
364.152	£7.99
LIB1436	

ISBN: 978-1-78219-900-7

All rights reserved. No part of this publication may be reproduced, stored in a retrieval system, or transmitted in any form or by any means, without the prior permission in writing of the publisher, nor be otherwise circulated in any form of binding or cover other than that in which it is published and without a similar condition including this condition being imposed on the subsequent purchaser.

British Library Cataloguing-in-Publication Data:

A catalogue record for this book is available from the British Library.

Design by www.envydesign.co.uk

Printed in Great Britain by CPI Group (UK) Ltd

1 3 5 7 9 10 8 6 4 2

© Text copyright Christopher Berry-Dee 2015

The right of Christopher Berry-Dee to be identified as the author of this work has been asserted by him in accordance with the Copyright, Designs and Patents Act 1988.

Papers used by John Blake Publishing are natural, recyclable products made from wood grown in sustainable forests. The manufacturing processes conform to the environmental regulations of the country of origin.

Every attempt has been made to contact the relevant copyright-holders, but some were unobtainable. We would be grateful if the appropriate people could contact us.

DEDICATION

To the twenty-nine lives lost to the three serial killers featured in this book:

Dzung Ngoc Tu (25)
Paula Perrera (16)
Debra Smith Taylor
Leslie Shelley and April Brunais (14)
Tammy Lee Williams (17)
Robin Dawn Stavinsky (19)
Wendy Baribeault (17)
Carmen Colon (10)
Wanda Walkowitz (11)
Michelle Maenza (11)
Laura Collins (26)
Yolanda Washington (19)

Judith Miller (15)

Teresa Kastin (21)

Jill Barcombe (18)

Jane King (28)

Sonja Johnson (14) and Dolores Cepeda (12)

Kathleen Robinson (17)

Kristina Weckler (20)

Lauren Rae Wagner (18)

Kimberly Martin (17)

Karen Mandic (22)

Diane Wilder (27)

Timothy McDowell (28)

Gerard George Lowe (33)

Sheila Damude (49) and Darin Damude (22)

CONTENTS

AUTHOR'S NOTE

I started corresponding with the three serial killers featured in this book as far back as the early 1990s, and subsequently worked with them for many years. Given that, by their very nature, they are, or were, all psychopaths and born-again pathological liars, the reader may not be surprised to discover that various other accounts of their lives and crimes may be found in other publications and on the Worldwide Web. What an offender says one day he may well change to something else the next day, ad infinitum, as the police, their legal advisers and the judiciary will confirm.

Michael Bruce Ross, Kenneth Alessio Bianchi and John Martin Scripps have formed chapters in two of my previous books: my international bestseller *Talking With Serial Killers* and its sequel, *Talking With Serial Killers 2*. I also made TV documentaries with the cooperation of Ross and Bianchi – these DVDs are available online.

'Time and tide wait for no man', so a popular saying goes, and this applies to the study of the criminal mind. And, since those early 90s, and the publication of the two aforementioned books, Ross and Scripps have been executed, while Bianchi still rots in prison. However, the passing of time can be a good thing, for it allows a cooling of tempers and perhaps a more measured view of the enormity of their sickening murders. With this in mind, therefore, my publishers and I felt that now is the right time to revisit these three men; to re-evaluate their heinous behaviour; to consider much else that has been written about them; and to combine everything into this reassessment, which I have called *Emissaries of Satan*.

Not surprisingly, other accounts concerning these three serial killers have appeared since my two original volumes were first published, and I have striven in this book to acknowledge this where possible, albeit with a caveat: I cannot always verify the accuracy of that information, simply because much of the source of this material is unknown to me, to the degree that it was not until my copy-editor brought various issues to my attention that I was aware that it even existed.

I have rectified this omission as best as I can, to leave you with this: to verify any accounts of their lives and crimes given to me first-hand by Ross, Bianchi and Scripps, I visited *every one* of their crime scenes in the US, Thailand and Singapore. I spoke to most of the law-enforcement officers concerned, prosecution and defence attorneys, judges, scenes-of-crime technicians, correctional staff, the offenders' families, likewise, where possible the victims' tragic nearest and dearest. Added to which were the thousands of official documents and photographs supplied to me concerning each case, in order to separate the truth from hearsay and fiction.

My two *Talking With Serial Killers* books are among required reading for students at the FBI's Behavioral Science Unit, Quantico, VA, so I truly hope the reader will find *Emissaries of Satan* a valuable and worthwhile upgrade, too.

CHRISTOPHER BERRY-DEE

ACKNOWLEDGEMENTS

As bizarre as this may seem, special thanks have to go to the three serial murderers who make up this book for without their cooperation *Emissaries of Satan* could not have been written: Michael Bruce Ross has since been executed, by lethal injection, in Connecticut; Kenneth Alessio Bianchi now sits in a special housing unit at the Washington State Penitentiary, while John Martin Scripps was hanged in Singapore.

In part, much credit is due to my long-time TV documentary producer, Frazer Ashford, who made it possible for me to finance my interviews with Ross and Bianchi. Also to the *Mail on Sunday*, who commissioned me to investigate the killings committed by John Scripps, and to APTV who screened my exclusive report on Scripps's hanging for worldwide news release.

For my work with Michael Ross: thanks go to the

Connecticut State Police Detective Michael Malchik; the New York State Police; Crystal Run PD; the Connecticut Department of Corrections, Warden J. Kupec; the officers at the Osborn Correction Institution, who made my visits to interview Ross on death row secure; and to New London County State's Attorney, the late C. Robert 'Bulldog' Satti.

For my work with Kenneth Bianchi: much appreciation to the Los Angeles PD, specifically Detectives Leroy Orozco and Richard Crotsley; to Judge Roger Boren; to the Bellingham PD with Chief Terry Mangan, Investigator Robert Knudsen, Detectives Terry Wight and Fred Nolte; to Chase Riveland, Director of Washington Department of Corrections and the officers at WSP; and finally Frances Piccione (formerly Bianchi).

For my work with John Scripps, thanks to the family of John Martin Scripps; HM Customs & Excise (Special Investigations); the Singapore Police; Royal Thai Police; Royal Canadian Mounted Police; the Singapore Supreme Court; Changi Prison; the staff at the River View Hotel, Singapore; the staff at Nilly's Marina Inn, Phuket; the Singapore *Straits Times*, the *Mail on Sunday*, the BBC and APTV.

Where other credits are due they can be found throughout the text, while other extracts are drawn from *Talking With Serial Killers* and *Talking With Serial Killers 2,* published by John Blake, London, in 2003 and 2005 respectively.

INTRODUCTION

MURDER CROSSROADS

For some individuals along the road of life there's a place called 'Murder Crossroads'. This is where two lives meet: one comes to a terrifying end, and the other takes a permanent detour, perhaps to end up on death row. And the statistics are chilling. At any one time, there are over 3,700 men and women awaiting execution in super-max facilities across the US and, on average, they will have killed three times their number.

To qualify for a cell on 'the row', the crime committed has to be one of 'aggravated first-degree murder'. The law in the US requires that the aggravating circumstances have to be proved, whether rape or burglary, or simply trying to avoid being given a speeding ticket by a cop when a murder plays a part. The killing of a police, fire or correctional officer qualifies for aggravated first-degree homicide, as does, in certain circumstances, causing a victim to suffer agonising physical pain and tortuous mental anguish before death supervenes.

The case of James Leroy Brett, who once lived on death row at the Washington State Penitentiary at Walla Walla, and whom I interviewed several years ago, serves as an example. Brett explained that he had been convicted of the shooting to death of a businessman, Kenneth Milosevich. The aggravating circumstances were that the murder was committed: (1) to conceal his own identity; (2) in the furtherance of robbery in the first degree; and (3) in the course of, in furtherance of, or in the immediate flight from the burglary in the first degree and kidnapping in the first degree. Brett was convicted on 11 June 1992, and was sentenced to death seven days later. Upon appeal, his sentence was commuted to life.

But what is death row like? I have visited many death rows, however, one of them that stands out in my mind was at the now closed Osborn Correctional Institution, Somers, Connecticut, where I spent some time interviewing Michael Bruce Ross, the first killer in this book.

Michael Ross has since been executed by lethal injection, and he was monster, and these types of men and women are not normal human beings for they have carried out serial murder, mass-murder, spree killing, necrophilia, dismemberment of bodies, both dead and alive. They bludgeoned their victims; they have buried them or dumped them in slow-moving rivers while they still clung on to life. They have suffocated them, strangled them and choked them to death, forcing debris down their throats, sadistically watching their victims' faces contort into grotesque masks of death.

Some of these killers have stabbed, hacked, filleted, and even eaten body parts of their victims, some of who were only a few months old. They have raped their victims, tortured them, even set fire to them. These men have trawled the highways and byways, and they have all met their victims at 'Murder Crossroads', and many have ended up on death row.

Once a prisoner is on 'the row', there are only three ways out: commutation of sentence, death by natural causes and execution. The first of these, commutation of sentence, is dependent upon a successful appeal. As a safeguard against any possible miscarriage of justice, the US has put in place an appeal process – which may stretch over a decade – and, monster or not, every killer is given the chance to argue the fairness of their trial and conviction. In the majority of appeals the best the convicted killer can hope for is to be allowed to exchange the death sentence for one of life and different colour fatigues.

'The Row' is the ultimate leveller. There is no colour or class distinction and, as one inmate pragmatically put it, 'There are no rich men on death row.' Not as noisy as the Special Segregation Units – which house the continually disruptive, mentally unstable and most violent prisoners, who shower visitors and staff with foul language, excrement and urine – death row can be as quiet as a tomb. In this dread place, the men and women sit quietly, reflecting on the years and the pitiless chains of days and nights, the iron struggle, the ruthless discipline and institutionalised regime, which culminates in a final walk along the 'green mile'.

Finally, it the odds are stacked against the condemned, he will come to another crossroads in his life – his last one. It is here that he will meet his own executioner, shortly, thereafter, The Grim

Reaper. There are those who walk bravely to their deaths, even enjoying a hearty last meal they will laugh and joke to the end. Others choose to go down the hard way, fighting and sobbing in terror as they are dragged towards the machinery of death, as did John Scripps.

Many of the killers I have interviewed over the decades have expressed repentance at the last moment while others have stayed stoically silent. One man responded to the death row warden when asked if he had any last words. 'Get on with it, will ya. You're wasting my fuckin' time.'

And, as an aside; I have lost count of the number of times I have been asked: 'Christopher, did you ever feel scared or threatened by these killers when you interviewed them, often alone with them while they were unshackled?' The answer has always been 'No!'

Serial killers, you see, are bullies and cowards by their very nature. They stalk and entrap their vulnerable, weaker, often trusting if not gullible victims, at a time and place of their own choosing. Hookers, the elderly, children, hitchhikers; sometimes young males who are plied with drugs to render them helpless before the torture and killing begins, are the usual serial murderers' *modus operandi* victimology stock-in-trade.

Of the some 30 plus male serial murderers I have personally interviewed, not one of them, not a *single* one, would have dared front up to a man during an argument. Period. In the case of Pee Wee Gaskins' rape and killing of a three-year-old girl, yes, but when he was cuffed too tight upon arrest, he complained he'd been abused by police.

And the list is endless, amongst them being:

Bianchi, Ross, Scripps, Ted Bundy, Arthur Shawcross, Ian Brady, Frederick West, Henry Lee Lucas, John Wayne Gacy, mass murderer Ronald DeFeo Jr. Even the monstrous Harvey Louis Carignan, aka 'Harv' the Hammer', who was built like a shed, never had the 'bottle' to get into an altercation with a man – yet he raped and killed around 50 young girls with as much compassion as one swats flies. Instead, these cowards – for there is no other way to describe them – do their work then scuttle away to hide from the law. You will see much evidence of this in *Emissaries of Satan*. So, tis no wonder that their ilk are segregated from the main prison population when they are incarcerated, for the other inmates would kill these sado-sexual killers in a heartbeat and, with guards turning a blind eye, win first prize, too.

Yes, they have threatened me with ice-cold stares… a kind of demonic 'huff and puff or I'll blow your house down,' while looming over me with their fists clenched tight and their faces white with fury. But, one simply smiles back and tells them to 'shut the FUCK UP and sit down.' They have *always* complied, and now you know the reason why.

MICHAEL BRUCE ROSS

MONSTER AND MANIPULATOR

Several times during 1993 and 1994, I visited Michael Ross on death row at the now closed Somers Prison, Connecticut.

After a long walk through the main prison, and the climbing of many stairs, I finally arrived at a brown-painted steel door upon which was crudely stencilled in white 'DEATH ROW'. When it was opened, I was instantly struck by the sweet stench of cheap disinfectant combined with the stale odours of human sweat, urine and fried food. The smell permeated every brick. The tier was deathly quiet. Of the seven inhabitants, five had been allowed recreation because of my visit. Robert Breton and Michael Ross were in their cells. Breton glanced at me as I walked past. I nodded respectfully, ever mindful that he was just a short walk from the electric chair in which he might sit one day. (Connecticut has since abolished 'Old Sparky'. Execution is now carried out using lethal injection.) It was a dreadful place, devoid of sunlight and fresh air; it was far more claustrophobic than the row depicted in the movie *The Green Mile*, more on a par with the cellblock in *The Silence of the Lambs*. And, when I approached the cell of Michael Ross, everything started to matter – then he smiled, to greet me like a long-time friend for, as we will soon learn, Michael was always a rather amiable young man – when he wasn't killing young women, that is.

★ ★ ★

'I have dealt with a lot of criminals in my years as a police officer and if anyone deserves the death penalty it is Michael Ross.' So said Detective Mike Malchik of the Connecticut State Police Serious Crimes Squad to me in September 1994

OSBORN CORRECTIONAL INSTITUTION, SOMERS, CONNECTICUT

> There was nothing they could have said or done. It was me . . . it wasn't them. They were dead as soon as I saw them, I think. They've got me on death row as some kind of big punishment, and uh, for some of us death is not a punishment . . . living *is* the punishment.
>
> *Michael Ross to the author, Monday, 26 September 1994*

According to the state of Connecticut governor's website, Connecticut's correctional system began with the Old Newgate Prison in East Granby. The name of the prison had been taken from London's 'New Gate', which in turn had originally been a gatehouse in the massive fortified wall that surrounded London, for Newgate had been a gatehouse gaol since the reign of King John.

Initially operating as a copper mine, when the venture didn't prove profitable, the colony of Connecticut began to use the disused tunnels as a prison. It was used to incarcerate convicts during the Revolutionary War and, in 1790, became the state's prison for men until 1827, when a new penitentiary opened in Wethersfield.

Recognised as the oldest town in Connecticut, Wethersfield held four trials and three executions for witchcraft in the seventeenth century. Mary Johnson was convicted and executed in 1648, Joan and John Carrington in 1651. Landowner Katherine Harrison, deeply unpopular with her neighbours, was convicted of witchcraft in 1669; her case was overturned, however, and she was released in 1670. She was banished and her property seized by her neighbours. Standing on land bordering on the town's cove, Wethersfield served the state as its maximum-security facility until 1963, when it was replaced by the Connecticut Correctional Institution (CCI) at Somers. In 1994, the facility was reorganised into a level-3 medium-security institution and renamed the Osborn Correctional Institution (OCI), which sits on 1,400 acres at 335 Bilton Road, Somers, Tolland County, just a mile south of the Massachusetts border. While in operation, it housed around 1940 prisoners, and when I interviewed Michael Ross it incorporated death row – which has since been moved to the more recently opened Northern Correctional Institution (NCI) close by.

The first of 126 officially recorded executions carried out

in Connecticut took place when a Native American, called Nepauduck, was hanged for murder on Sunday, 30 January 1639. The last hanging, at Wethersfield, was that of 30-year-old gangster/murderer John Simborski, on Tuesday, 4 April 1936, after which the gallows were discontinued and replaced by an electric chair.

Using an idea put forward by a dentist, Alfred P. Southwick, two of Thomas Edison's employees, Harold P. Brown and Arthur Kennelly, developed the electric chair utilising the more powerful alternating current – invented by Edison's rival George Westinghouse. The first inmate to be 'electrized', to see if it worked, was one William Francis Kemmler, an inmate at Auburn State Prison in New York, who had got himself into this unfortunate fix by bludgeoning his girlfriend to death. The experiment was not a success. On the morning of 6 August 1890, Kemmler, dressed in a suit, tie and white shirt, looked remarkably composed as he sat down, but was immediately ordered to stand up by Warden Charles Durston so that a hole could be cut in his suit through which a second electrical lead could be attached. With his hands immersed in buckets of salt water, the switch was thrown while 1000 volts, enough to kill a horse, passed through his body for 17 seconds. He gasped a great deal, lost consciousness and even began to smoulder a little, but conspicuously he failed to die. After confirming that Kemmler was still alive, the attending physician, Dr Spitzka called out, 'Have the current turned on again, quick – no delay.'

In the second attempt, Kemmler received 2,000 volts. Blood vessels under the skin ruptured and bled. An awful odour began to permeate the death chamber as the flesh and hair under the electrode on his head and around the base of his spine singed. In all, the entire process took eight minutes, during which time several of the witnesses made a bolt for the exit for this was truly a messy, ugly death, leaving one reporter who witnessed it saying: 'It was an awful spectacle, far worse than hanging.' For his part, Westinghouse later drily remarked, 'They would have done better using an axe.'

Eighteen men would sit in Connecticut's 'Old Sparky'; the first to take his seat being 45-year-old steamfitter, James McElroy, on Wednesday, 10 February 1937, the last was 36-year-old gangster, Joseph L. Taborsky, electrocuted Tuesday, 17 May 1960. When Wethersfield closed, the electric chair was dismantled and moved to a room at the end of the death row segregation block at the Osborn Correctional Institution. It was never wired up – and was replaced by the lethal injection gurney in 2004, at a cost of some $200,000.

Michael Bruce Ross would later earn the notable distinctions of being the only person in Connecticut to be strapped down and executed by an infusion of lethal drugs, and he could be the last to be executed there. 'The Nutmeg State' abolished the death penalty on 25 April 2011, though prospective in nature, meaning that this does not apply to those already sentenced to death. At the time of writing, there are currently eleven men on 'the row'.

EARLY DAYS

Born in the Windham County town of Putnam, Connecticut, Sunday, 26 July 1959, to Daniel Graeme Ross and Patricia Hilda Laine, Michael was their first child. The couple's marriage was a stormy one, with Patricia, who came from a broken home and was abandoned by her own parents to live in an orphanage, being a borderline schizophrenic who never hid the fact that while at high school she was forced to get married because she became pregnant with Michael. From the outset, her baby was an unwanted child.

A mix of lower middle-class normality and mental instability, the Rosses owned a chicken farm in Brooklyn, Connecticut, ten miles from the Rhode Island border, and after giving birth to Donna Marie (May 1961), Kenneth Thomas (9 September 1962), and Tina Marie (November 1963), along with undergoing two abortions, Patricia Ross abandoned the family, only to return home like a bad penny. A schizophrenic, she was twice institutionalised in the state mental hospital at Norwich.

Family and friends have described Patricia as a woman who could be charming one minute, cold and calculating the next. A number of people who knew her witnessed at first hand a volatile, manipulative woman who would take out her resentments on her family, especially Michael, whom she blamed for ruining her life.

During my lengthy interviews with Michael Ross he recalled his mother's mood swings, which all the children feared. They couldn't understand how she could laugh after making them ill by feeding them bad meat. Or why she would ruin her two daughters' clothes with a box of dye. Spiteful, vicious and sadistic, Patricia tried to trick young Michael into shooting his pet dog, after convincing him that it was suffering after a short illness. He even claimed that she even set his mattress on fire on the front lawn because she had caught him masturbating. She would administer enemas to him, deprive him of access to the toilet, and then berate him when he soiled himself. So, by all accounts, she was the 'mother from hell'.

Yet the four kids loved their mother, simply because she was their 'mom'. They grew to accept her mood swings, and learned to keep out of her way when she was angry. Like unwanted pets, which return even meagre scraps of affection with devotion and loyalty, the children had to love her just to survive. Michael Ross explained this to me:

'We had what we called "Mom drills". The first person up in the morning would go downstairs while the rest of us kids would wait and be real quiet and listen to what type of reception we'd get from our mother. And, if we got one kind of reception, we'd know how to act. An' I'll give you an example. See, one day my sister, Tina, was setting the table, and, uh, there was six of us in the family, you know. So, she opened up the dishwasher to get six glasses, three in each hand. You know how you do it. You know, the glasses clink together. My mother went off. She was screaming and yellin', so we knew that was a bad day coming. You just knew how she was but we loved her.'

The Ross children had little time for fun and games, and were even discouraged from having any friends, or participating in after-school activities. With these restrictions in place, they had bonded into a tight-knit group for self-preservation and mutual support, although Michael said that he was alienated because his brother and sisters erroneously believed that he was favoured as a 'Mommy's boy'.

As a young boy, Michael had exhibited symptoms of emotional turmoil, including bedwetting, sleepwalking, talking in his sleep, recurrent nightmares and trichotillomania, which is the compulsive desire to pull out one's hair. In early adolescence, he was diagnosed with attention deficit disorder for which he was medicated with Ritalin. Around the same time he started to have aggressive sexual fantasies and to engage in compulsive masturbation. At the age of fourteen, he was discovered rubbing his penis against a naked seven-year-old girl – his sister – for which he was hit with a board and forced to be his sister's 'slave' for a day.

Michael explained that he was very proud of his father, and the family egg business 'Eggs Inc.'. The farm at 71 Vina Lane, just of Route 205, would become the most important part of his formative years. Indeed, by the age of ten, he had his own set of chores, and, at his mother's insistence, only he was allowed to wring the necks of sick and deformed chicks. Although the lad was a hard worker, he was a mixed-up kid who desperately wanted to live up to his father's high expectations of him, while, at the same time, he was very much seeking the approval of his schizoid mother, and constantly vying for her rare affection.

When I asked him if he was physically abused as a child, he had this to say:

'It's hard for me to tell you what was wrong with my family because I don't know anything different. That's how I was raised. I was beaten sometimes but I don't think that was it. It was more emotional abuse, an' like I mean with my dad when we were beaten, we would have to go out an' pick up a stick out of the garage where we had a woodpile. An' what you would do was to go out and you couldn't pick one that broke 'cos if it broke he'd get pretty mad. But, you didn't pick yourself a club. You know, you didn't want to get the hell beaten outa you. An' so I had my own stick put away, hidden away in the back so that people coming in and out to get firewood wouldn't inadvertently take it. But, I mean there is something wrong there when a kid goes to the wood house and picks up his stick; his own special stick for getting beaten. And, you know if you got beat you didn't scream because my father just got madder.'

So, Michael says he loved his parents despite the physical and psychological abuse they handed out, but the effects of such treatment on the developing mind are often irreparable unless drastic countermeasures are taken to remedy the problems. But, if we look deeper into Michael's formative years we also learn that as a very young and unwanted child, he had been packed off to an orphanage because his mother could not, or did not want to, look after him. He was simply in the way. When he returned home it was readily apparent that he had suffered severe and traumatic abuse at the orphanage and that he was significantly affected by his parents' abandonment.

Years later, in mitigation for his terrible crimes, Michael Ross claimed that he was raised in a 'pathological, alcoholic and abusive family unit'. His mother was an alcoholic and she lacked the necessary mothering skills to raise him properly. He alleged that his father almost never worked or supported his family and drank excessively on a daily basis. Added to this, Ross said that he was subjected to verbal, physical and emotional abuse at the hands of both of his parents, and that he was the product of a broken home that lacked 'the necessary love, affection, support and nurturing that is critical to proper social and childhood development'.

Many psychiatrists and psychologists now generally agree that if contact and interaction with others in a peer group are restricted during the early stages of infant development, the ability to interact successfully at a later stage in life is retarded. That is, the infant and child must experience love and feel valued, or the limbic nuclei in the brain will not develop normally and gross mental abnormalities may result. Children will lose the ability to form emotional attachments with others, or any attachment that does come about may only be superficial, and this abnormality may last for the rest of their lives.

Michael Ross certainly had this problem, and it is not surprising to learn that, during an FBI study of serial sexual murderers, it was found that 53 per cent of the subjects' families had a history of psychiatric problems, 42 per cent of the subjects had been subjected to physical abuse, and 74 per cent had a psychological abuse history.

But was Michael telling the complete truth when later, through his lawyers, he tried to mitigate his many sexually related offences? He argued that as a teenager he worked and contributed to the household: however, this merely related to him doing his fair share of work around the family farm. He claimed that his formal education ended before completion of the eighth grade, but this certainly did not prevent him from gaining a place at the prestigious Cornell University, with his above-average IQ of 122. Ross also claimed that he worked hard to support his family for nineteen years, which is a complete falsehood, and yet not once volunteering the fact that his parents had generously supported him throughout his time at Cornell. 'He always had plenty of money in his pocket,' claimed one of Ross's girlfriends at the time. 'His parents had bought him a decent car, he was always well-dressed, and I never recall him saying that he was supporting them.' The icing on the mitigation cake came when he told the trial court that he'd had 'a long history of steady employment while leading a productive life'.

As we will learn, Michael's first job started in June 1981 and lasted a mere four months before he was fired in October after being arrested for sexual assault. His second stint of employment commenced in March 1982, and he was sacked that May after being arrested for attempted rape and assault of an off-duty policewoman. In the May of 1983 he started working for the Prudential Insurance Company of America before he was arrested on suspicion of serial homicide on Thursday, 28 June 1984. In reality, Ross only enjoyed 20 months' paid employment during the three years following his graduation from Cornell – hardly earning enough to support even himself let alone his mother and father.

CORNELL

In September 1977, after a period of schooling at the ironically named Killingly High School, Michael's future looked decidedly bright as he drove his car onto the Cornell University (CU) campus in Ithaca, New York. Graduating sixteenth, he had overcome long odds, and was justifiably proud of himself, as only 10 per cent of Killingly High's vocational agriculture (vo-ag) students went on to college. Fewer still attended Ivy League establishments.

Michael's grandfather, Karl G. Ross, highly respected and deeply religious, had graduated from the University of New

Hampshire in 1931, majoring in poultry husbandry. Employed by the A. D. Pierce Hatchery for more than 33 years, much of that time as general manager, he was a former president of the Connecticut Hatchery Association, going on to become a founding partner of Eggs Inc, where he stayed 13 years until his retirement.

Following in his family's footsteps, at Cornell, Michael Ross enrolled as an Animal-Science major in the College of Agriculture and Life Sciences (CALS), and started a course of study that would well suit his ambition to become the third generation to run the family poultry business. This was an obsession with Michael and, for a time, his fraternity brothers even called him 'The Egg King'.

Ross now joined AgPAC, the Agricultural Student Union Council, and attended the Collegiate Future Farmers of America Council. He was a student teacher, counsellor, researcher teaching assistant, and a study group leader around this time. Alpha Zeta, one of the two campus fraternities dedicated to agricultural activity, recruited him, and he pledged to them in 1977. He lived in the fraternity house with his brothers, who were mostly young men with small-town farming backgrounds, throughout his junior and sophomore years.

During his incarceration for serial homicide, a number of Michael's old Cornell friends said that he enjoyed the house and its social life, and the chance to share common interests. His classmates, though, also recall that Michael was a loner, aloof and somewhat arrogant at times.

Marc Baase, a transfer student who roomed with Ross at Alpha Zeta when both were sophomores, remembers him as welcoming and friendly. 'He kind of followed his own drum,' says Baase, now a floral designer in Lancaster County, Pennsylvania. 'He didn't form close friendships with his fraternity brothers,' Baase adds, 'in part because he spent most of his time with a succession of girlfriends.'

By far the largest university in the United States, with a population of over 21,000, the student body at Cornell was three times larger than the entire population of Brooklyn, and the campus became a large playground for Michael Ross. Now free from his mother's unpredictable influence, he could do whatever he wanted without fear of reprisal. He literally went crazy with all the fun he was having, plunged headlong into party life to the extent that he started taking the extremely addictive drug, Ritalin, three times a day to control his hyperactivity. He would continue to use this drug for a further six years. He drank heavily and he started to experiment with sex, often sleeping with different girls four nights a week. 'There was always a certain obsession on his part,' recalls Basse, 'that seemed to be such a big issue, a constant topic – needing a woman, needing to have a girlfriend. He would become obsessed about the relationship.'

During his first junior year at Cornell, Michael met his first true love, a pretty girl called Connie Young who had joined the Reserve Officers Training Corps (ROTC). They met at a party, and he walked her home through the moonlight, and they kissed as they watched a team of divers swimming in the shimmering water of Beebe Lake – a location he would revisit later under the most heinous circumstances. The couple strolled to the statues of the college's founding fathers, Andrew

Dickson White and Ezra Cornell, and he explained how they were supposed to move together and shake hands when a virgin passed between them. On this occasion, the statues apparently did not move, for 'Connie was hotter than a kitchen stove', Michael recalled.

Connie remembers the bespectacled Michael as, 'a go-getter', and a guy who always liked to be at the centre of attention. At first she accommodated this behaviour because he seemed a worthwhile prospect. She certainly overlooked the 18-year-old's arrogance and constant boasting about his father's egg farm. In Connie's eyes, he was handsome, if just a little lanky and nerdy. He was articulate, took her dancing and to dine out. She recalls that he always had money when he needed it and, for his part, he enjoyed taking her to places, almost as a trophy, to show her off. To everyone who knew them, they seemed the perfect couple, and most were thrilled when they became engaged.

For a short period, Connie shared his bed, and then the arguments started. Michael's fraternity brothers threw him out of the house because he was breaking the rules by sharing his room with a female. As a result of this, the couple rented a small apartment where Michael withdrew into himself. The schooling pressure, combined with the adverse side effects of the Ritalin, and the demands made by the close relationship with Connie had started to take their consequences. Added to this were his parents' escalating marital problems, which were clouding his judgement over the future, as home issues were never far from his mind. Mentally, he was strung too tight and falling apart like a cheap watch.

Connie's distress over her lover's change of attitude came to a head when he started to miss classes. She was a dedicated student, trying to cram four years of education into three, but Michael Ross seemed to have lost interest, and he started to hang around their apartment all day, watching television and reading pornographic magazines. He changed his major to Agriculture Economics, and his grades plummeted. He became bone idle, expecting Connie to do all the housework and cooking and, despite the fact that she was exhausted after studying, he demanded sex with her at least four times a day.

Initially, Connie complied with his demands for fear of rejection. She loved him deeply, even allowing him to have rough sex with her, although it hurt her badly. Then, as the day-to-day events became even more unpleasant, she started to wonder if marrying Michael was such a good idea at all. He was, she now believed, sex mad, and getting worse. With his graduation approaching in the spring of 1981, Michael could not face the prospect of leaving Connie behind at Cornell. He became even more restless and agitated, withdrawing for much longer periods into a fantasy dream world of his own.

Even as a pre-teen, he had had constant fantasies about women in which he would take them to what he called 'a special, underground place', where he would hide them, and keep them so they could fall in love with him. From juvenile criminal records, it is known that, at the age of 15, he molested several neighbourhood girls. Now an adult, Michael's fantasies grew even more sexually extreme and progressively more violent. During these fantasies, he explained, he was always the assailant and, by the time of his graduation, Connie had joined his faceless dream victims. He terrorised his fantasy girls and humiliated them by forcing them to undress and drop to their knees in front of him and give him oral sex. Michael told me that he gained enormous sexual pleasure and relief from raping his fantasy victims. He savoured the sense of domination that accompanied their fear, and he reasoned that he had control of real women, too, even though these bizarre thoughts were still locked away inside his mind.

Whatever dreadful thought processes were developing inside Michael's head during that period in his life, it seemed that there was a meeting between his distorted subconscious thinking and the bland reality of everyday life. It was as if Dr Jekyll had finally met Mr Hyde. This is where the two roads met, for not only did Ross overlay the beautiful face of Connie onto his fantasy victims, his demands for kinkier sex from her began to spiral out of all control. Added to this, the priapic Michael was masturbating himself raw – something he would later do up to forty times a day while in prison, his counsellor Anne Conoyer explained to me. Although he did not know it, he was suffering from 'satyriasis', an abnormally intense and persistent desire in men for sexual intercourse. In women, the compulsion is called 'nymphomania'.

More and more, Michael found himself wandering aimlessly around the campus. He became aroused by stalking female co-eds, staying just far enough behind them to remain undetected: 'This turned me on so much I always had a hard on,' he said during one of our interviews. To release this almost uncontrollable compulsion, he had to masturbate ever more frequently, or else tip right over the edge, and act out his fantasies in reality.

Finally, weeks from graduation, Michael crossed that threshold. In late April 1981, he found himself near Beebe Lake running up behind a co-ed, and then dragging her into a small copse where he forced her to act out his fantasy of stripping naked before him and giving him oral sex. After he ejaculated, he ran off into the night, swearing to himself that he would never do such a terrible thing again.

Just three nights later, he was revisited by the same uncontrollable demons. Overcome with sexual compulsion, he attacked another undergraduate student near the Fureles Observatory just a few hundred yards north of Beebe Lake. During this assault, he slipped a rope around her neck, enjoying the heightened power this restraint bestowed on him. The terrified co-ed was like an animal he could control with a quick tug of his hand. Fortunately, someone approached the scene before he raped her and he fled into the shadows, his sexual frustrations still boiling inside him.

Michael has said that he firmly believed that these outrageous acts would cease after he left Cornell, and he prayed that he could last out the final month without attacking anyone else. At the same time, he says he also felt cheated out of the ultimate sexual satisfaction, which had been denied him during the last attacks. Weighing up the pros and cons on his mental balance sheet, he said he was compelled to satisfy himself fully, at least once, before he graduated, but he promised himself that this would have to be the final attack, after which he would never hurt a woman again. Then, on Tuesday, 12 May 1981, a young student didn't come home. A few days later, the *Ithaca Journal* printed a missing persons notice with a small photograph of 25-year-old

Dzung Ngoc Tu, who was last seen reading a submission paper in Warren Hall, variously described as 'The Most Satisfactory Building at Cornell'.

DZUNG NGOC TU

Dzung had emigrated from Vietnam to America when she was ten years old. Her father, an economist, took a job with the World Bank, and in the summer of 1969 her family left their war-ravaged country for Bethesda, Maryland, just outside Washington, DC. 'My parents were looking for a better life for their children, as opposed to an uncertain future in the old country,' recalls Dzung's older brother, Lan Manh Tu, now a real estate appraiser in the Annapolis area. She learned English rapidly, became an honours student at the Walt Whitman High School, and enrolled at Vassar College, in Poughkeepsie, New York, in pursuit of an economics degree. Indeed, the reader might be interested to learn that according to the *Hartford Courant*, this bright, young lass attended the London School of Economics (LSE) for a year.

Dzung was a delicate woman; a year younger than most of her classmates, and so tiny – barely five foot tall and ninety-five pounds – her friends felt great, motherly affection towards her. 'But there was a spine of steel in her, too,' recalls Victoria Balfour, her Vassar College roommate in 1973–74. 'Dzung could take care of herself.' At Cornell, Dzung was finishing her first year in the agricultural economics graduate programme; her plan was to return to Vietnam and use her degree to help spur her country's redevelopment.

'Dzung was a model daughter and sister,' says Lan. She sponsored orphaned children in Africa, joined Ithaca's 'Big Brother/Sister' programme, and 'helped kids with terminal cancer as a hospital volunteer . . . one thing I wanted people to know about her that she wasn't just some tragic victim,' added Lan. 'Her life was really good up until the night of her death.'

Dzung's body was discovered on Sunday, 17 May, in Fall Creek Gorge, caught on rocks beneath the rain-swollen Beebe Falls. Her skull was fractured, and investigators first suspected that she had jumped from the Triphammer footbridge, but she left no suicide note. Friends, colleagues, and family members said that that there were no signs she had been depressed. 'It seemed very unlike her,' recalls Steve Payne, MBA, who was head resident at Cascadilla Hall when Dzung roomed there during the fall semester. 'She was friendly, outgoing. She was a very happy person.'

'Within days,' recalls Cornell University Police senior investigator Scott Hamilton, then a uniformed patrolman with Cornell Public Safety, 'suspicions turned elsewhere. Dzung didn't fit the classic profile of a student that would commit suicide, and yet we didn't uncover any evidence that she had any particular enemies.' Former Tompkins County District Attorney Joseph Joch announced on Saturday, 23 May, that foul play was likely. For a while, Dzung's boyfriend was briefly named as a suspect and he retained a lawyer. An autopsy was ordered, but after a week in fast-flowing water, the body was in poor condition. 'We saw no physical evidence of rape,' Joch remembers. 'For all practical purposes, it looked like she was just thrown off the bridge.'

On campus, edgy students suspected that Dzung's death was linked to the recent campus rape incidents, and Hamilton claims that his police department also looked, in vain, for a link. 'We had a gut feeling something wasn't right,' he says, 'but I can't go to court on my gut feelings.' Meanwhile, the Class of 1981 graduated, the campus emptied, and the investigation foundered. No further rapes were reported over the summer, and the case faded from the headlines. Choosing his words somewhat injudiciously, Joch told the media, 'After seven months it was pretty much dead in the water. There were no leads to follow. We were stumped.'

In 1982, Joch left the DA's office to open a private practice. For Cornell, Dzung Ngoc Tu remained, officially an unintended death. At no point in their investigation had Michael Ross ever surfaced as suspect, Hamilton says. 'There wasn't anyone saying, "Look, we should look at this guy, because we've had no complaints against him before". Nothing!' In the spring of 1981, Ross had been an undergraduate, a senior, with no personal connection to Dzung beyond the fact that they were studying the same subject. Years later, authorities would learn that Michael had been working at a student job grading her papers in Warren Hall on the night she disappeared. 'It was a total shot in the dark . . . you could have talked to everyone on campus,' Joch argues. 'This fellow just fell between the cracks.'

It would be years before Ross's name was officially linked to Dzung Ngoc Tu's death. It has been erroneously claimed by various sources, and in publications, that in 1987 he confessed to a prison psychiatrist, that he had, during his senior year at Cornell, raped a Vietnamese girl and tossed her body off the footbridge. The fact of the matter, is, however, much different, for Michael made no such admission of guilt to *any* prison psychiatrist before my interviews with him. He confessed the crime on camera to me, then later to the police.

Prior to my interviews with Michael Ross, he had refused to cooperate with any psychiatrists, or the police, who were, in 1994, still totally unaware that he was linked to Dzung's death. Indeed, his confession to the murder came about during a filmed interview I had with him in which he merely hinted at the killing of a Vietnamese girl while he was studying at Cornell. When pressed for more detail, Ross clammed up, claiming that he needed clearance from his attorney before saying anything else. It would take much negotiation before Ross finally 'gave it up' – all to be recorded on film, for the public record.

Here, published for the first time, is Michael's recollection of Dzung's Tu's murder:

'Let's get this straight. I didn't exactly kill her. Maybe you people like the technical stuff. She drowned. Huh, don't just take my word for it. Look at the autopsy reports. The ME stated there was water in her lungs. She was alive when she hit the water. An' I'll tell you this ... um ... well, the investigators never bothered to interview me even though there were plenty of people in the hall who saw me looking at Dzung's papers. There were hundreds of students who knew me but the police never came around.

'It was dark when we had finished talking, I offered to walk her back and mentioned the other attempted rapes going on, and she agreed, so we went along talking. There was no intention on my behalf to hurt her at the outset. Have you ever seen a spider crawling up a pane of glass ... it gets halfway up then sometimes slides back down? That's how I felt. Trying to stop myself from doing these terrible things and almost getting there, an' then sliding down again.

'Uh, we got to the health centre and that's when I snapped and dragged her across the road into the woods there. She didn't seem startled and didn't struggle at all . . . like she didn't believe it was all happening and stuff. Then she said something like, "Please don't do this, Michael." I dragged her through the woods by her hair. It was easy because she was so little. I didn't tie her up, and she didn't put up any kind of fight. I felt really cheated and disappointed 'cos this was not they way I wanted it. I wanted the kick of having her fight for her life.

'Yes! I raped her. What more do you want to know? Rape isn't nice, especially for the victim. Ha-hah! I was trying to strangle her but just lost interest. She lay there. Passive. So, I just lifted her up and heaved her over the footbridge into the water. At that time, everything was a blur. My heart was beating real fast. So, to be honest, Chris, I was not sure if I had killed her or not. But, I kinda guess the fall would have made sure she was dead . . . sounds terrible, doesn't it?

'So, I want to get it on the record. I didn't technically kill her, and I can't be tried for a capital felony. It has to be second degree, 'cos it was unintentional. That's what my attorney says, anyway.'

THE ROLESVILLE RAPE

Somewhat spitefully, considering that Dan and Patricia had generously financed their eldest son's education, Michael claimed that his parents attended his graduation ceremony only for appearance's sake and he decided, from that moment, not to return to the family farm. By a stroke of good fortune, despite his poor grades, in June 1981 he managed to land an enviable job with Cargill Inc. of Minnetonka, on the outskirts of Minneapolis.

Cargill is an international agricultural business best known for grain sales, and Ross was employed at one of the firm's more modest operations, in Louisburg, a rural town about 30 miles northeast of Raleigh, North Carolina. As a production-management trainee in the poultry products division, Michael was taught how to supervise the care and management of a quarter of a million laying hens. It was a job well suited to him and, by all accounts, his career prospects with Cargill were excellent.

During the transitional period between graduation and full-time employment, Michael tried to persuade Connie to transfer to North Carolina University, where, he suggested, she could complete her studies. Over the preceding months, their relationship had so deteriorated that he was now paranoid about the separation and feared that she would soon be gone for good. Nevertheless, he was secretly hopeful they would marry one day. For her part, Connie had strong ideas of her own, and marriage was no longer among them; besides, the leggy co-ed was now dating someone else.

Then a bomb dropped on Michael's world. He learned over the phone that his mother and father had split up for the third time, with Mr Ross leaving the family home and business to its own devices. Now, with no one to run Eggs Inc., the highly volatile matriarch flew to Louisburg, and Michael was pleased, if not surprised, to see his mother so quickly after learning the bad news. Mistakenly, Michael thought this visit was a sign that his relationship with his parents might improve. Even that they intended to get back together. At the very least, he wanted to believe that his mother could keep the egg farm going until he returned home to take charge, if only for his father's sake. This thought, however, was the furthest thing from Mrs Ross's devious mind, for she had, in fact, come to visit her son for one reason only. She needed Michael to sign over his shares in Eggs Inc. so that she could dispose of the company, becoming rich in the bargain.

Rather naively, Michael allowed himself to be duped into signing the share transfer, and soon after learning of the true reason behind his mother's impromptu visit, he felt that he had betrayed not only his father but also himself.

Then life was made even worse when Connie flew to North Carolina with more bad news. For her, the trip was a short one. She explained that she didn't like Michael's parents, and even if he did end up running the egg business, this wasn't exactly her idea of a future. The finality of the relationship hit home on Tuesday, 25 August 1981 when, at Raleigh Durham Airport, the couple fell into each other's arms, sobbing their farewells. For an hour Michael hung around the airport hoping to see Connie rush back to him, but it was not to be. Despite the fact that she had removed her engagement ring, he simply could not bring himself to believe that his relationship with Connie was finished, so he was understandably distraught as he started to drive back along Highway 401 to Louisburg.

At around 6.30 p.m., having covered just 16 miles, he passed through the small town of Rolesville where he spotted a young woman pushing her seven-month-old child in a buggy along

Main Street. Within milliseconds, his uncontrollable sexual urges surfaced again and, after parking his car, Ross ran up to the woman and offered to carry her groceries.

It was still two hours till sunset in Rolesville; a friendly town of around 3,200 inhabitants nestling in northeastern Wake County, where violent crime was relatively unknown – until Michael Ross drove in, that is! The 21-year-old mother, used to such a secure environment, did not hesitate when this helpful and seemingly decent young man approached her. She thanked Ross for his offer and passed over the heavy bags. They walked to her home several blocks away and, as they entered the backyard, Ross suddenly dropped the bags, whipped off his leather belt, and wrapped it around the woman's neck. He dragged her into a nearby soya bean field, where he threatened to smash the baby's head against a tree if it didn't stop crying.

This innocent woman now became a repository for the months of Ross's pent-up anger and sexual frustrations. He smashed his fists into her face, and he choked her with the belt, forcing her to her knees to beg for mercy. Then, with his hands tightly grasped around her neck, he ejaculated.

Ross explained to me that after regaining his breath he sat back on the ground with his victim squirming around in front of him. Somehow, he says, he felt cheated, for he wanted to satisfy his perversions by ejaculating as she died and not beforehand. Enraged, acting like a wild animal, he ripped off the woman's clothes, beating her again and again before reapplying his grip around her throat while the baby screamed nearby. Then a switch flicked inside his head. He stopped and as suddenly as he had appeared Michael Ross vanished. It was over an hour before the woman regained consciousness – at approximately the same time as Connie's flight landed at JFK Airport, New York. Painfully, she crawled across the street to a neighbour who summoned the local police chief, Nelson S. Ross. Officers arrived almost immediately. In a blaze of red and blue flashing strobes, cruisers raced throughout the area and roadblocks were set up on the county line, but Michael was long gone. He was not charged for this offence until he was arrested in Connecticut, three years later.

When I asked him if he recalled the Rolesville attack, Michael said, 'I don't really remember her, or any of my victims for that matter. It's like an old black and white movie; a collage of strange faces, that's all. Nope, I couldn't remember this woman if you had showed me a photograph of her the next day.'

Then he made this deadly cold statement: 'There was nothing she, or any of them, could have done when I zeroed in on them. They were dead. All over. That this one lived ain't got nothing to do with me. That she lived? Well, that was purely an act of God.'

When asked if the Rolesville victim had fought back and tried to escape, Ross replied, 'Nothing. She could have got away or something, but it never happened. I can't remember. Like with the Vietnamese girl, I can't remember any kind of struggling with her or anything like that. I can't remember, uh, any kind of fighting at all. I do recall, with the Rolesville victim, saying that I would smash the baby's head into a tree or a wall. So, I would imagine I probably said things equally horrible to, uh, the other ones that would make them stop and think not to do anything.'

Thereafter, Ross simply carried on his daily existence as if nothing untoward had happened in Rolesville. Then, on Tuesday, 17 September 1981, his parents filed divorce papers at the Windham County Superior Court. A week later, Michael's employer, Cargill, sent him on a field trip to Illinois, where he would visit the Chicago Commodities Exchange. Before this trip was over, Ross would be arrested for the first time.

THE LASALLE ASSAULT

Ross had decided to look over the Cargill operation in Seneca, which is about 75 miles southwest of Chicago. He rented a car at O'Hare International Airport, and headed out across the flat, central Illinois farm country. Just before 11 p.m. on Monday, 28 September, an attractive 16-year-old LaSalle City girl was walking along a road that threaded through a cluster of houses when she noticed a car slowly creeping past her. She had noted the car several times beforehand, and now she was becoming frightened for her safety.

Without warning, the teenager was suddenly grabbed from behind and a handkerchief was stuffed into her mouth. She was dragged into nearby woods where the attacker wrapped a belt around her neck and asked her for money. She gave him the 22 cents she had and, when he loosened his belt, she let out a piercing scream. She was now moments from a terrifying rape, probably murder, when salvation arrived. A woman living nearby had just switched off her television with the intention of going to bed when she heard a noise that made her blood chill. Opening her kitchen window, she heard a gurgling sound and rustling noises in nearby bushes, so she called the police. Luck was now on the teenager's side, even more so because fate decreed that a passing patrol car was only 100 yards away, and it arrived at the scene in moments. When Ross saw the beams of police torches sweeping the woods, he hurried back to his car, but this time his luck had deserted him.

Sergeant Lewis of the LaSalle Police explained how Ross had got himself arrested. 'What happened is, when we took the girl home, Ross had his car parked on the same street she lived on. And, on the way home, she saw the car, and said to us, "That's the car, that's the car." And, so pretty soon we are looking at the car, and he comes up and says, "What's the problem?"'

After Michael's arrest, for unlawful restraint, Sergeant Lewis said that he was puzzled by the contradiction, between Ross's demeanour, and what he had done. 'He was real humble,' Lewis recalled. 'He wouldn't look you in the eyes when you talked to him. He was a very educated and talented kid. He didn't appear to be the kind of guy who would go out to other towns and do this kind of stuff. He more or less kept his mouth shut, and he was subdued and spiritless when we took him in.'

On the downside for the LaSalle attack Ross was fined $500 after pleading guilty to assault, then on Tuesday, 8 October, his employers got wind of the case and fired him. On the upside, and with no alternative, he returned to Brooklyn where he attempted reconciliation with Connie. Indeed, he was very pleased when she invited him to spend Christmas with her at her parents' home in Vermont. He was even more delighted that they had also been invited to share the New Year with his mother – the Mother from Hell – and, as might have been expected, visiting Mrs Ross was an unmitigated disaster. His mother could not stand the sight of such a beautiful, upper-class young woman under her roof, and Michael was very upset by the fact that his father had been reduced to living in a run-down shed nearby. The hoped-for rekindling of his relationship with Connie failed for the second time, and she went off to Ithaca, New York, to visit a 'friend'. This was the catalyst that precipitated Ross into rape and killing again. Daniel's son would murder in the small town of Danielson.

TAMMY LEE WILLIAMS

Attractive, dark-haired, 17-year-old Tammy Lee Williams lived with her family on Prince Hill Road, Brooklyn, which was only 1.6 miles from the Ross's' egg farm. A free-spirited lass, who had quit high school, she came and went as she pleased, and it wasn't unusual for her to walk along Route 6 to visit her boyfriend who lived in Danielson, just under five miles away.

At 10.15 a.m. on Monday, 4 January, Tammy left her boyfriend's apartment to walk home, first promising him that she would telephone him to let him know that she had arrived safely. She did not fulfil this promise because she encountered Michael Ross on her journey. He was surprised to see the teenager walking along a busy road on such a bitterly cold day. The local weather station was recording highs of 2 degrees with lows ranging down to minus 8 degrees C, the ground was as white and hard as cast plaster, and it would take another couple of hours before the sun poked through the clearing clouds.

As was his developing modus operandi as an 'opportunist serial killer', Ross pulled his car over and ran up to Tammy offering her a lift. 'She was walking in the same direction as I was driving,' he later explained to me. 'That was west out of Danielson. At first she refused so I told her that my parents owned Eggs Inc., that I could drop her off anywhere en route. She thought about it for a few seconds, so I asked, "Where are you going?" and she replied, "Prince Hill Road." An' I knew the place so I told her, "That's just near to where I gotta go." And, she still refused so I lost it . . . I dragged her screaming and hollerin' and struggling into nearby woods, and I forced her to strip and get to her knees.' Ross raped Tammy and strangled her before hiding the body, under a pile of rocks and brush, in a swamp. He boasted that it took him all of eight minutes to throttle her to death, because he kept getting cramp in his hands. Each time this happened, he had to release his grip and massage his fingers before finally throttling the life out of her. With a sick smile on his face, he seemed proud of the fact that when he snatched Tammy from the roadside, it was in broad daylight with scores of cars driving past. 'A good few drivers must have seen me and her together,' he said. 'They were blind if they didn't . . . hey, and no one even saw my car, or so the cops say.'

Tammy's father reported his daughter missing the next day. On Wednesday, 6 January, a motorist found Tammy's pocketbook – brand-new, a Christmas present from her parents – lying along Route 6, at the junction with Brickyard Road. Michael Ross later explained that he had thrown the pocketbook out of his car before arriving back at his mother's place, shortly after the murder.

'She was missing almost two and a half years,' recalls Steve St John, Tammy's uncle. 'It was really devastating. We all went out and searched. Come to find out two years later I could have walked right over her body . . . She was a sweetheart . . . she was a typical teenager, with a family that was separated and she hoped they would eventually get back together. She was a very outgoing person.'

Tammy's mother had remarried, to a pilot, and had the opportunity to travel with him to a new posting in American Samoa. Tammy went along and lived there, and later in Hawaii, with her mother and sister. 'My daughter was a good daughter,' said Tammy's mother, Norma Deems. 'I kinda spoiled her.'

According to the *Hartford Courant*, while Tammy loved the exotic travel, she missed her hometown friends and longed to return to Connecticut, so, aged 14, she returned and moved in with her father and stepmother, on Prince Hill Road. St John recalls that, 'Tammy was very bright, but bored with school, so she sort of dropped out,' adding, 'she loved being with her friends. She had a very outgoing personality. But the scary thing is that she knew him [Michael Ross]. It really changed the lives of everyone in our community. You never used to lock your doors. We used to let the kids go out and play, be by themselves and walk to school. That all changed.'

After his arrest, on Saturday, 30 June 1984, Michael Ross took police to the decomposed body of Tammy Williams, and confessed later that she had recognised him and that she had pretended to enjoy the violent rape to avoid being killed. He also said that he returned to the copse several times during the weeks following the murder in order to masturbate over the body.

During January and February 1982, Ross's thoughts continually returned to Connie. Acting on impulse, he decided to drive 300 miles to Ithaca and visit her without prior warning of his intentions. On arrival, he found Connie in bed with another man. He stormed off in a rage and headed south in search for yet another girl to kill.

PAULA PERRERA

It was Tuesday, 2 March 1982. Sixteen-year-old Paula Perrera left Central Valley High School, in Montgomery, New York State, early, ostensibly because she didn't feel well. In fact Paula often bunked off school, and hitchhiked regularly to see her boyfriend, Jackie Eull, who worked at the McDonald's restaurant in Scotchtown. A colleague of Eull recalls that, 'Paula would show up unannounced while he was working, and he'd say, "How'd you get here," and she'd give some bullshit story, but we all knew she was hitching rides. Period.'

The petite, curly-haired blonde was the daughter of Michael and Christine Null Canavan. Born Wednesday, 4 July 1965, Paula was now a junior varsity cheerleader at Valley Central High School. Her sweet, soprano voice got her into the choir; she enjoyed the school's nightclub and her tiny size landed her roles in school plays. After she played a little lamb one Christmas, 'Little Lamb' became her friends' pet name for her. 'Even at 16, people often mistook Paula for a 12-year-old,' recalls school friend, Nancy Atkins.

'Paula was the girl everyone wanted to hang out with in school,' remembers another former classmate, Barbara Willard, who met Paula in the fourth grade. 'She loathed cliques and bent her ear for everyone. She lived in a carefree adventure land, rarely scripted and sometimes reckless. Me, Nancy and Paula would ride our bikes for miles around Orange County. One summer, we rode for so long we got bad sunburn. We looked like lobsters.'

The inseparable threesome shared 'lots of secrets and cried together,' says Nancy. 'For months at a time, we'd be Spanish gang-girls, sashaying around in crazy outfits, defending our turf. But, when she got heated up over one of her principles, she grew 10 feet tall. Having Paula on your side was like having a professional boxer behind you. When kids on the school bus poked fun at her clothes and her pals wanted to strike back, she'd answer, "That would make us as bad as them."'

And when the seasons changed, Paula didn't need good weather to find an escape hatch from her troubled family life; one where her single mother struggled to pay the bills while working two jobs, and raising four children in the blue and white trailer home at 206 Valley View Park, in Scotchtown.

'One day, she was an actress going off to Hollywood,' says Barbara. 'Then she's thinking about being a singer in Nashville. Her home life wasn't the greatest so she always put herself in this fantasy world and thought of things she would probably never be.'

But Paula's biggest adventures were the ones she embarked on by thumbing a ride, and this *did* worry her tight-knit circle of friends. She got a kind of kick out her hitchhiking trips, and – taking her inspiration from the journalist Charles Kuralt's regular feature 'On the Road' on *CBS Evening News* – described to pals the motorists she met along the way, as reported by the *Hartford Courant*. 'She'd tell us these stories about the people she would meet,' explained Barbara Willard. 'And, we'd be like, "OK, that's great this time but don't do it again." We really told her that she was pushing her luck. We begged her not to do it again, and she replied, "I only get into cars with nice people.'"

On that fateful Tuesday, Paula asked a school friend for a lift, but he couldn't oblige. 'I have a really important test,' he replied. With no money for a bus fare, she started hitchhiking and she was last seen alive around 12.30 p.m., near the Montgomery Auto Shop, on Route 211. A credible witness would later claim that he saw Paula, who was wearing a three-quarter-length coat, white slacks, brown shoes and carrying a tan shoulder bag, get into a light-coloured car. Paula's mother reported her 16-year-old daughter as missing to the Crystal Run Police later that day.

Although Ross had always been the prime suspect in the Perrera killing, there was never quite enough evidence to charge him with her murder; a situation exacerbated by the fact that Ross had refused to be interviewed by the police investigators while on death row. This changed when Michael was subsequently interviewed by me as part of my research for a TV documentary.

The night before the interview, my motel receptionist called my room to explain that investigators from the New York State Police based at Crystal Run wanted to speak to me urgently. They had got wind that I was to meet and film Michael Ross the next day, then, in a quiet corner they handed me documents, a photo of Paula, and a newspaper article concerning the homicide.

The detectives explained that Paula's family needed much-needed closure; that the police suspected Ross as the girl's killer; that he had refused to talk to them – as was his legal right. Indeed, this was their 'Last Chance Saloon'. Could I extract a confession from Ross, as in please?

My producer, Frazer Ashford, flipped. Ever mindful that serial killers are a litigious bunch, a furious argument broke out between us. 'We're here to film a serial killer, not solve a murder . . . we'll get sued for entrapment, for Christ's sake!' He went to bed fuming. Now things for me got very serious indeed.

I cannot divulge my technique in this book – mainly because it is often used by law enforcement as a training aid – nevertheless, at the interview, which was recorded on film, I subtly coerced Michael into confessing the crime, going on to give details that only Paula's killer would have known. (At the same time he also confessed the murder of Dzung Ngoc Tu). As a tailpiece, there was no entrapment, I can assure you of that. Frazer and I are still working together and are great friends. Michael's full confession in document form – in which I am referred to – along with the scenes-of-crime photographs are now in the possession of DCI Martin Brunning, Bedfordshire, Cambridgeshire and Hertfordshire Major Crime Unit, who assisted me in a previous book, *Love of Blood*, concerning the British serial killer, Joanne Dennehy.

Nonetheless, Michael explained to me that he was driving the 320 miles east from Ithaca, New York, to his home in Connecticut, and exited at Bloomingburg to pick up Route 17K as a shortcut to Interstate 84. Just at the very moment that Paula walked out of the school gates and stepped across the road, Ross spotted her and offered the girl a lift. Then, on a wooded stretch of highway called 'Crystal Dip', at a patch of marshy ground where people often dumped trash, Ross stopped and dragged Paula out of the car.

'What did you do with the body, Michael?' I asked.

'I raped and strangled her and sodomised her. Left the body by a low, stone wall. There was a willow tree near by. Then I drove off along I-84 and threw her purse out of the window.'

'What was Paula wearing?' I asked.

'I can't remember,' he said, with a dismissive wave of his hand.

With that he took the documents from my hand and, without looking at them he tossed them on the floor, adding, 'Well, it is just another murder, isn't it?'

New York State Police soon characterised this as a confession. It gave them legal cause to compel Ross to give up a blood sample that yielded his DNA. The DNA was matched with DNA extracted from semen found in Paula's body.

On Thursday, 3 December 1998, Ross disregarded his own lawyer's advice and made a formal confession to two Middletown-based State Police Investigators, Charles Auld and Steve Riordan. Ross talked for two hours. There was just one break. Then he talked until he was all 'talked out' and had answered all the detectives' questions. Auld later recalled that 'Ross said that he didn't want someone else to be falsely accused and convicted of the crime.'

Paula Perrera's half-naked body had been found almost in sight of her home 17 days after she had gone missing. Following a service at St Columba Roman Catholic Church, in Chester, she was buried at Pine View Hill Cemetery, Wawayanda, Orange County.

A year after my interview with Ross I received a letter from the New York State Police thanking me, on behalf of Paula's family, for bringing them closure in the case. In early 2014, I received yet another letter from the NYSP. It was accompanied by the complete transcript of the interview Ross gave to Charles

Auld and Steve Riordan, along with a presentation NYSP mug to add to my collection of many others from around the world.

SUSAN ALDRICH

Michael Ross started work at Ohio Fresh Eggs Inc. on Friday, 5 March 1982. The large poultry operation, based in the small town of Croton, northeast of Columbus, Ohio, hired him as a co-supervisor for 30 employees. He was also responsible for 14 hen houses and one million birds.

A fellow supervisor, Donald Harvey, remembered Ross, saying, 'He was a disaster in the job, and we were planning to fire the guy pretty soon. He was very bossy. And he just didn't relate to you in giving an order. He just didn't know how to come across. He wanted everyone to know that his education was much higher than theirs, and that they were just hourly paid workers and high-school dropouts.'

On Sunday, 25 April, Ross spotted pregnant Susan Aldrich in a laundromat at Johnstown, six miles south of Croton, and followed her home. She was completely unaware that she was being stalked and he was ignorant of the fact that she was an off-duty Licking County police officer. Around midnight, he knocked on her door and told her that his car had broken down and asked if he could borrow a torch. A short while later, he returned and asked to use her telephone. As soon as Susan turned her back, he reached over her shoulder, cupped his hand over her mouth to prevent her from screaming, and forced her to the floor. She struggled, and managed to shout out, saying that her husband was also police officer, and that he would be home at any moment. After giving her a severe beating, Ross ran back to his car, ripped a parking ticket from the windscreen and drove off.

Ross had been parked close to the laundrette, and it was here he got the ticket. Police also found a witness who saw him running from the direction of Susan's home towards his vehicle, so they put two and two together and traced the owner through the Vehicle Licensing Office. In an act of poetic justice, it was Susan's husband who arrested Susan's attacker.

Ross was sacked from Ohio Fresh Eggs Inc on Monday, 3 May, and bailed to his mother's home before sentencing. While there, he visited a psychiatrist at the Learning Clinic in Brooklyn, hoping to win a little sympathy from the doctor, who might have influence with the court. Nevertheless, if Ross now believed that his bad luck had bottomed out he was in for yet another shock for the following month proved yet another disaster for him.

Although he had returned a number of photographs to Connie, she still had his engagement ring and he wanted it back. However, the day before he turned up to collect it, she set off across country to marry her boyfriend. When Ross learned of this, he was furious. But, if that slap across the face was hard to take, a family development enraged him even further.

It seems that financially his mother's divorce had paid off handsomely. When Patricia flaunted her new lover before speeding off in her flashy new Cadillac, it proved too much for Michael. These two emotional setbacks coming so close together were sufficient to set him off on the murder trail again.

DEBRA SMITH TAYLOR

The last time anyone could recollect seeing 23-year-old Debra Smith Taylor alive was around midnight on Tuesday, 15 June 1982. She was driving home with her husband when their car ran out of fuel on Highway 6, near Hampton, just eight miles east of Mrs Ross's home. A state trooper came across the stationary vehicle, and drove the couple to the Sunoco petrol station in Danielson, where the boyfriend of one of Ross's earlier victims, Tammy Williams, had lived. The trooper recalled that the Taylors were arguing, and that Debra was so annoyed that she said that she would find her own way home. After leaving her husband to his own devices, she walked across Danielson Town Green, to the bandstand, where she gratefully accepted the offer of a ride home from a bespectacled young man who had walked up and spoken to her.

On Sunday, 30 October, two hunters discovered the remains of Debra Taylor in one of the large tracts of woodland east of Route 169, in Canterbury. The spot was less than ten miles from the Ross's egg farm. The body was so decomposed that identification was only possible by means of dental records and items of jewellery.

★ ★ ★

During the first week of August 1982, Ross had returned to Ohio for sentencing over the assault he had committed on Susan Aldrich four months previously. The psychiatrist who had examined him concluded that Michael was an 'over-achiever with too much spare time on his hands', and in his report suggested that Michael should find a hobby, such as learning how to fly. But the judge wouldn't buy any of it, and packed Ross off to the Licking County Jail, in Newark, where he would serve a six-month term for the assault on Susan Aldrich. He was also ordered to pay a $1,000 fine. Daniel Ross collected his son from prison on Wednesday, 22 December, drove him back to Connecticut, and offered him a place to stay.

Michael Ross had misrepresented himself when he applied for work at Ohio Fresh Eggs Inc. by declaring that he had never been in trouble with the police, and he did exactly the same thing again in May 1983 when he applied for a job with the Prudential Insurance Company of America. He would become one of the forty agents selling health, life, automotive, property, casualty insurance and securities, from the company's office in Norwich, Connecticut. With steady money in his pocket, Ross rented an apartment at 58 North Main Street, in Jewett City. He settled in and his landlady remembers him as a decent, smart and extremely affable young man, whom she enjoyed having around her large, Victorian-style house.

Ross's female work colleagues also took an immediate liking to him. They thought of him as sweet and probably inexperienced in romance. He dated when the opportunity arose, and when he met recently divorced Debbie Wallace, while out canvassing for business, he reasoned that his past problems were now well behind him.

During this relationship, Ross says he spent a great deal of time masturbating, fantasising and stalking women. Some he followed at random. With others he set out to learn their daily schedules.

According to Michael, he slipped into apartments, just to watch women undress and get into bed. And he raped once during this time, allowing his victim to run away. The attacks were of course reported to the police, but as was the previous case with Dzung Ngoc Tu, Ross never became a suspect. Indeed, he never even came on to the law's radar.

Although he was often out until all hours of the morning, Debbie Wallace was totally ignorant of Michael's perverted behaviour. She believed that he would make a good father to her three children; however, like Connie, Debbie was stubborn, independent and strong-willed. She was a spitfire, full of energy, and sex with Michael was excellent. Their relationship was volatile, too, and their frequent arguments often ended in physical violence.

During Thanksgiving 1983, the couple had a furious fight over dinner arrangements. From the outset, the 'Mother from Hell', Patricia Ross, had never liked Connie, and she didn't approve of Debbie either, so she invited her son for a meal but refused to extend the invitation to Debbie. Ross did not know what to do. He felt torn between the two women, so he and Debbie fought and the outcome was that he spent the holiday alone.

ROBIN DAWN STAVINSKY

Around the time Ross was learning the insurance business – giving a new meaning to the term 'The Man from the Pru' – 19-year-old Robin Dawn Stavinsky was moving from Columbia to Norwich, where she hoped to find a job that would pay enough to allow her to enter college.

In August 1993, Robin took a job as a switchboard operator at D.P.M. Enterprises, Inc., Norwich. At 9.30 p.m. on Wednesday, 16 November 1983, the attractive blonde disappeared after apparently arguing with her boss. Although it was cold and dark, Robin refused a lift from a workmate and, in what proved to be a fatal mistake, decided to walk to her boyfriend's house.

That evening, Ross was driving along Route 32, when he saw Robin storming along the roadside. He stopped, climbed out of his car and approached her with the offer of a lift. When she rebuffed him, he became angry and dragged her struggling into a patch of dense woodland just a few hundred yards from the offices of Connecticut State Police Major Crime Squad, at Uncasville. Ross had started to strangle Robin as soon as he grabbed her, and by the time he was ready to rape the young woman, she was barely conscious. Ross later recalled that by now he was no longer excited by the idea of sex, and his satisfaction came only from the act of killing, and by reliving the moment, occasionally driving to the murder scene to masturbate until the body was discovered eight days later.

A jogger, running through the grounds of the Uncas-on-Thames Hospital, just three miles south of where Robin worked, found the partially clothed corpse under a pile of leaves. Police retrieved the remainder of the dead woman's clothing, from a river, after Ross's arrest.

Robin died of manual strangulation and was asphyxiated. The strangling cut off the blood supply to the brain by compressing the arteries on either side of her neck.

Such a death could be as quick as twenty seconds or could take longer.

The evidence of Medical Examiner Dr Arkady
Katesnelson at Ross's trial

The brutal murder of Robin Stavinsky was to prove a dreadful watershed in Ross's killing career. To begin with, he had murdered out of fear of recognition should his victims survive. Now he was seeking his ultimate sexual thrill – that of ejaculation as his victim's death supervened. So far, the murders had provided him with only part-realisation of this fantasy. The overwhelming emotions, topped with feelings of power, domination and the act of murder were there, but he felt that Robin Stavinsky had short-changed him. She had provided him with none of the sickening criteria because she had collapsed limp and helpless as he dragged her into the scrub. Nevertheless, he strangled her and raped her after death. When arrested, he told Connecticut State Police Investigator, Mike Malchik, that, 'She was strong. She had been one hundred per cent unwilling to engage in sex', but that he had been able to force her because he was bigger and stronger than her, and had intimidated her.

However, Ross told me later, 'She told me that I was going to get caught. I was surprised, ya know. It was a pretty good thrill, but not the best. She writhed around a lot, gurgling an' stuff, so I had to stop to massage my hands 'cos I got cramp in them. I got a kick out of that.'

A former star track and field athlete at Windham High School, Robin was a 1981 state champion in the discus. At her funeral, one of her former teachers described her as a hard-working young woman with a lot of potential. She is buried in Hartford, Connecticut. Her simple grey headstone, reads:

Robin Dawn Stavinsky
Jan 11. 1964
Nov 3. 1983
Loved and Missed

LESLIE SHELLEY AND APRIL BRUNAIS

If all of the above recollections of homicide most foul by Michael Ross are not disgusting enough, nothing will prepare the reader for the gruesome details of this man's rape/murders of two schoolgirls as related by him exclusively to me during our filmed interviews and in correspondence, for, on Easter Sunday 1984, two 14-year-old schoolgirls disappeared in eastern Connecticut.

Leslie Shelley and April Brunais, inseparable friends and neighbours in the town of Griswold, New London County, had decided to walk into Jewett City to see a movie. Both girls were aware that their parents would not permit them to walk back during the hours of darkness, so each said that the other's parents had agreed to drive them home. This childish deception would cost them their lives. As darkness fell, the girls phoned their homes, and both were ordered by their parents to walk back along Route 138 as punishment. It was a decision that their mothers and fathers would regret to their own dying day.

At 10.30 p.m., when neither girl had returned, their concerned parents called the police who made the initial mistake of listing the youngsters as 'runaways'. The exact time Ross stopped and offered the girls a lift is unknown.

It is known from Ross, however, that April, who was the more assertive of the two, climbed into the front passenger seat, while the petite and fragile Leslie sat behind. They asked him to drop them off at a service station at the end of their street, and both children were understandably startled when Ross drove right past, and despite their protests that he had missed their turning, he wouldn't stop. Michael explained that April pulled out a small steak knife she had in a pocket and threatened to stab him if he didn't pull over, but Ross yelled at her and nearly drove off the road, at which point she panicked and gave him the knife.

Driving five miles east on Highway 138, he headed for Voluntown, and the nearby Beach Pond – a vast expanse of water with a dam holding back the Pachaus River, which separates the states of Rhode Island and Connecticut. Parking at a still unknown location, Ross ordered April into the back seat. He tied Leslie up with an elastic belt she had been wearing, and then he took April Brunais out of the car. During the incident April became 'mouthy', recalled Ross, but Leslie Shelley urged her friend to do exactly everything he wanted. He forced April to remove her jeans and cut the material into strips with the steak knife. Then he bound the girls' hands and feet and shut Leslie into the trunk of his car. Ross dragged April a few yards and forced her to her knees. There can be no doubt that the terrified Leslie overheard her friend arguing with Ross, for April put up a spirited fight for her life before he raped and strangled her to death.

Ross now turned his attention to Leslie. He later admitted to me during his filmed interview – a copy of which was later used at his trial – that the girl made a great impact on him.

'She was delicate with wispy blonde hair,' he stated. 'She was calm as I talked to her in the car. I told her that I didn't want to kill her, and she cried when she found out that her friend was already dead. Yes, I suppose she started shaking and appeared resigned to her fate when I rolled her over. This is the murder that bothers me most. I can't remember how I strangled her, but her death was the most real and hardest to deny. With the others, it was like someone else did it, and I watched from afar through a fog of unreality. This was real but somehow not real. Her death? Um . . . It wasn't someone else and for the first time I saw it was me. I watched myself do those things and I couldn't stop. It was like an invisible barrier was between us. I didn't want to kill her.'

At this point during the interview with me, Ross showed the first signs of stress and remorse. He stopped talking, lowered his head, and sucked in a lungful of stale prison air. When he resumed his sickening account of the murder of Leslie Shelley, there were tears – but how genuine – in his eyes.

'I couldn't do anything but watch as I murdered her, and you want to know something outrageous? Well, I cried afterwards. You know something else? Well, ah, I don't know but nobody knows this. Well, I wanted to have sex with her straight after I raped and killed April, but I couldn't get it up. So, I had to sit back with Leslie for an hour, just talkin' an' stuff. Then, because she started crying, saying that she would be in trouble for being late home, I had to kill her. But I anally raped her, after death, to release the tension. Then I re-dressed her. You see, nobody has been told this before.'

(Note: It has since been suggested that no evidence of 'post-mortem anal rape' was found by the medical examiner to support Ross's disgusting claim. However, by the time the bodies of April and Leslie were discovered, they were almost skeletal and any possible intimate trace evidence had long gone.)

Then Ross smiled sheepishly before adding, 'You see, they call me a serial killer, right? Well, I've only killed eight women. Big deal. There are a lot more guys you could meet and they've killed dozens more. An' in that context, I'm a nice guy. I'm such a nice guy really.'

With that, he burst into an uncontrollable fit of laughter, before explaining that he had dumped the bodies of April and Leslie at another location near Beach Pond, occasionally revisiting the site to masturbate over their remains.

'I'd just sit there, just to look at their decomposing bodies. Like my childhood fantasies, they were there for me and they gave me pleasure when I needed it,' Ross explained.

Michael Ross took the police to the bodies of April Brunais and Leslie Shelley shortly after his arrest on Tuesday, 28 June 1984. They were found in a culvert, by a sparsely populated road, near Preston. The precise location of the actual murder scene has never been established, and this was put down as an 'oversight' by the Connecticut State Police, later proved in court to be a deliberate attempt by them to avoid a jurisdictional boundary dispute with the Rhode Island law-enforcement agencies who had to foot the bill for this homicide investigation.

★ ★ ★

Leslie Shelley's mother and father, Edwin and Lera waited twenty-one haunting years to witness their daughter's killer's execution. During an interview on 12 May 2005, Edwin said, 'Can you imagine how scared that little girl was, and people tell me to turn the other cheek.'

The Shelleys by then had both retired; Edwin had worked as a postman until 1992, while Lera had worked as a mental nurse at the state hospital in the grounds of which Robin Stavinsky's body had been found. Reminiscing over their beloved daughter as they fished off a wooden bridge above Kinne Brook, near their house. They recalled Leslie's one and only home run in softball when she was thirteen; how she liked to wait up for her mother to finish the nightshift so they could play cards and talk, how stubborn she was, but 'just a little sweetheart and pretty as a picture'.

Edwin Shelley, who later watched Ross's execution, remarked bitterly that Ross was 'so brave, since Leslie was all of ninety pounds'. A former navy man with tattooed forearms. According to the *New York Times*, 'Edwin did most of the talking while Mrs Shelley, her grey-threaded hair drawn back into a tight bun, mostly looked down. Her tears dropped into the water.'

In the months and years after Leslie died, the Shelleys turned their grief into action. They met with the families of Ross's victims and with relatives of other victims. They met with state legislators and worked to establish a prison psychiatric review board. And they persuaded state officials to hire victims' advocates for each county.

'The media will be on one side and Ross's family on the other, and we'll be right here – dead centre!' said Edwin, lining his feet on the slats of the bridge and motioning an alignment for his next cast with an invisible Michael Ross, as again reported in the *New York Times*.

In November 2010, five years after Ross's execution and facing another Thanksgiving holiday without his daughter, finally Edwin Shelley had had enough, and passed away. 'I think it just accumulated to the point where he just couldn't take it any more,' said Jennifer Bennard, Leslie's sister and April Brunais's best friend. 'He really had just given up. He had stayed around long enough to see Ross executed and I think it just ate him too much.'

Edwin Shelley's life is now over, but his family believes his reunion with Leslie has just begun. 'There is a lot of comfort knowing that my dad is up there with my sister, and I made that comment to my mother when I set up the funeral arrangements,' Jennifer recalled. 'I said, "That's a great birthday present for my sister. She'll have her dad buried right next to her."'

Edwin Shelley was buried on what would have been Leslie's 41st birthday. Among the condolences was this from Edwin's granddaughter, Heather La Fleche: 'My grandfather was one of the strongest, bravest people I know. He kept our family together during the biggest tragedy our family had to experience. He did his best to cope the best anyone could expect, but I guess in the end it just wasn't enough. We will all miss him during the Thanksgiving holiday season and always.'

How heart-breaking life can be!

★　★　★

Ross was now nearing the end of his run for he was completely out of control, and his work at the Prudential Insurance Company was suffering as a result. Faced with the prospect of dismissal, as he was failing to bring in new business, Michael was also coping with his turbulent relationship with Debbie Wallace, which had taken a more active turn. Debbie's father had died while she and Michael were on vacation. After the funeral, on the return journey, they had argued. A major rift followed, they split up and, once again, he felt alone and rejected.

WENDY BARIBEAULT

For 17-year-old Wendy Baribeault, Friday, 13 June 1984 was the final day of her examinations at the Norwich Free Academy, 305 Broadway, where she was a junior student. After she had finished, she went home to 24 Round Hill Court, Lisbon, and left a note for her mother saying that had decided to catch a bus into Jewett City to visit a convenience store. It was about 4 p.m., a fine afternoon, so Wendy, dressed in a white T-shirt with black sleeves, blue shorts, blue socks and red trainers, decided to walk back home, south along Route 12. As she approached a rest area, a mere few hundred yards from the cul-de-sac that led to her house, a young man approached her. He was about six foot, in his early twenties, bespectacled, clean-shaven, dark-haired, slim, bookish-looking and wearing smart, casual clothes. He walked alongside her for a short distance trying to persuade Wendy to accept his invitation to attend a work's barbecue that evening. She politely refused. Several witnesses driving past would later recall seeing a man of this description briskly walking in the direction of a young woman, and one person noted a 'Japanese type of blue hatchback with a rear windscreen wiper' parked close by.

The following day, Wendy having failed to return home, her mother reported her missing, offering a $1,000 reward for any information regarding Wendy's whereabouts, and hundreds of police and local residents launched a search of the immediate area. Two days later, Wendy's half-naked body was found by a firefighter. The corpse was in dense woodland, partly hidden under branches and stones taken from an ancient stone wall. She had been raped and strangled.

Ross gave me two conflicting accounts of what he had intended to do that day. First, in an audiotaped interview with me he explained that before going to work he cut himself while shaving, and blood seeped on to the collar of his only clean shirt. After phoning in with the excuse that he was ill, he dressed himself in smart, casual clothes, and hung around his apartment, reading pornographic material and masturbating, after which he went for a drive. Later, when I interviewed him, this time on camera, he changed his story. He *had* gone to his office in Norwich, but the colleague he was working with had called in sick, so he went to a print shop to collect some flyers, then started to drive home, and that is when he spotted Wendy Baribeault walking along Route 12.

After swinging his car round and parking in the rest area, he hurried up to Wendy, and after she refused his invitation to go to a barbecue, Ross dragged her into nearby woods, where he rolled her over on to her stomach before strangling her. He ejaculated almost immediately, so he throttled her again. She struggled and kicked, and her body twitched. Michael had cramp in his hands as he fought to strangle the life out of his victim. When he stopped to massage his fingers, she heaved and squirmed under him until he reapplied his grip. Finally, a kick of her legs told him she was dead.

Here, published for the first time, is Ross's account of Wendy's murder.

'When I attacked her, I don't believe I was in control. I don't think I could have stopped. Ah, the very reason I say this is that there was a clear point to me after she was dead when I was feeling – well I wasn't really feeling anything. Uh, uh, I knew what was going on. I saw what was going on. It was more like watching the old films kids see in high school or elementary school. They have been played so many times, they are all spliced together, and it would be going along and it would jump. I'm not saying I wasn't there, or a multiple personality, or any of that kind of crap. I was there. I did it but I wasn't one hundred per cent there.

'It was the same with all the victims. There was nothing they could have said or done. It was me . . . it wasn't them. They were dead as soon as I saw them, I think.

'I felt like was on the edge, ya know. Like I was in one of those flytraps, an' the fly struggles but keeps sliding down. I felt I was right on the edge, Chris. It wouldn't take much to push me over . . . I was very frightened back then.'

Ross's words tailed off to a hush. For a few moments the interview room went deathly quiet. Somewhere along a corridor outside, a door slammed shut. Michael looked down at the floor. He seemed lost in another world . . . was this a sign of remorse? Then, in an instant, something switched on inside his head. 'Ya know, at the trial the doctor for the state got into a real mess,' Ross said. 'He got all confused about the marks around Baribeault's throat. He couldn't explain the multiple bruising. I thought this was real funny 'cos I knew that she had struggled and I had to reapply my grip several times 'cos my hands cramped up. Yes, I thought that was real funny.'

With that, Ross leaned back in his chair and laughed and laughed and laughed.

CONNECTICUT STATE POLICE DETECTIVE MIKE MALCHIK

'Ross is the most nondescript person,' Detective Mike Malchik, arresting officer, Connecticut State Police Serious Crimes Squad, said to me in 1994. 'Very non-threatening. He's very articulate. He's got a good personality. At the time of his arrest, many people were shocked. He worked in the insurance industry where he had a great deal of contact with the public, and no one expected, at least, that he was capable of these heinous crimes.'

* * *

Known for disarming suspects, using his boyish smile and supportive manner, former Connecticut State Police Detective Mike Malchik has used his investigative skills to crack even the toughest of homicide cases, including 40 or more considered 'unsolvable' by his colleagues. A legendary lawman in 'The Nutmeg State', Malchik often worked alone and unpaid on these jobs, such was his dedication to law enforcement. Tall, lean, blue-eyed and blond-haired he is one of those types women are meant to drool over at the movies – sadly for the ladies he has been married forever, with adoring children – and lives in an upscale home surrounded by meticulously clipped green lawns.

Mike is a very humorous fellow when making TV. I recall that after a very strenuous day of take after take, he turned to me and, with a wry smile, said, 'Okay, so where is the glamour in all of this ... the big limos and make-up? I thought champagne at least ... Where's my cheque?' And that is Mike Malchik the professional man – unassuming as the front man to the tenacious, serious crime investigator standing behind the façade.

Mike had already found strong links between the murders of Debra Taylor and Tammy Williams, and when he placed Robin Stavinsky and Wendy Baribeault into the equation, he knew he was looking for a sexual psychopath and a serial killer who would not stop murdering until he was arrested and brought to justice.

Mike Malchik's experience in homicide cases was such that he did not need to consult the FBI for advice, but to confirm his belief he spoke to a colleague at the National Center for the Analysis of Violent Crime, Virginia. Malchik knew what type of suspect he was looking for. He would be a young, dark-haired Caucasian male in his late twenties or early thirties. He would be of the 'white-collar' type, who worked in Norwich yet lived further south, and would frequently travel along Route 12 between his place of work and his home. Griswold was a good bet for the suspect's locus and now there was the extra bonus of knowing, thanks to the witnesses who came forth, that the man drove a blue car of foreign make.

Using what Mike calls 'basic common sense', he reasoned that whoever had murdered Wendy Baribeault would want to flee the crime scene and get home as quickly as possible, which bolstered his idea that the killer was a local man. He phoned the Vehicle Licensing Department and asked them for a printout of all vehicles, and their owners, in the area. For this service, the VLD charged the Connecticut State Police $12, which turned out to be a cheap investigative tool. When the list of some 3,600 cars rolled out of his fax machine, Malchik started looking for a blue, foreign make of car. Number 27 on the list was a vehicle owned by one Michael Bruce Ross who lived in Jewett City.

When detective Mike Malchik showed up unannounced on Thursday, 28 June, flashing his badge at the door of Ross's lodgings, Michael invited the cop in for coffee. It was only basic courtesy.

'You have a very nice home,' Malchik said.

'What were you expecting it to look like?' Ross asked. 'The Munsters'?'

Malchik had a few questions. 'That your blue Toyota out front?'

Ross answered in the affirmative.

'Where do you work, Mr Ross?'

Ross explained that he was an agent for the Prudential Insurance Company of America, in Norwich. That he had moved to Jewett City, in May.

The sleuth knew that the description of a blue car didn't exactly match that of Ross's vehicle. Malchik was looking for a hatchback with a rear wiper and, while Ross certainly had a blue Toyota, it was a sedan and had no rear wiper blade. After a few more moments of general conversation, Mike actually felt that the clean-cut and personable Ross could not have been a serial killer. Then, as he was about to draw a line through Ross's name and rejoin his colleague, Detective Frank Griffen, sitting outside in their car, Malchik was asked a question. Ross wondered if such a murderer would be declared insane and escape the electric chair if convicted? It was such a pointed enquiry that it prompted Malchik to pause at the door of Ross's sitting room, for a gut instinct now prompted him to ask Ross a question of his own. In the manner of the late Peter Falk, acting out his role as Columbo, Mike stopped as he was leaving and turned back to ask, 'What were your movements on Friday, 13 June, the day Miss Baribeault went missing?' Ross immediately reeled off his movements for that day almost to the minute, with the exception of the hour encompassing 4.30 p.m.

Seemingly satisfied, Malchik said goodbye for the second time, then as he walked down the path the penny dropped. Malchik thought it remarkable that anyone could recall his, or her, exact whereabouts, along with solid timings, two weeks after an event, so he reckoned that 13 June must have been a special day for Ross. Then there was the time when witnesses had seen Wendy walking along the road with someone resembling Ross following her. Ross had not mentioned the time around 4.30 p.m. Malchik stopped in his tracks and asked Michael what he had been doing on the two days either side of this critical date. Ross couldn't remember a thing. The detective was stunned, for the implication was now obvious: Ross had tried to alibi himself for the day of the murder, and in doing so had proved himself too clever for his own good.

Malchik then asked his suspect to accompany him to the nearby murder incident room, which had been set up in the nearby Lisbon Town Hall. Ross was not under arrest at this time and voluntarily agreed to go along for the ride. To him, being driven in an unmarked police car would be 'fun', so he changed into a white, short-sleeved shirt, and dark, lightweight slacks – the very same clothes that he had worn when he killed Wendy Baribeault – for the three-mile journey.

★ ★ ★

'There was nothing threatening about Michael Ross. No signal to anyone that there was a dark side … anything that they should be afraid of. He could conceal that until the time came for him to attack these innocent young women,' Detective Mike Malchik told me.

Once he was seated in the makeshift police interview room, Ross was soon rambling on about his life to the amiable cop. More used to listening than talking, Malchik was now privately convinced that he had a serial killer sitting in front of him. But in the bustling confines of the command post, obtaining a full confession was another matter entirely. At one point, just as Ross was about to make some serious admissions, a cleaner burst in and started to mop the floor. This unexpected intrusion broke the spell and Malchik had to begin coaxing his suspect again.

Suddenly, Ross asked, 'Mike, do you think I killed Wendy?'

Malchik said that he believed so and formally arrested Ross before giving him the Miranda Warning. Asked if he wanted an attorney present, Ross waived his legal rights and confirmed that he did not wish to consult a lawyer.

During a subsequent prison interview with me, Ross explained, 'I remember the detective coming to the door. He was looking for a blue hatchback with a rear wiper, and I didn't have a blue hatchback. I had a blue sedan with no wiper. And, uh, he was getting ready to leave, and I told him something. I don't remember exactly what I said, but something that made him pause. And he said he had better ask me a few more questions and then afterwards he was getting ready to go, an' I said something else, so I guess I didn't really want him to leave.'

Ross then went on to say, 'You know, it's not exactly the easiest thing in the world to do. You know, "Hello, Mr Police Officer, I killed a load of people." You know, it was hard for me. If you actually listened to the audiotape confessions, ah, it was very difficult for me to admit that I did it, and then I had one got out. Then, he would have to kinda get the next one out. Then I would talk about that one. Yes, it was hard at first saying I killed this one, or that one. I mean I told 'em about two they didn't know about [Leslie Shelley and April Brunais]. I mean they didn't even question me about them 'cos they thought they were runaways.'

When I asked Ross why he had confessed to the murders of Leslie Shelley and April Brunais when he hadn't even been asked about them, the killer complained. 'Well, the police said that there was something wrong with me, and there was a place called Whiting for insane criminals. Yeah, I fell for that one, an' I thought I was going to get the help I needed and that's what I wanted to hear. "Hey, you have got something wrong with you and we are going to do something about it 'cos the murders have to be stopped." Yeah, Malchik said all the right things, so I thought, "What the hell," and I gave 'em everything.'

To be fair to Mike Malchik, he did honour his promise to

Ross; the murders did stop, and the law eventually did something about Ross's problem – justice would later execute him!

NEW LONDON COUNTY STATE'S ATTORNEY C. ROBERT 'BULLDOG' SATTI

Windham County Prosecutor Harry Gaucher only charged Ross with the 1982 murders of Tammy Williams and Debra Smith Taylor. Whether it was because of lack of physical evidence to support the rape portion of an aggravated capital felony charge, which carried the death sentence, or Gaucher's anxiety about losing his case at trial, he allowed Ross to plead guilty solely to murder with a maximum tariff of 'life'. Sitting on Saturday, 13 December 1986, the trial judge sentenced Ross to two consecutive life terms. He should serve no less than 120 years behind bars.

The murders of Wendy Baribeault, Robin Stavinsky, April Brunais and Leslie Shelley, however, fell under the jurisdiction of a more tenacious prosecutor. New London County State's Attorney, C. Robert 'Bulldog' Satti, was of the 'hang-'em and whip-'em' brigade, and wanted to be the first prosecutor for decades to light up a convicted killer in Connecticut's under-used 'Ole Sparky'.

Father of five, C. Robert Satti, Sr was the New London County state's attorney from 1975 to 1995. Born Sunday, 15 April 1928, in New London, to Dr C. John and Dorothy Heffernan Satti, his father was a former Secretary of the State of Connecticut, his grandfather, Charles Satti, being one of the first Italians to arrive in New London. 'Bulldog' was educated at St. Mary's Grammar School, Bulkeley High School, the University of Notre Dame – where he was a 'Bengal Bouts' boxing champion – and Fordham

University Law School. He served in the United States Marine Corps during the Korean War and remained in the reserves attaining the rank of Major.

After returning to New London, he practised law with Justice Angelo Santaniello. He was then appointed as a police court prosecutor and later became an Assistant State's Attorney working with Edmund O'Brien. He was appointed the first full-time State's Attorney for New London County in 1975. He served in that capacity until his retirement in 1995, after 41 years as a prosecutor.

Although Satti had worked on countless cases, his wife, Maureen I. Griffen Satti, says that the Ross murders were amongst the most notable, and the ones that really affected the whole family as well. 'This one was very much part of my life, to be honest with you,' she recalled. Her son, former Mayor William Satti Jr, said, 'It was my father's life from 1984 until his passing in 2002.'

Speaking from the family home overlooking a cove near Ocean Beach Park, His widow explained that her husband would spend countless hours preparing for the case, including nights and weekends. He would meticulously take notes during the trial and use that information for more questioning the next day hoping to tie up any loose ends and prevent Ross from avoiding execution because of a mitigating factor. 'I travelled with my husband to Bridgeport almost daily,' she recalled, 'to watch him at work during the first trial. Because of the local publicity surrounding the case the prosecutors stayed in an hotel during the week.'

Maureen remembered that her husband was very concerned

about the victims' families, who had to drive a 142-mile round trip from eastern Connecticut to Bridgeport for the trial. Every evening, he would meet up with them after the day's testimony had finished. Satti knew that the families were emotionally wrecked by the killings and he feared one of the fathers might even try to shoot Ross when he entered the courtroom.

Satti explained to me during an interview at the New London County courthouse, that he knew that he was up against a death penalty statute that tipped the balance in favour of life imprisonment. But the attorney stuck to his guns; agreeing with Mike Malchik, he strongly believed that if ever there was a man worthy of 'the chair', it had to be Michael Bruce Ross. But, apart from the morality of executing a man in liberal Connecticut, there was something else to consider. 'Old Sparky' had not been used since Joseph 'The Chin' Taborsky had been 'electricised' in it on Tuesday, 17 May 1960, and if there ever was a botched execution that one was.

* * *

Taborsky, a gangster spree killer, dubbed by the media the 'Mad Dog' murderer, had waived all appeals and walked bravely to his death before offering to donate his eyes for medical research. He also told a rather superstitious fellow death-row inmate, called Benny Reid, that he would be reincarnated as a 'big fly'.

Reminiscent of that grim scene in the film *The Green Mile*, where Edward Delacroix is electrocuted, Taborsky was strapped down, the metal helmet, which looked like a mixing bowl, was placed over his head and a black mask draped over his face.

The execution itself at the old Wethersfield Prison took mere minutes: three 30-second jolts of 2,000 volts were poured into the victim's body. 'It was all very gruesome,' recalled the journalist Gerald Demeusy years later. 'Every hair on the guy went up in flames. I can't think of a case where we didn't have that. So, if you want to say that Taborsky burned to death, or want to say flames engulfed him, it's true. But that's the way it is with the electric chair. It touches off the hairs . . . on the head, on the legs and anywhere on the body. The other unnerving thing about it was that these guys were going through these spasms like they were coming back to life. Every time the executioner turned the rheostat wheel to give them another 30-seconds of juice, the guy would sort of come back to life. Then you have the fear that maybe they're not going to kill him.'

After three blasts of current, and constant thrashing around, Taborsky's heart was still beating. The doctor who was required to pronounce death said, 'This man is still alive.'

'Meanwhile,' Demeusy continued, 'the blue smoke reeking of burnt flesh and hair was descending, and all the reporters were sinking lower and lower in their seats to avoid breathing it in. My concern was, "Jesus, what if he comes back to life?" We sat there and the doctor kept checking his stethoscope for about two minutes, and finally said, "This man is dead," and when his shirt was torn open, his skin was blue. The witnesses couldn't scramble out of there fast enough.'

The other thing that Demeusy vividly remembered was, ' . . . the man who pulled the switch looked like Elmer Fudd [a Looney Tunes character]. He was bald-headed, slightly built, the last guy you would think was an executioner. According to the warden, he also did executions at Sing-Sing.' But this was not quite the end of the saga, for moments after Taborsky died, a scream came from one of the cells: there was a large fly on the ceiling of Benny Reid's cell. 'He was hospitalised for three months for psychiatric care,' Demeusy recalls, 'and his sentence was commuted to life.'

★ ★ ★

After Taborsky's execution, Connecticut's electric chair had been moved from Wethersfield Prison when it closed down in 1963, to the Osborn Correctional Institution, where it had since fallen into disrepair. A special room for the chair was built, but it was never connected to the power supply. Department of Corrections spokeswoman Connie Wilks, and other officials, explained that there was no one left in the state system who remembered how to carry out an execution. They didn't know how the electricity was fed into the 5-foot-tall oak chair, let alone how an occupant would be strapped into it, or how much voltage was required to execute someone. 'It may need readjusting,' Connie Wilks said with some degree of understatement.

After I visited Michael Ross in his cell on death row, I walked the few yards to the door that led into the execution suite. There, in the middle of a 12-by-19-foot concrete-block room, sitting on a rubber mat, was the chair with a black leather seat and headrest. Half-windows on one wall would allow witnesses to view an execution, and a severed black electrical cord trailed beneath the chair. Small fingernail gouges are visible on the arms, and on the right arm is scratched the word 'help'. Connie Wilks was anxious to point out that she didn't know the etching was there, adding, 'Convicts would not have had time to have done this.'

As it turned out, if they had wanted to electrocute Michael Ross, the state would have had to pay out at least $30,000 to make the chair serviceable, redecorate the witness viewing area and death house suite, and then find someone who knew how to use it. Finding someone to sit down in the chair would prove to be no problem, for Ross shared death row with a select group of other candidates, waiting in line.

For their part, the defence attorneys had to convince a jury that Ross was not legally responsible for the crimes to which he had confessed. Making their job tougher was the fact that Ross didn't qualify for an insanity defence. Moreover, the case had received so much pre-trial publicity that, in the summer of 1987, the venue was moved to Bridgeport, where the prosecution would argue that Ross was a rapist, a cold-blooded, calculating monster, who had planned his assaults and had murdered his victims simply to avoid being arrested and being sent to prison.

STITCH-UP AND COVER-UP

It is a rare thing for defence and prosecution psychiatric experts to agree on both a diagnosis and its ramifications, but if the Ross case was in any way unique, it was in that there was psychiatric consensus that he was a paraphiliac and suffering from sexual sadism, a mental disorder that resulted in a compulsion in Ross to 'perpetrate violent sexual activity in a repetitive way'.

Unknown to the trial jury, forensic psychiatrists, from both sides, had also agreed that the crimes committed by Ross were a direct result of the uncontrollable sexual aggressive impulses to which he was *also* prey, making him, in some way, a victim, too. Significantly, this was an extremely important factor, for although Ross was completely unaware of it at the time this was a consideration leaning favourably in his direction. But the prosecution, aware of the damage that could be caused by its own psychiatrist effectively giving evidence against the state by concurring with the defence, decided to present no psychiatric witness at all. This was a slippery move and gave State's Attorney, 'Bulldog' Satti, blue water to sail into. Hence, the jury was kept in the dark as to a probable mitigating factor that could have removed the threat of the death penalty from Michael Ross.

Satti was assisted in no small part by a close friend, the presiding judge, Judge G. Sarsfield Ford, with both men having graduated from the Notre Dame University. Judge Ford rolled his eyes, clipped his fingernails and read his mail as the defence psychiatrist gave his evidence at trial. His look of boredom demonstrated entirely inappropriate behaviour towards the defence team and their witnesses. He lashed out and badgered one of Ross's sisters when she testified as to the childhood abuse her brother suffered, firing questions at her, which amounted to an attempt to discredit her testimony.

A psychiatrist called Borden claimed that Ford would whisper disapproving comments to him when he took the stand for Ross. Dr Berlin was later quoted as saying: 'The doctors who were testifying to things that might have mitigated in Michael Ross's behalf were not dealt with in a polite and respectful fashion by the judge.' Dr Berlin later filed a complaint with the Judicial Review Council, but everyone closed ranks and the imputation against Judge Ford dismissed.

With the psychiatric consensus now reached, the state's only hope of obtaining a conviction and death sentence was to muddy the waters and inflame the jury members' passions so they would ignore any defence evidence of psychological impairment. In Ross's case, as one might expect, this was quite an easy thing to do.

Satti's suggestion to the jury was that Ross had been examined by a psychiatrist who had found him *not* to be suffering from a mitigating psychopathology, which was patently untrue. The state psychiatrist had, indeed, examined Michael Ross and had concurred, in every single respect, with his counterpart for the defence. Amazingly, the defence failed to ask why the state's psychiatric expert was not made available to testify. Had they done so, it would have become apparent that he had withdrawn from the case – a damaging admission for the prosecution.

In June 1987, after four weeks of testimony, the eight men and four women of the jury took just 87 minutes to convict Michael Ross of capital felony murder. At the penalty phase, three weeks later, it took them under four hours to prove that Connecticut's death sentence could be imposed. On Monday, 6 July, twenty days before his 28th birthday, Ross was condemned to death for killing Wendy Baribeault, Robin Stavinsky, Leslie Shelley and April Brunais.

During my investigation into the life and crimes of Michael Bruce Ross, I met most of the principal players, and one of them was Dr Robert B. Miller, the psychiatrist employed on behalf of the prosecution. He was clearly a shattered man. Dr Miller confirmed to me that he had, indeed, concurred with the psychiatrist for the defence's assessment over Ross's state of mind, and, in his report to the State's Attorney Robert Satti, a year before the trial, Dr Miller had concluded: 'Were a specific diagnosis be attached to Mr Ross's condition at the time of his offences, it would be in *DSM-111, 302.84, Sexual Sadism.*' In something of a climb-down, Dr Miller later added, 'notwithstanding this diagnosis, I believe that Mr Ross could still conform his behaviour to the requirements of the law.'

In simple terms, and bearing in mind that Michael Ross could become the first person to be electrocuted in Connecticut in decades, Dr Miller explained that he had suffered sleepless nights, having been influenced by the media reports of the case, and the awfulness of the crimes. This, he told me, had coloured and tainted his otherwise professional opinion. His conscience had weighed heavily on him, for his diagnosis could help a man into the electric chair. 'This was something,' Dr Miller said, 'I could not live with. If the state had its way, they might as well use me to pull the switch.'

To try to rectify his error of judgement and to clear his conscience, just two days before the trial Dr Miller wrote a letter to Judge Ford explaining his reason for having to withdraw from the case, but the judge refused to show this letter to the jury. In due course, this distasteful issue was brought before the State of Connecticut's Supreme Court for a ruling, and 'Bulldog' Satti and his team would come in for a roasting. For a man such as Robert Satti, who enjoyed 'neighbourly barbecues', this was an event he did not want to attend. This time around, instead of him taking meat off of the grill, he would become the prime cut.

An *amicus curiæ* (friend of the court) brief had been filed by a group of eminent psychiatrists from Connecticut. They were connected to neither the state nor the defence, but they became involved because – as the brief stated – there was 'concern that the psychiatric issues had been distorted at both the guilt and penalty phases of the trial'. They summed up their point of contention perfectly: 'By distorting Dr Miller's diagnosis thus leading the jury into believing that Mr Ross could control his behaviour, when in fact he and all the other psychiatric experts were of the view that Mr Ross could not, the court allowed the jury to be effectively misled.'

The Supreme Court decided that this amounted to 'constructive deceit', for the trial jury had been led to believe that there *was* a difference of opinion between the state and defence psychiatrists, when there was *not*. This resulted in: '. . . rulings that improperly excluded evidence, disingenuous summations, and instructions that allowed the jury to draw inferences that were insupportable,' said one irate judge. To any reasonable person, the only inference that could be drawn was that the state had rigged the case in their favour.

In July 1994, in their summation, the justices ruled in Ross's favour, to the effect that his illness, that of sexual sadism, was a mitigating factor after all. 'The state,' they said, 'was able to seize upon inflammatory connotations of the sexual sadism diagnosis to turn a legally mitigating factor into an aggravating factor . . . and the judgment of the court is reversed.' With the death sentences overturned, the court ordered a new penalty phase, one applicable to a natural life sentence.

With no state psychiatric experts to disagree with the defence, the law now pronounced that Ross had mitigation for his crimes; that he was suffering from overpowering, uncontrollable, sexual urges and, that all of the rapes and murders were one continuous act.

Of course, Ross claimed successfully that he was not only unable to control his sexual desires, but also the need to inflict suffering as well. In other words, he was a walking time bomb, requiring just the slightest jolt to set him off. But was there any real substance to his claims that the problem was like an intrusive roommate who lived inside his head? There is some sense in thinking that people like Michael Ross are, simply, 'wired up' all wrong.

WIRED UP ALL WRONG?

The hypothalamic region of the limbic system is a primitive and important part of the brain, and the hypothalamus serves the body tissues by attempting to maintain its metabolic equilibrium, thus providing a mechanism for the immediate discharge of tensions. It appears to act like an on/off sensor – on the one hand, seeking or maintaining the experience of pleasure and on the other, escaping or avoiding unpleasant, noxious conditions. Hence, feelings elicited by this part of the brain are very short-lived and may disappear completely after just a few seconds, although they may last much longer.

So the limbic system mediates a wide range of simple emotions. Because it controls the ability to feel pleasure and displeasure, it is able to generate and use these emotions to meet a variety of its needs, be they sexual, nutritional or emotional. That is to say, it can reward or punish the entire brain, and thus the individual. If, for example, the hypothalamus experiences pleasure, be it from satisfying a craving for chocolate or from satiating a desire for drugs or sex – even the need for sadistic sex and murder – it will switch on 'reward' feelings so that the person continues engaging in the activity desired. If it begins to feel displeasure, it will turn off the reward switch. But, if the switch jams halfway, so to speak, the limbic needs go unmet, and the individual will experience depression, anger or even homicidal rage.

The person who feels sexual desire and abstains may feel tension. Paradoxically, the only way to reduce this tension is by increasing it until orgasm, and thus tension release is obtained. Under normal circumstances, this would be considered acceptable. However, if satyriasis becomes linked with extreme sexual fantasies and sadism, a very different problem emerges altogether. Wrap this package up with an anti-social personality disorder, and an unstable situation is created which could erupt, for no apparent reason, at any time.

Even in perfectly normal people, emotions elicited by the hypothalamus are often triggered reflexively and without an understanding of the consequences. The hypothalamus seeks pleasure and satisfaction, and whether the stimulus is thirst or sexual hunger, the basic message from the hypothalamus is 'I WANT IT NOW!' There is no consideration for the long-term consequences of its acts because it has no sense of morals, danger, logic or right and wrong.

If the limbic system is physically damaged, feelings of love, hate, affection or even sexual responsiveness and desire may be abolished, or become severely abnormal. However, it is not necessary to suffer physical damage to this area to experience these types of altered responses, for electrical stimulation of the limbic centre can also cause feelings of violence, which can lead to murder. Moreover, if certain regions in the limbic system (such as the amygdala) are damaged, heightened and indiscriminate sexual activity can result, including excessive and the almost constant need for masturbation – a need which Ross exhibited to the end of his life. And, it is interesting to note that the FBI found that 81 per cent of the serial murderers they interviewed indulged in compulsive masturbation.

Like the hypothalamus, the pleasure principle, or the drive to fulfil needs and obtain pleasurable satisfaction, is present at birth. Indeed, for some time after birth the infant's search for pleasure is unrestricted and intense as there are no forces other than 'mother' and 'father' to counter it, or help it achieve its strivings. If the child's bonding with its mother is satisfactory, and it is brought up in a healthy environment, then the child goes through a healthy development process. If the opposite occurs, the child may be psychologically damaged beyond repair.

Put another way: imagine a complete amateur building a complex computer without any previous experience and little understanding of the complicated instruction manual. Inevitably in such a case, there will be a pile of bits and pieces left over, and when the machine is switched on it is bound to malfunction, and continue to produce erroneous calculations, no matter what inputs are entered via the keyboard. While the computer might appear normal from the outside, the electromechanical switching systems, and the machine's 'brain' inside are inherently flawed. For basic functions, it might work quite well some of the time, but it will break down when more complicated calculations are required of it. This seems to illustrate what had happened to

Michael Ross. From a very early age he exhibited many traits that indicated he was wired-up all wrong.

'I'M NOT AFRAID OF DYING'

During one of my interviews with Ross, he explained to me that he was not afraid of dying in the electric chair. He said that living was too good for him, but he was worried that, if the fateful day ever arrived, he would say the wrong thing, or show weakness in the face of death. He was also afraid of something he claimed was worse than death.

'I've always felt that I had to be in control of myself and, even to this day, I feel I need to be in control,' he explained. 'What scares me the most isn't prison, or the death penalty, but insanity. I'm scared of losing touch with reality. Sometimes I feel I'm slipping away, and I'm losing control. If you are in control you can handle anything, but if you lose it, you are nothing.'

When I asked if he had feelings of remorse for his crimes, Michael replied bluntly. 'Nope! I don't feel anything for them. I really wish I did. I don't feel anything. I feel really bad for the families. Like I can see Mrs Shelley, the mother of one of 'em girls I killed, on the witness stand crying. And, then there's Mrs, ah, I can't remember her name, but I can think of another one on the stand describing her daughter. She went to the morgue [to see the body]. But the girls themselves I feel nothing for, and I never have.'

Ross then explained why he hadn't turned himself in to the police when he started to commit his earlier offences, way back at Cornell University, when he knew he needed help.

'I made myself believe that it would never happen again, Chris.

And, I know it sounds hard, but looking back, I can't understand how I did it. It was a fluke because I really didn't do those things. Even sitting here now, I know if I was released I'd kill again. There's no reason to think otherwise. But I can't, as I sit here now, picture myself wanting to do that. I can't really see myself doing it. I mean, it's like being on different levels.'

When asked if he had any detailed memories of the murders, Ross chuckled, and then said:

'Yes and no! I used to fantasise over the crimes every day and night. I would masturbate to the point of, um, actually having raw spots on myself from the friction. I would bleed. It's weird. I get a lot of pleasure from it. It is a really pleasurable experience. But, when it's all over, it's a very short-term thing. I guess it's like getting high. You know I've never used drugs, but you can get high, then you come down and crash. That's almost how it is. It's not an easy thing to live with.'

An inevitable question was to ask him what had been going through his mind when he was raping and killing his tragic victims. Michael's reply was, 'Nothing.' But, after a moment's reflection, he contradicted the earlier reason why he killed, saying:

'That's what's so weird about this thing. Everybody seems to think, you know, the state's theory that I'm a rapist and I kill them so they can't identify me. Look, most of the time it's broad daylight. I mean, I'm not a stupid person. As sure as hell wouldn't do it that way. There was nothing going through my mind until they were already dead.

'And then it was like stepping through a doorway. And, uh, I remember the very first feeling that I had was my heart beating. I mean *really* pounding. The second feeling I had was that my hands hurt where I always strangled them with my hands. And, the third feeling was, I guess, fear, and the kind of reality set in and there was this dead body in front of me.

'And, again, I don't want to mislead you, Chris, because I knew what was going on, but it was like on a different level. I mean it was like watching it. And, after it was all over, you know, it kinda sets in, an' that's when I would get frightened an' stuff. I would hide the bodies and cover them up, or something.'

LIFE ON DEATH ROW

Before I visited Michael Ross in his cell, which was truly an ancient dungeon, with the bars and door painted a muddy brown, I had to pass through the general prison. Indeed, the entire inmate population was under lock-down, the only men out and about were cleaners, and even they had to put down their mops and press their noses against the walls when I passed them by. Eye contact from the prisoners was absolutely forbidden.

As each door was unlocked then locked behind us, we took a creaking lift to the second level, which housed the most violent and disruptive prisoners. The racket sounded like Bedlam. Yet another door opened and we climbed a flight of stairs where there was a door, upon which was crudely stencilled in white, 'DEATH ROW'. Only Ross and Robert Breton were 'at home'. Because of my visit, Sedrick Cobb, Ivo Colon, Richard Reynolds, Todd Rizzo and Daniel Webb had been given extra yard-time and were enjoying fresh air in a small exercise yard.

Robert Breton had been sentenced to death in 1989. He was convicted of two counts of murder and one count of capital felony murder for beating and stabbing to death his 38-year-old ex-wife, JoAnn Breton, and their 16-year-old son, Robert Jr. In the early morning of Sunday, 13 December 1987, Breton entered the Waterbury apartment his ex had rented after their divorce eleven months earlier. Surprising her while she slept, he slashed at her with a sharp, 5-inch knife and pounded her with his fists. JoAnn scrambled across the room. He ex-husband followed her and killed her by thrusting the knife through her neck, opening a major artery. Robert Jr. heard his mother's screams and ran into her room, where his father attacked him. Bleeding from his arms, hands and fingers, the lad tried to escape down a flight of stairs. But, his father pursued him, overtaking him at the bottom of the staircase and continuing the attack. Robert Jr. bled to death from a wound that severed his carotid artery. Police found him, clad only in his underwear, at the bottom of the stairs, his head propped against a wall.

Of the other death-row inmates, Sedrick Cobb was sentenced to death in 1991. The former deliveryman from Naugatuck was convicted of the rape and murder of 23-year-old Julia Ashe, whom he kidnapped from a Waterbury department store car park on Saturday, 16 December 1989. Cobb first flattened one of her car tyres using a valve stem remover and, when she returned, he offered to help her change the wheel, which he did. When he asked Julia for a lift to collect his own vehicle, she obliged. He then forced her, at knifepoint, to drive to a road where he raped her, following which he bound and gagged her with fibreglass tape and carried her to a concrete dam. He pushed her and she plunged 23 feet into the shallow, icy water below. She managed to free her hands by rubbing the tape across wire mesh protruding from the concrete and gouged her face trying in vain to remove the tape across her mouth. When she tried to crawl up the bank to safety, Cobb forced her, face down, back into the water. Her ice-encrusted body was found on Christmas Day.

Ivo Colon had been sentenced to death in 2000. He was convicted of capital felony murder for the beating to death of his girlfriend's two-year-old daughter, Keriana Tellado, in Waterbury. He killed the 32-pound girl by beating her head against a bathroom wall, holding her up by her hair when she could no longer stand. The child's mother, Virginia Quintero, who did nothing to stop the fatal beating, was later convicted of manslaughter, and in 2006 was sentenced to five years' imprisonment. She has since been released.

Richard Reynolds, a Brooklyn, New York crack dealer, was sentenced to death in 1995 for the murder on Saturday, 18 December 1992 of Waterbury police officer, Walter T. Williams. Officer Williams had stopped Reynolds, and when the cop went to search him, Reynolds pulled a gun from his pocket and shot the 34-year-old officer once in the head. Prosecutors proved that before firing, Reynolds bumped into Williams to see if he was wearing a bulletproof vest.

Todd Rizzo was sentenced to death in 1999. The 18-year-old former US Marine was convicted of killing 13-year-old Stanley Edwards, of Waterbury, with a 3-pound sledgehammer in September 1997, because he wanted to see what killing someone felt like.

Daniel Webb had been sentenced to death in 1991. He was convicted of kidnapping, attempted rape, and murder for the slaying of Diane Gellenbeck, a 37-year-old Connecticut National Bank vice president. Webb, driving a car he had borrowed from his girlfriend, abducted Diane from a downtown Hartford parking garage at midday on Saturday, 12 August 1989, while she was on her way to a meeting. He drove her to Keney Park, in the city's North End, attempted to rape her, and then shot her five times when she broke free and tried to run. Witnesses testified that the last shots were fired at close range as she crawled across the grass. Webb fired the final shot, point-blank, into her face.

★　★　★

Ross claimed that death row in Connecticut was not as rough as some other death rows, 'especially the ones down South, but it's no country club either,' he explained. His cell measured 7 foot by 12 – large by most prison standards – and was furnished with a metal bunk, a desk, and a combination toilet and sink. He would spend up to twenty-three hours a day alone in the cell, his only sight of the outside world through a three-inch by three-foot slot window, which boasted a view of the glinting razor wire fencing and recreation yard.

Connecticut death-row inmates eat all of their meals in their cells. The food is delivered in Styrofoam boxes with a plastic spoon – no knives, not even plastic ones, are allowed. Some of the main prison population eat their meals at tables in the dayrooms, 'like civilised men', complained Ross, but this is a privilege not afforded to death row inmates, I would learn.

The men are allowed one hour of outside recreation five days a week. The yard is approximately 20 foot square with 30-foot-high concrete walls and chain-link netting across the top. Not so much as a handball is allowed – the only activity for exercise is jogging in circles. Recreation begins at 8 a.m., which means that the men can only 'see' the sun on the walls, but 'officially' they are locked back up in their cells before the sun rises high enough that they can actually stand in its rays. However, during the period that I was interviewing Michael Ross, he always seemed slightly tanned, certainly brown enough to have a white area around his wrist where he had, until recently, been wearing a watch.

'The exercise regime is so poor,' lamented Ross, 'that only two of us go outside on a regular basis, no one else bothers.' So, the fact that Cobb, Colon, Reynolds and Webb were having extra 'yard time' when I visited death row proved to be a rare event indeed. I sensed that a few strings had been pulled, with an extra perk or two thrown in to entice this deadly foursome into the yard – we were a British film crew after all! Since then, death-row inmates socialising in the yard has been stopped. Today, it is 'individual recreation only'.

Out-of-cell time for these men was between 6 p.m. and 8 p.m. in a small dayroom on 'the mile'. The condemned could use this period to make reverse-charge telephone calls – two 15-minute calls a day – and death-row inmates have absolutely no contact with other inmates in the institution. Death rows throughout the United States are effectively Super-Max units within Super-Max facilities. No one has ever escaped from Connecticut's death row.

When Michael Ross first arrived at Somers, he was placed in the 'Death Cell', a cell directly adjacent to the execution chamber intended to house a condemned man during the last twenty-four to forty-eight hours before meeting his Maker. Ross made much of this, complaining:

'A guard was posted at a desk directly in front of my cell for twenty-four hours a day, seven days a week. I had absolutely no privacy. I got dressed in front of the guard. I used the toilet in front of the guard. Everything I did, including masturbating, was in front of the guard. And everything was written down in my very own "Death Row Log Book". What time I woke up in the morning. What time I ate my meals and brushed my teeth. Everything. You cannot imagine what that absolute and total lack of privacy does to you. You cannot imagine how it begins to destroy your very sense of humanity, like you are an animal in a cage on display at a zoo. No wonder I spiralled into a clinical depression and had visions of my own execution.'

Warden Robert J. Kupec, who died 27 August 2000, justified this initial intensive scrutiny of Michael Ross to me in 1994:

'Mr Ross was and still is, by his own admission, a highly unpredictable and dangerous person. His own lawyers claimed that he is insane. When he arrived here, he was the first man to have been sentenced to death for years. He was the state's only convicted serial killer and a high-profile inmate. Our responsibilities at this facility focus on ensuring the safety of our correctional staff and the welfare of our inmates. With Mr Ross, there was the very real risk of self-harming or even attempting to commit suicide. Back then, our death row unit was empty. Yes, I agree that housing him so close to the electric chair may not have been appropriate, but for the reasons I have already explained, we had financial constraints in place. Why police an entire unit when just the one cell was more economical?'

Michael was kept under personal 24/7 observation for almost a year, then, as death row filled, the guard was replaced with a CCTV system that monitored the inside of his cell, 'for my privacy,' laughed Ross. 'In reality,' he added, 'it was because I wasn't a disciplinary problem, and it was cheaper to monitor me by closed circuit television at a desk at the front of the unit than to post a guard on a single inmate for 24 hours a day . . . And, actually, it gave me less privacy, for at the other end of the camera was a monitor viewed by anyone who happens to pass by, including female officers. The camera lasted years before I was finally able to convince them that it was an unnecessary invasion of my privacy. Now I am on death row proper with the other guys who have come here. The guards still make their rounds every half-hour or so, but at least now I know about when to expect him, or her, so I can time when to use the toilet, get dressed, or jack-off.'

Ever boastful, Michael Ross claimed that he had 'received more publicity than any other inmate in the prison system. Naturally, I stood out,' he said, adding, 'prison is a bad place to stand out.' In a rambling account of his alleged inmate infamy, this is what he said in his essay *A Time to Die*.

Most people here are anonymous. Few people know who the other inmates are or what they did, so they are not judged by their crimes, but rather by what kind of people they are. If they are jerks, they tend to be treated as jerks. If you stay by yourself and don't bother anyone, you tend not to be bothered. But if you stick out, everyone jumps on you. For some people it's a way to deal with their own insecurities – by putting you down they are boosting themselves up. For some people it's a way to divert attention from themselves.

I've found that those who yell 'Tree Jumper' the loudest are quite often rapists themselves.

Then there are those who join in to be part of the crowd. These are the ones who are friendly when they are alone with you, but suddenly can't stand you when others are criticising you. And finally, there those who are just so damn miserable that they can only feel better by trying to make others miserable too.

Not everyone fits into one of these categories. I have made some friends. Most of them are people who don't believe everything they read in the newspaper or hear through the grapevine. They are the ones who tend to approach people with an attitude of 'how you treat me is how I treat you'. Unfortunately, people like these are few and far between in prison. But at times they can be like a breath of fresh air. When someone simply says, 'Hey, Mike, how's it going?' or 'Hey, Mike, hang in there,' it can mean a lot, especially through the rough times.

And, there have been rough times. I have received a great deal of harassment from my fellow inmates, and also from the guards. Whenever I went somewhere in the prison, to medical or visiting, there were always the stares, the whispers, the threats. 'Hey, man, do you know who that is?' 'He's the one who killed all those girls.' 'I wish they would let that SOB into population, then we could teach him a lesson'. 'Ripper!' 'Child rapist!' 'Hey, Tree Jumper, we're gonna kill you!' 'If it was my sister, you would already be dead.' And the ever-present sound of mimicking the electric chair: 'Bzzzzzzzzzzzzz'.

Any reader of these claims made by Michael Ross may be forgiven for believing every word. Certainly, much of the US media did by publishing his account, without contradiction. However, the truth is somewhat different as I can now confirm.

Upon his arrival at the Osborn Correctional Institution, Ross was classified and housed as 'Security Level 5'. For the initial years of his incarceration, he was completely isolated from any other prisoner held at the facility. He was several years into his term before another inmate joined him on death row – Robert Breton (No. 163703), who arrived on 15 December 1987. Breton's CT Department of Corrections 'Inmate Records' show Breton to be a well-behaved, compliant inmate, who kept himself to himself. The other death-row men who joined Ross similarly appeared to have accepted their fate. 'There has never been any trouble on my row,' maintained Warden Kupec, when I interviewed him. 'Any allegation that Mr Ross has been subjected to inmate, or correctional staff abuse, is only in his mind.'

That Michael Ross was abused and threatened by inmates from the general prison population as he attended visits from his attorney, family, and me, can also be dismissed as pure fiction, and complete rubbish for the following reasons.

When a condemned inmate is moved around the prison, it entails a *complete* 'lock-down' of any inmate not performing highly monitored duties. The routes from death row to the medical or interview room, are planned with military precision. The very few inmates Ross *might* have seen en route would have been trustee cleaners, who were ordered by his guard escort to, 'Stop. Drop that mop, an' nose against that wall!' 'Trustees' have earned the very much-valued privilege of being allowed to work 'out-of-cell' and gain extra TV time, along with other bonuses. Trustees also provide a conduit between the prison population and their guards so that grievances can be easily resolved by keeping 'things sweet'.

At every visit I made to see Michael, it took at least two hours before the facility was 'sanitised'. And, contrary to Michael's claims, death-row inmates – considered as 'Dead Men Walking' – are given the highest respect amongst general prison populations throughout the US of A.

Having walked to many a death row, and back, in penitentiaries throughout America, I can testify that every door, every corridor, every stairwell and every lift is monitored every second by CCTV. While in transit around the prison, each death-row inmate is leg-ironed and cuffed to a body-belt then chained to a guard, while other officers surround him every step of the way. And, this was the procedure with Michael Ross. He would shuffle along surrounded by four immaculately dressed officers wearing starched shirts, knife-edge creased trousers and spit-and-polished boots, and every moment of CCTV footage is made available to an inmate's attorney, should it be required to prove an allegation of abuse by officers or inmates. As Warden Kupec told me: 'Our responsibilities at this facility focus on ensuring the safety of our correctional staff and the welfare of our inmates' – and I know this to be true. However, even though it was clear that Michael Ross was inventing psychological and physical abuse that could not have happened, he went on to claim:

I have been assaulted on several occasions, I've been hit with bars of soap, doused with cups of urine and faeces, had my food messed with by the guards, who spat on it or put hairs in it. I've had to go to the free-world hospital twice. Once I was stabbed fifteen times by an inmate with a pair of barbershop scissors taped to his hand. I had been set up by a guard, who let a non-death-row inmate out to attack me. The other time, I was beaten by an inmate in a stairwell and received stitches. Fortunately, for me, things have settled down considerably for me since those early years. I still get the stares and the occasional comment, but things are much quieter these days.

It was now clear to me that Michael was living in his own fantasy world; for when I asked him to show me the scars of this alleged scissor attack, he refused. 'You'll see the photos of the stabs in my medical notes,' he said. I had full access to his medical papers and there was nothing there to confirm his claim. So, perhaps Michael lived in a world where his father was not so bad at all? Perhaps he had a tough upbringing, and maybe his mother was all he claimed she was – the mother from hell. And, I did write to Michael's father to try and iron out a few issues and received no reply.

Ross was proud of his 'house' – the name convicts give to the tiny spaces they live in. It was piled high with books and writing materials; indeed, he boasted about the fact that he had been allocated the empty cell next to his, where more of his books were stored.

He explained that when first came to death row his father had bought him a colour television set, on which he could receive six local broadcast stations. He now had a typewriter that he was using to submit to various publications – mostly anti-death-penalty pieces, but more recently he had branched out into more spiritually based articles. He claimed that he was now a devout Catholic, regularly meeting two priests over the years and saying the rosary each morning. He told me how he was translating reading material into Braille for the blind, sponsoring an impoverished child from the Dominican Republic. He bragged about the dozens of pretty young women who courted his attentions, one of whom was as gorgeous as a starlet. She had even signed her photograph, 'With love'. Her letters indicated that she would marry Michael in a flash, but he would have probably strangled her in an instant.

'Look, Chris,' he said, waving a large bundle of letters and envelopes in the air. 'Women, women, everywhere, but not one to fuck and not one to kill.' Then he laughed. 'But I did have a fiancée,' he said. This was a Susan Powers from Oklahoma who broke up with him in 2003, but continued to visit him right up until his execution – in fact she witnessed it.

With a white towel around his neck, which he used frequently to wipe his forehead and hands, he pointed to his bunk set against the far wall. 'That's where I escape into the real world outside,' he said. 'I put my Walkman headphones on and listen to my music. They say that music soothes the savage soul, and classical music does relax me. I spend many hours listening to this music with my eyes closed, and then I am away, flying like a bird. It is how I cope with life here.'

THE OBNOXIOUS ROOMMATE

Michael Ross was not unique among the serial killer breed but, to his credit, during the period I had been corresponding with him, and throughout the visits I made, it became apparent that he was struggling to understand why he had been driven to commit such terrible crimes on young women. Indeed, to the very end, when it was obvious that the thing he feared most – insanity – had all but taken him over, he strove to understand the forces that propelled him into such severe antisocial behaviour in the first place. In fact, at one time during his incarceration he volunteered for a series of treatments, which included chemical or surgical castration – the latter being refused by the state.

Many acknowledged experts seemed to believe that the castration process could separate the beast from the decent Michael Ross, a sort of chemical version of religious exorcism, if you will. Then, when refused castration by any means, for a lengthy period Michael was prescribed Depo-Provera to reduce his enormous sex drive. And, when I started researching this drug, things became very ominous, indeed, for he was being used as a human guinea pig with a nod from one of the largest drug manufacturers in the world.

In short, Depo-Provera is a long-acting reversible hormonal contraceptive birth control drug that is injected at 150 milligrams every three months, and its side effects are numerous, and as various, if abused. Nonetheless, the highly respected John Hopkins Hospital latched onto Ross's condition and Ross became this willing guinea pig. He started receiving 700 milligrams weekly. In men, Depo-Provera significantly reduces the body's natural production of the male sex hormone, testosterone. For some reason, whether because of some abnormal biological hook-up in his brain, or some sort of chemical imbalance, Ross claimed the treatment was affecting his mind more adversely than the average male's mind.

At the same time, Ross was also prescribed Prozac, a powerful anti-depressant and, as one might expect, the cocktail of these two drugs certainly reduced his abnormal sexual urges. Unfortunately, excessive use of the Depo-Provera caused him to balloon in weight by several stone, the result being that he suffered pathological changes in liver function and hormone levels and his depression, quite understandably, reappeared.

Before these drugs were prescribed, Ross claimed that he masturbated constantly. Once, when in the company of a female nurse, he experienced an overwhelming desire to kill her. In an interview with this author, Ross said:

I had been having thoughts and urges of hurting this one young woman in particular, a nurse who had always gone out of her to help me. She always had a smile, and was always friendly to me, even though she knew who and what I was. Here was someone I liked, and it was tearing me up inside. She had always helped me and how did I repay her kindness? By wanting to rape and strangle her. I felt uncomfortable whenever she was around, and I felt so guilty and ashamed that I could hardly look at her. Fortunately nothing ever happened, and she never found out what was going through my mind. Could I have actually killed her? Yes! It could have easily been the wrong time for her and the right moment for me. But then a door opened and we walked out. Thinking about it now, she was a bit overweight for my taste, anyway.

Ross added, 'You know that everybody has had a tune that plays over and over again inside their heads, Chris. An' if you have this tune that plays all day, over and over, it can drive you nuts. An' just imagine having thoughts of rape an' murder, an' you can't get rid of it. Well, just like the tune, it'll be driving you nuts, 'cos no matter what you do to get rid of that tune, it's going to stay in your head. And, that's how I am. I don't want these thoughts.'

When I asked Michael if he thought this tune was, in reality, the monster, he replied very candidly:

'No, I think he's separate. He goes to sleep for a while and, uh, you never know where he's gone, and that's very true. I mean, sometimes he's there, and especially with the Depo-Provera, I can feel him back there –' he touched the back of his head – 'I don't know how anybody is going to understand this, but he used to be always in the front of my mind, and always intruding, like an obnoxious roommate, always butting into your business and you can't get rid of him.'

In a letter to me, and repeated in his essay A Time to Die, Ross described what happened to him when he became used to the Depo-Provera before it was withdrawn because of the side effects:

A few months after I started to receive my weekly injections, my blood serum testosterone levels dropped below prepubescent levels. During the last month my level was 12 ng/dl, with my normal range being 260–1,250 ng/dl; and as this happened, nothing less than a miracle occurred. My obsessive thoughts, urges, and fantasies began to diminish. I would do anything to clear my mind.

What Depo-Provera did was to move that obnoxious roommate down the hall to his own apartment. The problem was still there, but it was a whole easier to deal with because he wasn't always in the foreground. He didn't control me any more because I was in control of him. It was an unbelievable sense of freedom. It made me feel as if I were a human being again, uh, instead of some sort of horrible monster. For three years I had a sort of peace of mind.

'The medication gave me some relief but my body has adjusted to it now, and the thoughts and sexual urges have returned,' he said. 'Now, my obnoxious roommate has moved back in and things seem to get worse because now I saw what it was like without him. Today, I feel like a blind man from birth who was given eyesight as a gift, but it was soon taken away. It's really hard to understand what is normal for everybody else if you've never had it yourself.'

There was an alternative medication to Depo-Provera, but it lacked Federal Drug Administration (FDA) approval as a treatment for sex offenders, so the Department of Corrections refused to approve its use. From Ross's past medical history it was his high testosterone levels that had been the cause of his paraphiliac urges. 'Get that testosterone out of my bloodstream,' Ross argued, 'so that it can't reach my mind and I'm okay. It took more than a year of fighting by good people in the Mental

Health Department before I was allowed to receive the alternative medication, a monthly shot of Depo-Lupron, which I have been receiving to date.'

Michael Ross also believed that he was a victim, a victim of an 'affliction' no one would want. In his essay, he wrote:

One of my doctors told me that I am, in a sense, a victim. And sometimes I do feel like a victim, but at the same time I feel guilty and get angry for thinking that way. How dare I consider myself a victim when the real victims are dead? How dare I consider myself a victim when the families of my true victims have to live day to day with the pain of the loss I caused?

I asked Ross, what was an affliction? So what if he was really sick? Did that really make any difference? Did this absolve him of his responsibilities for the deaths of six totally innocent women and two little girls? Did this make his victims any less dead? Does this ease the pain of their families?

Michael went quiet and looking down at the floor, he quietly said 'No,' before adding: 'I close my eyes and I see the families of the women I killed. Even though my trial was over a decade ago, I can't make the visions go away. I can see Mrs Shelley on the witness stand testifying about the last time she saw her daughter alive. I can see the agony in her face and hear the pain in her voice as she described how she and her husband searched for their daughter, and I can vividly recall how I actually saw them searching along the roadway after her death. At the time I didn't know who they were, but I knew whom they were searching for.

'I close my eyes and I am haunted by the vision of Mrs Stavinsky on the witness stand testifying how on Thanksgiving Day she had to go to the morgue to identify her daughter's body. She was hurt bad. She testified as she broke down and cried. She was hurt real bad.

'It is hard for me to close my eyes and not see these people as they appeared during the court proceedings. I can still, eleven years later, very clearly see how they looked at me; I can still feel their anger and hatred. I tried very hard to pretend none of this bothered me. I put up a façade of nonchalance to show that nothing was getting to me. I intentionally chatted and joked with my lawyers and with the sheriff's deputies as if I didn't have a care in the world. But, although I tried very hard not to show it, I did see the families of my victims. And, it is their faces, their pain, that haunts me today.'

Ross said that he wished he knew how to tell the families how sorry he was, but there were no words to describe how he felt:

How do you tell someone you are sorry when you have stolen something so very precious from them? How do you tell them you are sorry when those words sound so inadequate that you are ashamed to even speak in their presence for fear of making things worse? I cannot even face them, never mind ask for their forgiveness. And, while I would really like them to understand what happened and why, I don't expect they will ever truly understand the insanity that drove me to kill their loved ones.

And that is the big question: was I really insane? The big

question that everyone is all riled up about is a question that in the end may not matter at all. Whether I was sane or insane can't change the facts of what happened, can't bring anyone back, can't ease the families' pain. And, it can't cleanse my guilt, or wash the blood off my hands. It can't change anything, or absolve anything.

I think that this is part of the reason why I volunteered for execution.

LIVING IN LIMBO LAND

For years, Michael Ross existed in a state of limbo because the Connecticut Supreme Court had reversed his death sentence after having found the one mitigating factor in this killer's antisocial behaviour. But he was not off the hook just yet. Following the evidence Ross gave to me on camera concerning the post-death sodomising of Leslie Shelley, in September 1994, I spoke to the soon-to-retire State's Attorney, Robert 'Bulldog' Satti, who obtained a copy of the film tape, and he flipped, going straight back to the courts to demand yet another trial for this disgusting offence.

I have been asked many times about how I reacted to this sickening confession blurted out by Michael Ross, and my answer has always been the same. 'I did not react at all, for had I done I would have played right into this killer's hands.' He wanted to shock me . . . to gain some kind of emotional control over me . . . that's what psychopaths thrive on. And, when one does not respond in the way these people want, they talk some more, and some more, until they are all talked out.

Generally, for his part, Ross was now volunteering for

execution, all of which confused matters further; the legal consensus being that nobody wants to die, so volunteering to be executed must prove that he was insane. 'I need to get it over with,' Ross explained. 'I don't want to put the victims' families through another court case again.' This invites the question, why did he allow his attorneys to argue the mitigation issue in the first place?

But with the dread spectacle of the botched Taborsky execution not far from their minds, would Connecticut execute their only convicted serial killer? The general thought was 'No!' Of course, at that time the death penalty was firmly on the statute book, but finding the will to use it was another matter. As a retired judge explained, 'Ross will probably outlive everyone else involved in his case. If he really wants to die that bad, then he should kill himself.' But help was on the way to assist Ross in his bid to be executed.

Satti had just about come to terms with the lashing he had received from the Connecticut Supreme Court Justices, but now in the knowledge that Ross had committed yet another heinous crime on Leslie Shelley after she was dead, the retired state prosecutor worked tirelessly with the killer for four years to fashion an agreement that would allow the death penalty to be imposed without going through another full-blown penalty hearing. As far as Satti was concerned – and his blood was boiling – if Ross wanted to die he would do all he could to help him, even to the extent of strapping the killer into the chair, then lighting him up.

That agreement was eventually signed off on Wednesday, 11 March 1998. However, on Saturday, 1 August 1998, Satti and

Ross hit a brick wall when a Superior Court judge rejected the agreement because he found it, 'unsettling that the prosecutor would work with Michael Ross and his wish to be put to death without more scrutiny'. The judge ruled that '. . . shortcuts on procedure where an individual's life hangs in the balance cannot be tolerated under our criminal justice system. It is unconstitutional.'

Previously, on 25 September 1994, one of the days throughout that month that I interviewed Michael Ross, he promised me that he would write to the prosecutor and literally beg to be executed. Michael kept his word, for that evening he typed a letter to C. Robert Satti, which said in part:

There is no need for the penalty hearing to go forward. There is no need and no purpose served in unnecessarily opening old wounds. There is no need and no purpose served in inflicting further emotional harm or distress on the families of my victims. I do not wish to hurt these people further – it's time for healing.

I had volunteered for execution precisely to avoid the situation that we currently find ourselves in. And I am willing to hand you the death penalty 'on a silver platter' on the condition that you will work with me to get this over with as quickly and painlessly as possible. There is no need to drag the families through more lengthy and disturbing court proceedings. Please allow me to go into the courtroom to admit my actions; to accept responsibility for my actions, and to accept the death penalty as punishment for those actions. I'm not asking you to do this for me, but for the families involved, who do not deserve to suffer further and who, in some small way, might gain a sense of peace of mind by these actions and my execution.

COMING DOWN TO THE WIRE

Michael Ross and his fellow death row inmates were transferred the few hundred metres from Osborn Correctional Institution to the newly opened Northern Correctional Institution in 1995. Over the next decade, and at a cost of millions of dollars of taxpayers' money, Ross went through several more court appearances, every time pleading to be executed.

On Wednesday, 6 October 2004, Ross fired his public defenders and hired T. R. Paulding, who had been his standby counsel in the mid-1990s. He then told New London Superior Court Judge Patrick Clifford that he wanted to waive further appeals and proceed to his execution. Judge Clifford questioned Ross at length about his knowledge of the appeals still open to him and, now satisfied that the prisoner had his wits about him, set Wednesday, 26 January 2005, as the execution date.

That January, Michael Ross's father, Daniel, and his sister, now Donna Dunham, entered the fray, issuing two separate lawsuits. Asserting themselves as 'next friends', Dan Ross and Donna Dunham first applied for writ of habeas corpus *allegedly* on Michael's behalf to block the execution, despite the fact that Michael had continually stressed that he wanted to die. On Friday, 7 January, US District Judge Christopher F. Droney rejected the application out of hand.

Subsequently, in the same US District Court on 25 January – and just a day from the execution – in response to a similar petition by Gerard A. Smyth, Chief of the Connecticut Office of the Public Defender, the court granted a stay. The Supreme Court overturned this stay in a 5–4 vote. The game was back on.

With the hours ticking down, Dan Ross then brought an action against various Connecticut officials asserting a constitutional right not to be deprived by the state of his association with his son, and alleging that the prison's conditions had made Michael incompetent to waive further proceedings. Added to which, Dan Ross argued, the execution would cause a wave of suicide attempts among other traumatised Connecticut prisoners. Attorney Mike Fitzpatrick claimed that Michael Ross was suffering from 'Death Row Syndrome'; essentially a condition that develops over a long period of time and is the product of sensory deprivation. 'If the government is going to kill someone,' he argued, 'they had better be sure he's in the right mind to make that choice.'

For my part, I had followed the mental and physical deterioration of Ross over the past years and he was now a shadow of his former self. Long gone was the 'tan' he enjoyed way back. His skin was almost transparent white. There was no life left in his eyes. What cynical humour he once had, had died. He was most certainly a 'Dead Man Walking'.

Attorney General Richard Blumenthal called the last-ditch lawsuits frivolous and said they 'seemed designed simply to derail or delay the criminal justice process, which should go forward to conclusion for the sake of all our citizens, most particularly the victims' families.' In a television interview with *Fox 5 News*, he added, 'I have great personal doubts about Death Row Syndrome or segregated housing units, but a court will have to determine whether this has so impacted Mr Ross's competence of waiving his rights by agreeing to die.' Then, just hours before he was scheduled to be strapped down onto the gurney, in another bizarre twist worthy of a novel, Ross's lawyer T. R. Paulding called off the execution after a searing telephone conference with a federal judge who threatened his law licence and questioned if Ross was really driven by despair over years of segregation. Paulding, it seemed, was under suspicion of a conflict of interest for not questioning his client's competency more thoroughly.

On Thursday, 10 February 2005, the Superior Court appointed Thomas J. Groark, Jr, as special counsel to investigate and present evidence that Ross was not competent to waive his appeals, but the new six-day evaluation in April led to another finding of competency. The findings were:

Inmate Ross's decision [to waive his right to further postconviction relief] is knowing and intelligent . . . his decision not to seek further appeals is both competent and voluntary. It was made un-coerced and made in full understanding of the significance and consequences of that decision . . . The record demonstrates that in this court [Supreme Court] and elsewhere, the rights of Michael Ross have been afforded extensive due process protections irrespective of whether he has sought or even affirmatively resisted such efforts. And, as the state continues to concede, Ross can, at any moment prior to his execution, reverse course and invoke his right to seek further proceedings to overturn his conviction or death sentence.

As if to underscore his wish to be executed, the court read out an affidavit submitted by Michael Ross: 'I wish to make it clear that I do not authorise, endorse, concur in, or approve of any legal petitions filed in any court anywhere in the time remaining between the execution of this affidavit and the moment of my execution unless they are filed by me or my attorney T. R. Paulding Jr.' Simply put, Ross was telling his father and sister to mind their own business and allow him to decide his own fate.

After 18 years on death row, Michael Bruce Ross's execution date was set for 2.01 a.m., Friday, 13 May. 'Old Sparky' had long since gone. Ross would be strapped to a lethal injection gurney and receive 'The Goodnight Juice', but if Michael thought that he had got his sister and father out of his hair, he was wrong.

'TURN ROSS INTO MOSS'

More legal drama started around 10.30 a.m., Thursday, 12 May, when Judge Droney refused to grant a temporary execution restraining order and rejected Donna Dunham's bid to intervene. She then instructed her lawyer to appeal to the US Second Circuit Court of Appeals in Manhattan. Those appeals were heard at 2.30 p.m., using an elaborate network of video relays connecting three locales: the appeals court in Manhattan, a small conference room equipped with monitors at the Hartford federal courthouse and a similar room in a federal court in Vermont, where Appellate Judge Peter W. Hall resided. At about 5.30 p.m., the Second Circuit rejected any appeals; however, appeals soon followed in the US Supreme Court, and all parties involved in the execution countdown remained on tenterhooks until just after 11 p.m.

According to a Connecticut Department of Corrections

spokesperson released to the media, most of Ross's last day was spent seeing visitors. He awoke around 5.45 a.m., and had a breakfast of oatmeal and grapefruit. He watched television and read newspapers until 8.10 a.m., when he was moved to the execution suite – a series of four contiguous rooms consisting of: the holding cell; the execution anteroom, in which the equipment used to carry out the punishment of death by continuous intravenous lethal injection is kept; the execution enclosure housing the gurney, and the witness observatory. He took with him a Bible, a book of verses, candy and a coffee cup. The holding cell resembled his former open-barred cell except that it was encased in Plexiglas with a circle of holes drilled midway down the front of the door so he could communicate back and forth. He was not allowed even to touch his visitors, however – previously he had at least been able to grip a visitor's hand. In an allusion to the cannibal psychiatrist in the film *The Silence of the Lambs*, Ross joked with visitors about the 'Hannibal Lecter' cell. Only priests were allowed physical contact – necessary so they could administer Holy Communion, which Ross received at 9 a.m. Later he received his last rites.

For lunch, he ate a cheeseburger and hash browns. At 3 p.m. he chose his last meal: nothing special – he wanted what all the other inmates would be having – 'turkey à la King with rice, mixed vegetables, white bread, fruit and a beverage'.

By now, a team of six primary officers (the Strap Down Team), along with a further six officers to assist if needed, plus the executioner – a medically trained officer to insert intravenous catheters into the appropriate veins – and a physician, who would certify death, were silently gathering close by. They had been practising many times over the past months and could deal with any eventuality that might occur. Now the prison went into complete lockdown and all inmates were confined to their cells. Outside, all of the towers were manned, and, to reduce the possibility of any confrontations, the Department of Corrections set up separate gathering areas for pro – and anti-death penalty groups.

Around 9 p.m. anti-death demonstrators gathered for a two-hour interfaith prayer vigil. At midnight, demonstrators on both sides would be permitted to march within 50 feet of the prison. High above them hovered 'Trooper One', the Connecticut State Police helicopter. It was prepared to chase away any aircraft that approached within 1,000 feet of the prison.

Around sunset, protestors, holding their up anti-death-penalty banners in the stiff breeze, were approaching the prison after marching for five days from a former colonial site at Gallows Hill, Trinity College, Hartford, where many of the Salem witches were executed. [Source NY *Times*/*Newsday*/*Hartford Courant*] 'Long story short, killing is wrong in any form,' 26-year-old Christine Elkovich commented succinctly. A 20-year-old student at St Michael's College in Vermont, Rachel Lawlor, was in the middle of her exams but felt compelled to come down and show her opposition to the death penalty. 'It's hard to believe it's really happening,' she said. 'It's hard to believe that Connecticut is murdering someone.'

Along the road that ran past the prison complex, perched at the top of a grassy slope about a mile from the Massachusetts border, drivers hooted and shouted their approval or disapproval as they passed groups of prison guards and police.

Robert Nave, director of the Connecticut Network to Abolish the Death Penalty, who led the march, also told the *New York Times*, 'A serial killer should not be allowed to dictate public policy. Michael Ross is totally in control,' adding, 'Because the crimes of Michael Ross are so heinous, people often confuse us with being advocates for him. We are fighting against poor public policy, which is state-sponsored homicide.'

Among the sombre protestors was Attorney J. Ullmann, head of public defenders in New Haven County. The previous year, Ullmann had defended a multiple murderer, Jonathan Mills, who was facing the death penalty and had succeeded in getting the death sentence commuted to life imprisonment without parole. Ullmann said people still could not believe it was happening. 'It's just that they're shocked. To me, as a human being, I feel I have an obligation to be here and help out. We know we're on the right side of this issue. To say it's the law – well, so was slavery at one time. This is another human rights issue and eventually we will prevail.'

Among those who had marched from Gallows Hill was 58-year-old Elizabeth Brancato from Torrington, whose mother had been murdered in 1979. To her the execution was state-sponsored homicide, and she had wanted to come as a member of a murder victim's family who opposed capital punishment. 'It feels like we're all doing it and in fact we *are* all doing it,' she claimed. 'It's not the state as some faceless entity. The state is *us*. Maybe that's why I've been doing this . . . to feel less a part of it.'

Of course, the state of Connecticut was not murdering anyone, if anything Michael Ross was committing suicide, and the state was merely helping him along his way.

Families and relations of Ross's victims were also gathering at the prison. Robin Stavinsky's stepsister, Jennifer Tabor, had been 12 years old when the murder had been committed, and she never thought she would be able to witness the execution of the man who took Robin's life. 'I had hatched a plan in which I would stand outside the gates of the prison on the morning of Ross's death,' she told a local reporter. 'I always pictured myself out there with the rest of the people, holding a big sign in favour of his death. In my prayers, I always promised Robin I would be there on that day.' However, instead of waiting outside, Jennifer was to get a front seat as an actual witness to the execution. She was there with her siblings, Debbie Dupuis and David Riquier, representing the parents who, after so many years of stress and heartache, were too exhausted to face the emotional turmoil.

Before leaving her home in Columbia for the ride to Somers, Tabor said she grabbed a photograph of Robin so she could have it in the observation room where she watched the execution. 'I just wanted to have it with me, have her with me.' As they drove up Shaker Road towards the prison, she was amazed at the groups of police officers gathered at every intersection. 'There were cops everywhere,' she said. The dozens of checkpoints they went through and a long line of orange traffic cones that glowed from her vehicle's headlights were 'intimidating'. When they arrived at the 'safe house' where correction officials had them wait before going into the prison, she saw about twenty people gathered inside. Jennifer recognised some of the faces from the court proceedings she had attended years ago. Others were strangers. 'It was real quiet,' she said. 'It was like a dream. It didn't seem real.'

Ross's last visitor was sent away at 1.30 a.m. Meanwhile, officials were busy making sure everything was in place. At 6 p.m., 9 p.m. and 1.30 a.m., the two telephone lines leading to the execution chamber had been checked just in case a last-minute reprieve came through. However, the 27th Governor of Connecticut, Mary Jodi Rell, said that in Ross's case no reprieve would be coming from her, as she had no power under state law to intervene.

At 12.30 a.m., with the temperatures dipping towards the low 40s, a bus arrived at the witnesses' 'safe house' to take them into the prison proper. An hour later, Ross was led to the execution chamber and strapped to a gurney. A catheter was attached to each of his arms – the left catheter would carry the final lethal dose.

The first injection into the right arm would be a sedative called sodium thiopental, administered in 2,500 milligrams in 50ml of clear sodium chloride to relax his body. This would be instantly followed by 100 milligrams of pancuronium bromide designed to paralyse him. The third and last step would be 120 milligrams of potassium chloride to stop his heart and kill him. When all of the drugs had stopped flowing, a curtain would be drawn across the viewing window. It would not reopen.

By now, over 300 people had gathered outside the prison, many in a silent, candlelit vigil, with Christopher L. Morano, the Chief State's Attorney, whose office prosecuted Ross, stressing the fact that as Ross had 'volunteered' to be executed he had the right, up to the very last moment – the point at which the injection was about to be given – to stop the proceedings and ask to appeal. 'Under the law, we have no option but to honour that if he does so. But that doesn't mean we will not do all we can to bring finality for the loved ones of his victims. He is now the master of his own fate.' Attorney General Richard Blumenthal had said in an afternoon news conference, 'Because of his status as a so-called volunteer, all Mr Ross has to do is say he wants to appeal and the machinery of death will stop.'

A man, who gave his name as 'Richard', had travelled to Somers from West Springfield, Massachusetts. He supported the death penalty, arguing, 'I'm really out here to protest against the protestors. I think it's hypocritical of these people that they defend the most outrageous cases.' Wearing a baseball cap with the legend, 'Grateful Citizens for the Appreciation of Veterans', he sat in his car at Parking Lot B, south of the Robinson Visitors' Center, where he set up a 4 foot by 7 foot handmade sign that said: 'Liberalism is a Mental Disorder'. It criticised liberal ideas such as defending mass murderers, burning the American flag and defending America's enemies. 'How can they defend a mass murderer tooth and nail?' he asked. 'They also defend America's enemies like Taliban and al Qaida as well as other anti-American causes.'

A group of teenage girls had arrived at the site to make their own signs and show their support for the death penalty. 'I was chanting all this day in school,' said 16-year-old Kaylah Winter, who was holding placard that read 'Turn Ross into Moss'. Her younger sister, 14-year-old Ashley, explained that they learned in school all about the Hammurabi Code, and that punishment should fit the crime. In unison, both girls agreed with this teaching, saying: 'You can't tell us that he wasn't competent to tell us he wants to die, but he knew he shouldn't kill those girls. He deserves to die. Like I said, punishment should fit the crime. Plus why should we keep him alive if it's causing our parents to pay more taxes?' One of the girls' friends, 17-year-old Lauren Mashiak, another junior from Somers High, was not so adamant. 'I am kinda sitting on the fence,' she said. 'I support the execution of Ross, but I'm not sure I totally agree with it on every case, but on this one I think he should die. Knowing that the dead girls were our age, knowing that he killed and raped them and stuff, I'm putting myself in their shoes.' Some distance away, David Cruz-Uribe, a 41-year-old mathematics teacher at Trinity College, Hartford, recited the Hail Mary, his fingers working the beads of a rosary. 'I'm not here because of Mr Ross,' he explained. 'He's not a nice person. I'm here because I oppose the death penalty.' Another teacher, 23-year-old James Russell from Longmeadow, Massachusetts, stated, 'The execution is a barbaric act that should not happen in a democratic society.'

* * *

Nine of Ross's friends and family would watch the execution at his request. They included Kathy Jaeger, a spiritual advisor who met with him frequently, Reverend John Giuliani, and Martha Elliott, a freelance writer who was working on a book.

Separated from Ross's 'team' by a heavy grey curtain, arresting officers detectives Mike Malchik and Frank Griffen took their seats along with five media witnesses, including Shelly Sindland, a reporter for WTIC-FOX 61, who were allowed to document the event with notepads and pens.

Edwin and Lera Shelley, parents of Leslie; Debbie Dupuis, the sister of Robin Stavinsky; Lan Manh Tu, the younger sister of Dzung Ngoc Tu, shuffled in. Dzung's aged father had been allowed into the prison but was not to witness the execution. 'I'm glad that we will never have to hear about him again,' he said later.

The blinds blocking the view into the execution chamber were opened at 2.08 a.m., revealing a dimly lit room. Ross was tightly strapped down on the gurney, his arms outstretched and secured with Velcro strips. A spotlight beamed down on his face. Asked if he wanted to make a final statement, he said, 'No, thank you', then he looked up at the ceiling. The Death Row Warden then placed a call from the chamber that lasted five minutes. It was unclear why the call lasted so long, though the execution procedure required a final check to see whether any stays of execution had been ordered.

Once the call was over, the warden nodded, and the machinery of death started. It was 2.13 a.m., Ross reacted visibly to the flow of chemicals. 'He swallowed hard. He definitely gasped and shuddered,' reported Shelly Sindland of Hartford-based WTIC-TV. 'You could see the life draining out of his face.' A member of one of the victims' families was heard to say sarcastically, 'Uh! Feeling some pain?'

Gerry Brooks, a reporter for WVIT NBC 30, said, 'It was very quiet in there . . . he never looked . . . he just lay there with his head back, looking directly at the ceiling. There was a gasp, there was a shudder, but that was it. The man barely moved other than shudder. And, at 2.15, the man was gone.'

Steve Kalb of the Connecticut Radio Network reported

that, 'Ross was strapped down, and his fingers were all taped closed at the end. He shuddered a bit after the first drugs were administered. He was flesh-coloured when we walked in – he was ashen when we left. It almost seemed surreal. His eyes were closed. It was like, "Go ahead let's end this."'

Ross's body was then removed from the prison by Dr H. Carver II, the States Chief Medical Examiner and two technicians for an autopsy.

A PAINLESS DEATH?

In the end, the man described as both monster and manipulator controlled his own fate. He had until the chemicals started flowing to call off the execution by saying he wanted to pursue more appeals. He did not. Osborn Correctional Institution Warden Christine Whidden announced Ross's death from a podium at 2.28 a.m. But was Michael Ross's execution as painless as most people might imagine?

A man familiar with the routine of carrying out executions by lethal injection was Neil Hodges, the former Assistant Warden in Charge of Executions, at 'The Walls' prison, Huntsville, Texas. When I interviewed him and asked about the reality of this method of judicial homicide, he said: 'People think this all painless and stuff like that. It ain't! Basically, they [the condemned] suffer a lot. They are sort of paralysed, but they can hear. They almost drown in their own fluid and suffocate to death really ...

'Yeah, we get problems. Sometimes the guy doesn't want to get on to the gurney. But we have the largest guard in Texas here. He gets them on that gurney, no problem. They go on that mean old table and get the goodnight juice, whether they like it or not.

An' we had times when we can't find a decent vein. Had one guy where we tried everywhere to get the right place' his arms, wrists and legs. Then he suggested we try a foot and it worked. Fuck, did he go through it. Pain? Of *course* there is pain. This guy went through thirty minutes of severe pain before the needle went in, and that's before the juice burned him out. But, so what! They ain't gonna do anything 'cos they are dead.'

★ ★ ★

I vividly recall that last conversation I had with a distressed Ross over the telephone just hours before he died. He asked me, 'Will it hurt?' 'Nope, Mike,' I replied. 'It would hurt if you remember it but you'll remember nothing.' Then his handset was taken away from him and slammed down.

The initial injection of sodium thiopental (Pentothal), a fast-acting anaesthetic, which takes effect within ten seconds, would have caused a slight pressure and his right arm would have started to ache. He would feel light-headed.

Then came the pancuronium bromide (Pavulon); it is a curare-derived muscle relaxant that paralyses respiratory function and steadily brings unconsciousness in around ten seconds. Ross would have pressure in his chest. It would have been a suffocating feeling, and this is what caused him to gasp for air. He was now dizzy and hyperventilating; his heart beating faster and faster as his entire nervous system came under attack. This is called the 'stress syndrome', a common feature during the first stages of dying.

As the poison permeated through his body, Ross entered

the second stage of death. He was unable to breathe or move, but he could see and hear. He was paralysed and not able to swallow at this point: a condition that leaves many witnesses to believe that death has now supervened. However, Ross was still alive, but his central nervous system was shutting down. His eyes dilated and the hairs on his skin stood erect as he was finally given a massive dose of potassium chloride. When injected intravenously in large doses, this drug burns and hurts, because it is a naturally occurring salt and instantly disrupts the chemical balance of the blood. It causes the muscles to tighten up in extreme contraction and the instant it reaches the heart muscle, it causes the heart to stop beating. While Michael Ross was sedated by the thiopental and couldn't draw breath because of the pancuronium, he was physically unable to scream in pain when the potassium was injected, sending his heart into a crunching, excruciating cramp.

★   ★   ★

Shortly after the execution, Governor Mary Jodi Rell said that Ross alone was responsible for his fate. 'Today is a day no one truly looked forward to – but then no one looked forward to the brutal, heinous deaths of those eight young girls.' She added, 'I hope that there is some measure of relief and closure for their families.' How right Governor Rell is too!

The Commissioner of the State Department of Corrections, Theresa C. Lantz, remarked that it was the Connecticut's first execution by lethal injection. 'We have drilled consistently for several months,' she said, 'utilising every contingency and scenario that we could possibly could, thirty times at a minimum. The employees involved with the lethal injection had been qualified by a state-licensed physician. It was reported in the *New York Times* that all who participated did so voluntarily, confidently and have full access to counselling and support services if they feel it is needed.'

Family members expressed a range of emotions after witnessing the execution. Some expressed sympathy for the Ross family, none of whom were present. 'I thought I would feel closure but I felt anger just watching him lay there and sleep after what he did to those women, said Debbie Dupuis. 'It was too peaceful.'

Lera Shelley remarked: 'My daughter and the other victims finally have the justice they deserve and now they can all rest in peace.'

Jennifer Tabor issued a statement, which was a mixture of compassion and grief: 'We feel sorrow for the Ross family and respect the grief at losing a family member. We know that the sadness of losing Robin will always remain, but now the anger caused by Michael Ross's crimes can begin to fade into a safe place. We hope the words, thoughts and life of Michael Ross will become a faint memory and the notoriety that surrounded him will finally end.'

Wendy Baribeault's cousin, Robert Baribeault III, was relieved that at last Ross had been executed, but 'His death will give us some closure, but will never bring back the lives he has taken', she told reporters from *Newsday* and the *Hartford Courant*, adding, 'There will always be an open wound in the hearts of the families and friends who knew and love these young ladies. To Michael Ross, may you rot in hell.'

After the execution, Ross's lawyer T. R. Paulding told reporters that his client wanted to help the families of his victims and had made a 'decision that required courage'. 'This was not an act of suicide,' he said, 'He sought to do what he thought was right . . . he simply stuck to his principles.'

THE COSTS

Whether one is pro or anti the death penalty matters little for the purposes of this book; however, let it be said that there is not a shred of evidence, anywhere, or from anyone, to confirm that the threat of the ultimate sanction has ever proved to be a deterrent to committing capital murder. We are all entitled to our own thoughts and beliefs, so while James Russell claimed that Ross's 'execution was a barbaric act that should not happen in a democratic society', we must also respect Wendy Baribeault's cousin, Robert, when he said, 'To Michael Ross, may you rot in hell.'

The cost of the human grief, suffering and loss caused by Michael Ross is incalculable, for his murderous legacy has lasted for years and will continue to do so for decades to come. While the protesters, waiting outside the Osborn Correctional Institution for the news of Ross's demise, were able to troop off, their personal lives untainted by Ross's murderous deeds, the families and close friends of the victims would carry their own tragic burden for the rest of their lives, some of them feeling a sense of 'what if' guilt.

What if Tammy Lee Williams's boyfriend had insisted on escorting her home that freezing cold morning, rather than allowing her to walk?

What if Paula Perrera's schoolmate had missed his important test to drive her back to Crystal Run? What if Debra Smith Taylor's husband, or the state trooper, had ensured that she got safely home, argument or not?

What if either of Leslie and April's parents had driven into Jewett City to collect the girls after the movie, rather than ordering the two 14-year-olds to walk four miles home in the dark as punishment? The answers are simple: all of these victims would be alive today.

The chances against any American citizen falling into the clutches of a predatory homicidal sexual psychopath are about 1 in 350 million, mega-considerably less than being killed in a plane crash at 1 in 2.5 million, or by lightning at 1.2 million. However, the chances dramatically increase when one is a woman, or child, out alone, especially at night.

There are also the financial costs to the public purse to be considered. *Each* of Ross's murders brought with them a police invoice estimated at $20,000. Added to which were the on-duty police costs of just under $500.000. Overtime costs were in the region of $121.000. Non-personnel services added a further $28,000, adding the rider that other costs would tally it all up at around a staggering $650.000– if factors such as 'patrol time/area altered to a specific pattern; training of investigative personnel; administrative staff time in managing the cases, and volunteer hours spent on the investigation by employees (paying just their expenses)', were included.

To keep Ross in prison under Level 5 Security for the 11 years until his execution would cost Connecticut $130.00 a day, and this did not include any medical expenses. But, all of this pales into insignificance when the bill for defending, prosecuting and putting Michael Bruce Ross through the legal system, is slapped down on the desk. Estimates vary from state to state, but it is commonly agreed that it costs a state approximately a median bill per case of $750,000 – and Ross had four cases to answer – to put an inmate to death, which is 70 per cent more than the cost of non-death penalty cases.

While this all may seem at odds with the cost of keeping an inmate alive in prison until he dies, the facts are that the greater costs associated with the death penalty occur prior to, and during trial/s, not on post-conviction proceedings. Indeed, even if all post-conviction proceedings (appeals, and in Ross's case, also competency hearings) were abolished, the death penalty would still be more expensive than alternative sentences.

Trials in which the prosecutor is seeking a death sentence have two separate and distinct phases: conviction (guilt and innocence) and sentencing. Special motions and extra time for jury selection typically precede such trials. More investigative costs are generally incurred in capital cases, particularly by the prosecution who have unlimited funds at their disposal. But, in Michael Ross's case, his main trial verdict was initially reversed to one of life imprisonment, causing the taxpayers to incur all the extra costs of a capital retrial and trial proceedings, which finally culminated in his execution.

That the cost of purchasing the drugs used to execute Michael Ross, amounted to no more than $89.00, seems too trivial to mention, however, this might all change. 'The Lone Star State' of Texas has purchased pentobarbitone (pentobarbital in the US), commonly known by the brand name Nembutal, and has sourced stocks to kill at least 15 inmates at a cost of $1,286.86 per injection, despite the Danish manufacturers claiming that it is unsafe for lethal injection and who have since restricted its use for such a purpose. Texas is going ahead regardless.

Michael Bruce Ross proved to be a very expensive serial killer indeed.

MAD, BAD OR SAD?

Michael Ross turned into a monster, and his own words leave an indelible mark: 'You know, they [the medical examiners] found strangulation marks around the neck of Wendy Baribeault. They called them "multiple strangulation marks" 'cos they were kinda all around her throat. An' they confused. I knew she was struggling and my hands kept cramping up. I kinda laughed at them for that. I thought that was funny.'

Yet his chilling sense of sado-sexual homicidal priorities was always masked by the impression he gave to others. Karen B. Clarke, an experienced New York journalist, who visited Ross in prison, reported: 'He looks so normal he could be the guy next door. If I was walking down a dark alley at night, heard footsteps behind me, and turned around, well, I would have been relieved to see Michael Ross. That's how normal the guy looks.'

And, there is Detective Mike Malchik's observation: 'There was nothing threatening about Michael Ross. No signal to anyone that there was a dark side . . . anything that they should be afraid of. He could conceal that until the time came for him to attack these innocent young women.'

As psychology student Sarah Newton points out: 'Serial killers do not go around dressed in hockey masks and carry a chainsaw.

Serial killers have the ability to blend into the background; they are, on the surface at least, just like us.'

Ross's landlady at 58 North Main Street, Jewett City, thought of him as an intelligent, affable young man, always anxious to please. None of his co-workers, at the few jobs he did have, suspected that the former Cornell University graduate was anything other than a regular guy. In reality, however, he was a wolf in sheep's clothing.

So, was there ever any real psychological mitigation for Ross committing his heinous crimes, and what turned him into a homicidal maniac in the first place? At one point during court proceedings, Ross's psychiatric experts argued in mitigation that all of his crimes were the result of one continuous act, which is, perhaps, one of the most ludicrous claims I ever come across. For most of the time, Ross behaved in a perfectly acceptable manner, and it was only when his homicidal fantasies got the better of him that he raped and killed. Between each homicide there was a cooling-off period and this is what defines a serial killer: three or more murders, with a period of days, weeks or months of inactivity separating the 'events'. This differs from a mass-murderer who kills all of his victims in a single act at one location, or the spree killer, who perhaps trawls a neighbourhood, hunting down numerous prey in a continuum of multiple homicides during a day.

Many psychiatrists and psychologists will argue that Michael Ross was insane, therefore not responsible for his crimes. Indeed, Michael's own medical experts put forward mitigation that Ross was a 'victim' of his own paraphiliac disorder, an illness over which he had no control, thus rendering him incapable of resisting the sexual compulsions that drove him to kill.

The famous legal precedent for criminal insanity came about during the M'Naghton case. On Friday, 20 January 1843, Scottish wood turner, Daniel M'Naghton, thinking he was aiming at the then Prime Minister, Sir Robert Peel – in the belief that the PM was conspiring against him – mistakenly shot and killed civil servant Edward Drummond. The court acquitted M'Naghton by 'reason of insanity', and he was placed in a mental institution for the rest of his life. The case caused a public uproar, so much so that Queen Victoria ordered the courts to develop a stricter test for insanity. Thereafter, the 'M'Naghton Rule' was a standard to be applied to a jury, after hearing medical testimony from prosecution and defence experts. The rule created a presumption of sanity, unless the defence proved that 'at the time of committing the act, the accused was labouring under such a defect of reason, from disease of the mind, as not to know the nature and quality of the act he was doing or, if one did not know it, that he did it not knowing what he was doing was wrong.'

In a nutshell, the M'Naghton Rule is still the standard for insanity for almost half the states in the US, with an amendment since taken up in Connecticut. Developed by the American Law Institute as part of the Model Penal Code, this new rule for insanity states that a defendant is not responsible for criminal conduct where '(s)he, as a result of mental illness or defect, did not possess "substantial capacity to appreciate the criminality of his conduct or to conform his conduct to the requirements of the law".'

As far as I'm concerned, the M'Naghton Rule could never have applied to Michael Ross. Of course he appreciated the criminality of his serial murders, and he agreed with this on scores of occasions. He knew the difference between right and wrong. As Mike Malchik proposed, when we visited the wooded murder site of Wendy Baribeault:

'Christopher. You don't just flick a switch and suddenly become "insane", then straight after a murder you flick the switch off again, and become "sane", and get on with your life as if nothing has happened till you spot another kid you decide to abduct, rape and kill again. Give me a break, please! It may wash with the courts just the once, but Ross killed all those girls. It just doesn't sit right with me.'

At this, Mike Malchik pointed to the place where Wendy's body had been partially concealed. Sweeping his arm around, he said, 'See there . . . that's where Mr Ross dragged Wendy off the highway into that clearing over there. Once he had raped and murdered that girl he tried to hide her body under the stones in this wall. Then he got outa there as fast as he could.'

State Prosecutor, C. Robert 'Bulldog' Satti, once shared Mike Malchik's sentiments with me: 'This is off the record, right? Okay! Well, here is the deal from my end. You go take a look at the autopsy photos of these women. You go interview their parents and loved ones. Then come back here and preach an insanity defence for Michael Ross.' Then he added, with anger written all over his face: 'Now, after that motherfucker's confession to you, that he anally raped Leslie after he'd killed her, that's another capital crime. I WANT THAT TAPE!' C. Robert Satti received a copy of the filmed interviews with Ross with my blessing.

There can be no doubt that Michael Ross started to have unhealthy sexual fantasies from an early age; fantasies that became so strong that this took him from sexual assault, to thoughts of imprisoning young women whom he would use as sex slaves, to stalking, voyeurism, to attempted rape, serial rape, murder and then into committing serial sexual homicide. 'Perhaps he was oversexed,' argues Professor Elliott Leyton, 'but there are millions of young men who are over-sexed and they don't go around killing people, do they?'

Likewise, when it comes down to Ross's dysfunctional upbringing, Elliott Leyton says much the same again. 'Yes, maybe Ross did have a less than perfect childhood. But, really, countless of millions of youngsters suffer some form of family abuse, often a lot more extreme than Ross ever did, and they do not turn into serial killers, do they?'

In his book, *Hunting Humans*, Professor Leyton says:

In our own society, an increasing number of people kill for the pleasure it appears to give them. Are they mad, or they acting out some analogous social message? The lesson here is that psychiatric analogy is a false one: madness is not like a cancer or any other physical ailment. Rather, it is a culturally programmed dialogue. It should not therefore be surprising that no matter how hard our psychiatrists search, they are unable to discover much mental disease among our captured multiple murderers (except in the nature of their acts). Therein lies the special horror, for the killers are as 'normal' as you and me, yet they kill without mercy, and they kill to make a statement.

I could not agree more.

NOTE: This chapter is based on video and audiotape interviews between Christopher Berry-Dee and Michael Bruce Ross within the Osborn Correctional Institution, Somers, Connecticut, during 1994, and several years' previous correspondence. Also in newspaper reports and Ross's essay 'It's Time for Me to Die' [published in the *Journal of Psychiatry and Law*, Winter 1998], and articles from the *Boston Globe, Hartford Courant, New York Times* and *Newsweek*.

As the direct result of this author's filmed interviews with Ross, the killer made full confessions to police concerning the murders of Paula Perrera, Dzung Ngoc Tu and the post-mortem rape of Leslie Shelley.

KENNETH ALESSIO BIANCHI

'THE HILLSIDE STRANGLER'

And there was war in heaven. Michael and his angels fought against the dragon, and the dragon and his angels fought back. But he was not strong enough, and they lost their place in heaven. The great dragon was hurled down – that ancient serpent called the devil, or Satan, who leads the whole world astray. He was hurled to earth, and his angels with him.

Revelations 12:7–9 (NIV)

Deep within the bowels of one of America's toughest penitentiaries breathes one of the most heinous sado-sexual serial killers in the black annals of criminal history, caged for twenty hours a day in a small cell No. 8 that is part of the three-floor Secure Housing Unit (SHU) where only the most dangerous and unpredictable killers are confined. With an operating capacity of 2,200, the Washington State Penitentiary (WSP) at Walla Walla is the second largest men's prison in the state. It also houses condemned inmates – it is the place where men are sent to die at the end of a rope or by lethal injection.

Gaining access to US correctional facilities can prove an almost impossible task, and it took me years of correspondence and in-depth research before I came face-to-face with Kenneth Alessio Bianchi. It is claimed that he is a 'multiple personality' – with several other evil personae living inside his head – that he is a real-life Dr Jekyll and Mr Hyde – perfectly normal one minute, the personification of evil the next. Some say that he is the Devil's spawn: 'Bianchi?' said Detective Sergeant Robert Winslow of the LAPD. 'Old Nick tossed-off against a wall and Kenneth hatched in the fuckin' sun.'

But most alarmingly – while behind bars Bianchi became an ordained priest; the Devil's son had wheedled his way into the Lord's House, soon to claim that he was sitting on the right hand of God. Now, at once preaching from the 'Good Book', this insidious creature's evil tentacles of thought started feeling their way around the cellblocks and exercise yards of the prison itself, affecting everyone, including the guards, to then slither over the high walls to infect society itself.

Of the several women he mentally inseminated, one went on to attempt to commit murder by proxy; another married this beast behind bars, while others of similar misguided moral compass queued up to bear his children. And, that's just the gals. This antichrist figure even conned the Christian Church; leaving one perfectly respectful pastor and his wife to suggest to the parole board that if, 'Ken were to be released, we would welcome him into our home and share our life with our two daughters.' I mean one could not make this up if one tried! But, is Kenneth Bianchi really an emissary of Satan, or just another sick and twisted sado-sexual psychopathic serial murderer?

I set out to seek the truth and the truth *will* out.

Apart from studying hundreds of Bianchi's letters, poems, his own deranged unpublished stories, visits to all of his crime scenes, interviews with cops, access to hundreds of case papers and CSI photos, attorneys, a trial judge, psychiatrists and psychologists, correctional officers, members of the Church, his adoptive mother and the woman who attempted to kill on his behalf, I have also interviewed 'The Beast' at WSP.

★ ★ ★

September 1996, Washington State Penitentiary, Walla Walla. My nerves are on edge. I am about to be locked into a small cubicle with a sado-sexual psychopath. He detests me; he hates me with a passion over a falling out during correspondence. Kenneth Bianchi is an exploitative homicidal maniac who ripped away the lives of some 15 young women, including two (maybe five) little girls, and dumped their bodies like so much trash.

Bianchi has, and has always had, an attitude problem. He is a human predator, an efficient killing machine; a first-strike weapon designed to approach a target with stealth and shower it with immediate, sustained destruction. He is a cold-blooded psychopath who once boasted; 'Put me with a young broad an' it'll be dead wrong for her and dead right for me.' That *is* an attitude problem!

I am about to get up close and very personal with this monster who recently vowed to tear my face off if I ever came into his space. Powerful, predatory, with dark hair, a heavily pockmarked face and ink-black eyes that never blink: the cold, wet eyes of a Great White shark, soon to stare deep into my head with his evil tentacles of enquiring thought.

An arm's length away, a touch away now, Kenneth Bianchi does not smile as he is escorted into the grey-painted cinderblock room. His cuffs and leg shackles are removed by a guard, who leaves and locks the steel door behind him. Bianchi sits down and his breathing is shallow. I can almost hear his mind working like the ticking of a clock, even a bomb about to explode, for his hatred of me radiates like red-hot coals.

Over a minute passes. Not a word is said. Tick, tick, tick, tick. His eyes are now starting to disturb me; the left eye seems to belong to some sort of long-dead entity, as if it belongs to an emotionless automaton – pure, distilled evil. The right eye is actually looking into my mind, a planning and calculating eye. I am now positive that there are two people inside Bianchi. Tick, tick, tick. One senses the ice-cold menace of a cobra about to strike.

There is only a rickety table between us. I lean back in my chair; I smile. 'You don't like me one bit, do you, Ken?' I ask.

There is no response. The skin on Bianchi's face is now stretched as tight as bat's skin. There is no movement from the man simmering a heartbeat away.

To break the ice, I rise to my feet and slowly walk around the table to him. I placed my right hand on his shoulder. 'Hey, Ken,' I whisper. 'You are some miserable son-of-a-bitch. C'mon, where is that fuckin' smile?'

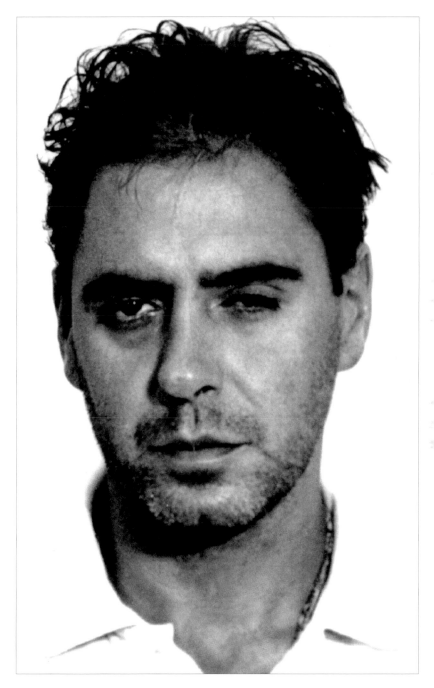

John Martin Scripps – 'Tourist from Hell'.

'The Hillside Stranglers' –
Kenneth Bianchi (*above*) and
his cousin, Angelo Buono
(*below*).   ©*Press Association*

Above: LA police investigate the car containing the body of Cindy Lee Hudspeth, a victim of the Hillside Stranglers, in February 1978.

©*Bettmann/CORBIS*

Below: Eagle Rock Plaza – the site of the abduction of two more victims, Dolly Cepeda and Sonja Johnson, in November 1977.

©*New Criminologist*

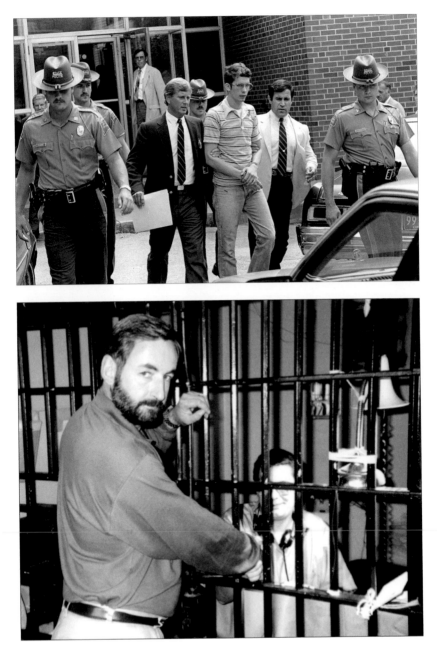

Above: Michael Ross – 'The Roadside Strangler'.

©*Press Association/AP Photo/John Duval*

Below: The author (*left*) with Michael Ross on Death Row. ©*Christopher Berry-Dee*

A switch seemed to flick inside his brain within a millisecond. The tension washed out of him in an instant and a cruel smirk slowly came to his thin mouth. It was this human contact, the physical touch and a dangerous up-close encounter – which could have played out either way – that now enabled me to have a 60-minute interview with the 'Hillside Strangler'.

When we parted, Ken stopped in his tracks, reeled around and snarled, 'Don't ever, *ever*, come near me again.'

I did – not once but twice.

★ ★ ★

In previous correspondence, Bianchi had boasted that he was a trustee; as such he was afforded special privileges, which included a very spacious cell, within the general prison population. However, the assistant warden had told me that he was held in a secure housing unit for highly dangerous sex offenders; that his cell was so small you could not swing a cat around in it. So, on my next visit to see him, as instructed by the guards who waited at the entrance to the tier, I slowly walked the yellow line down the SHU. Cross that line and the spittle, excreta and urine from angry inmates can spatter you. I stopped at cell number 8. Ken was lying on his bunk, radio headphones on. I stepped over the line and pushed my nose up to the bars on his door and called his name. He stirred. He ignored me. Then he flew at the bars in frenzy.

'You upsetting one of our guests?' came the shout from an amused correctional officer. 'You pissing off Kenny?' another guard chuckled.

'Yep. It seems like he's busted his radio against the wall.'

Thus poked with a sarcastically weighted verbal stick, Bianchi was now plaster-white with fury. 'Now, now, Kenneth,' I said, 'be a good serial killer and get back in your cot, you prick.'

'He ain't got no right harassing me,' he complained to an officer who was now at my side. 'He's invading my privacy and I am going to sue him and you for breaching my rights.' Bianchi knew all about his legal rights; oddly enough he studied law in prison and was now a member of the American Bar Association.

The guard butted in. 'This gentleman has every right to be here,' he patiently explained to Bianchi, who had now retreated to the back of his cell. 'The Director of Corrections says he has the right to be here. The Governor says he can be here, so I say he has *every* right to be here.'

Bianchi blustered. 'I am gonna sue all of you . . . you are going to lose your job. Your wife and kids are gonna go hungry, pal!'

'That's a threat against a correctional officer,' came back the guard. 'SHUT THE FUCK UP, BIANCHI. SHUT THE FUCK UP, or I'll write you up.'

The third and last time I saw Kenneth, it was 'yard time' and bitterly cold, wet and windy at the Pen. Bianchi spotted me watching him as he walked towards the yard in a procession of SHU inmates. He was wearing blue dungarees, and a black donkey jacket. This time mute, he turned up his collar, pulled his cap down over his eyes, and looked away. I was just a couple feet away from him now. Behind me were two correctional officers; built like brick ovens, they were just waiting for another chance to throw him into 'The Hole', and just the smallest infraction would have given them justification, with that 'No eyeballing' rule' even more strictly enforced for scum like him.

* * *

'One girl was killed and, when she was dead, I took her girlfriend [Sonja] into the bedroom and raped and buggered her before killing her. She screamed for her mom, and the last thing she saw was the face of her dead friend lying under the sheets next to her.'

So Kenneth Bianchi described to me the murders of Sonja Johnson, aged 14, and Dolores Cepeda, aged 12.

* * *

It had taken four years of continual correspondence with Bianchi before I was finally granted a rare interview with him. The meeting took place at the notoriously tough Washington State Penitentiary (WSP) in Walla Walla – a medium-size city that squats in dry flatlands just 13 miles from the Washington-Oregon border in the southeastern corner of the state. Walla Walla, incidentally, is an ancient indigenous name meaning 'Place of Many Waters'.

I had been in Washington State for a couple of weeks, and had interviewed most of the people who had been involved with him in the US Northwest, and now I had the run of WSP for five days. To get from SeaTac to Walla Walla, the 270-mile flight on an Alaskan Airlines twin-engine turboprop would take the plane within a mile of Mount Rainier, and I would be staying with an assistant warden during my visit.

EMISSARIES OF SATAN

Bianchi stands around 5 foot 11 inches tall, and he is extremely well built. A tough exercise regime had toned his muscles to perfection; back in 1996, he had a washboard abdomen and powerful shoulders, indeed, even today he might be classed as a fine specimen of a man. Ken's once rich, black mane of hair is thinning and turning grey; however, many women still think he is drop-dead gorgeous. But look into his eyes and you are looking into an abyss and that abyss is looking straight back at you.

TO THE DEVIL A SON

Nature seems at each man's birth to have marked out the bounds of his virtues and vices, and to have determined how good or how wicked that man shall be capable of being.

François de la Rochefoucauld, Moral Reflections, Part I

Kenneth Alessio Bianchi was born on Friday, 22 May 1951, in Rochester, upstate New York. He was the last of four children born to Florence King, an attractive, precocious 17-year-old 'go-go' dancer. She dumped him like an unwanted puppy shortly after giving birth. Kenneth never knew his genetic father, so, throughout his life, he would suffer the social stigma of knowing he was a bastard. Effectively, he had been dumped into a hand basket and shit-canned to Hell.

Within weeks of his birth, Ken was fostered out to an elderly woman who had little time for him, so she farmed him out to a number of her friends and neighbours.

Every child has a need to be noticed, understood, taken

seriously and respected by its mother and, as Dr Alice Miller says in her book *The Drama of Being a Child*, 'In the first few weeks and months of its life, the child needs to have its mother at its disposal, must be able to use her, and to be mirrored by her.' Therefore, it would be fair to say that, during this crucial period, Kenneth did not enjoy the benefits of having a mother. In fact, he did not have anyone to give him this vital attention. Indeed, it was quite the opposite, for he was shuttled from home to home, with each minder exhibiting different reactions towards him, ranging from short-term curiosity to unwelcome nuisance. So, in this respect alone, and in much the same way as so many other serial murderers, from day one, Ken was being emotionally deprived and damaged.

Italian immigrants Frances and Nicholas Bianchi, a manual worker at the American Brake-Shoe foundry in Rochester, adopted Ken when he was three months old. He was to be their only child.

Born in 1918, Frances had wanted a child since her late teens, but she could not conceive. Time dragged by and, now aged 32, she felt the only option open to her was that of adopting, to which her husband somewhat reluctantly agreed. Although a very sharp, intelligent and plain-speaking woman, Frances, unfortunately, was a hypochondriac who suffered a positive fiesta of maladies: headaches, fatigue, chills, shortness of breath, dizziness and shooting pains in the extremities and – not surprisingly in the circumstances – chronic depression. Nonetheless, she was successfully able to conceal much of this under a veil of overt assertiveness, which manifested itself in an over-solicitous and authoritarian manner.

In order to survive emotionally, Frances was capable of 'splitting off' from her weaker self. She used denial and repression, which broadly speaking means that when one is not happy with a situation, one puts conscious thought of it out of one's mind. This was her mental defence mechanism, a vital requirement as her husband Nicholas, although a hard worker and a loyal spouse, was weak-willed and had succumbed to the lure of gambling to which he lost the better part of his wages at the bookies. This further aggravated the family's weak infrastructure, especially as he was not able to pay off his gambling debts so the family was always on the move because loan sharks threatened to shoot him if he didn't pay up.

This confused package of mental and financial instability spilled into the Bianchi home on a daily basis, and it was Frances who felt it the worst, with her paranoia rubbing off on her adopted son. If Mrs Bianchi deserved anything from this unsettled and worrying existence, it was security, and she mistakenly reasoned that she would be better off if there was someone who really needed her and, in turn, she would satisfy her maternal instincts by having a child. However, Frances wanted a child for all the wrong reasons, and Ken was to become an object at her disposal, an object that could be controlled, manipulated and become totally reliant and centred on her. The security she could not find in her married life could be found in her adopted son, she thought. Therefore, Ken would have to pay a very high price, and he was forced to give Frances his undivided admiration and full attention during the years to follow if he were to survive psychologically himself. A hint of these troubles surfaced a year later when the adoption agency called on the Bianchi family to complete a progress report.

The adoption agency records reveal that, although Kenneth was a 'sturdily-built baby with bluish eyes and wavy brown hair [it was black], appearing happy, contended and alert', they describe Mrs Bianchi as 'over solicitous'. A footnote added that Nicholas Bianchi was 'quiet, unassuming, but very friendly, able to control his incessant stuttering, which has troubled him since childhood, only when Kenneth is around him'.

In 1953, with loan sharks forever chasing Mr Bianchi for his gambling debts, the family was forced to leave their home on Saratoga Avenue, in Rochester, New York, and move to nearby Glide Street, where they kept a low profile. The loan sharks soon caught up with them, so a year later they moved to Los Angeles where they stayed with Frances's sister, Jennifer Buono. By now, Ken had developed asthma.

While in California, he attended the Century Park Elementary School, at 10935 South Spinning Avenue, Inglewood, LA, where, aged five, he suffered the first of two bad falls. He tripped while running up a flight of concrete steps, cracking open his head, then, a month later, he fell headlong from playground equipment, hitting a number of steel rungs and breaking his nose when he hit the floor.

After this accident, he started wetting his pants during the daytime. He developed a facial tic, which was apparent when he was stressed, and he was significantly accident-prone; choosing to run rather than walk and always falling over.

During their time in Los Angeles, Nicholas Bianchi managed to save some money, which he used to pay off his gambling debts, so the family decided that it was now safe to return to Rochester. Ken's asthma had all but disappeared, although his mother noticed that her boy had become withdrawn. He would retire to his bedroom where he spent hours gazing vacantly at the trains as they passed the house. He was brooding, and something was stirring in both his conscious and subconscious mind. Then, as might be expected, Nicholas started running up large gambling debts again.

The family's stay at 529 Lyell Avenue – in the red-light district where serial killer Arthur Shawcross trawled for victims – was short-lived. The seedy street was lined with sagging houses, Laundromats, 'five and dime' stores, cheap liquor bars and seedy strip joints, while two-star hookers, with more tattoos than a fairground worker, plied their trade on every street corner. The impressionable six-year-old took it all in.

According to Ken, 'In 1958 we moved to a pink-painted house on Wildwood Drive, then in 1959 to 60 Villa Street, then on to Campbell Street,' and, all the while, Kenneth was changing not only any friends he had made, but schools as well.

In 1960, the nine-year-old was seen briefly at the Strong Memorial Hospital Clinic in Rochester. His appointment was prompted by a complaint from the Society of Prevention of Cruelty to Children. In a nutshell, this issue was based on school and adoption-agency evidence suggesting that the lad was not being properly cared for and, of course, there was every reason to believe this was the case. The report claimed:

Kenneth is a very anxious lad who has many phobias and counter-phobias. He uses repression and reaction formation.

He is very dependent upon his mother. She has dominated him, and indulged him in terms of her own needs. He is anxious, protective, and this clinging control has made him ambivalent. But he repressed his hostile aggression, and he is increasingly dependent upon her.

So, as early as the age of nine, probably several years earlier, there appear to have been significant indications that Kenneth Bianchi was made up of two opposing sets of attitudes and emotions. Echoing the psychopathology of his neurotic mother, he was mentally splitting in two. He had developed an alter ego, a multiple-personality disorder, and author Christine Hart formed this chilling observation of him after one of her lengthy interviews with Bianchi in prison during 2010: 'His right eye seems to have a perverted glint, while his left eye is blank and devoid of anything but darkness. There are definitely two entities living inside Kenneth's head,' she wrote, and, in part, I am inclined to agree with her for there is 'good' and 'bad' in all of us.

It could be said that Kenneth had for years been the victim of a subtle form of child abuse. Effectively he had been brainwashed and only a major change in his life would keep him from being emotionally scarred for life. Nothing did change. Indeed matters became worse when, in 1961, two doctors at the DePaul Psychiatric Clinic in Rochester saw Ken again. On this occasion, the complaint came from the Monsignor at Kenneth's school, because of his continual truancy and his inattentiveness (what would later become known as attention-deficit disorder). The facial tics and enuresis (wetting himself) were also cause for concern, as was the asthma, which had returned with a vengeance. Doctors Dowling and Sullivan strongly believed that he was suffering a great deal of stress at home and recommended treatment for the lad, but, after two visits to the clinic, Mrs Bianchi bluntly told the doctors that she didn't see the need for any more treatment, and refused to let the doctors see her son again, in doing so, putting the boy's mental health at grave risk.

In June 1965, disaster struck when Nicholas Bianchi died at work following a massive heart attack. According to Ken's unpublished manuscript, his father was on the telephone to Frances when it happened, and he collapsed with the handset clutched tightly in his hand.

Later that year, Frances and Ken moved house yet again, and once more he was uprooted from his school, moving to the McQuaid Jesuit High School in the same city.

In the same manuscript, Kenneth Bianchi devoted half a page at most to the subject of his father, whom he says he 'adored'; however, over five pages contain explicit details of his early sexual experiences, and this is all rather sinister for a convicted serial killer who is intent on proving his innocence for a string of sexually related homicides, which include the kidnap, rape, buggery, torture and murder of two little girls.

Nevertheless, the following is Bianchi's account and, although some might find this shocking, it is significant that he refers to girls aged around ten, as 'women'. He also claims to have been sexually active since the age of 11:

While my hormones increased, it was not until my sophomore year when I had my first sexual experience with a partner. It was when I was about eleven-years-old when

I had my first solo experience. My first love was blonde, thin build, and easy to speak with. She had a cute way of flirting, head tipped a bit. A beautiful smile across her face, she smelled divine, as women do.

Our first sexual encounter was at her home, with her parents and sister away. It was brief and I was so nervous my hands shook. I tried my best to be patient and gentle as I assumed a man should be. I'm certain I was hurried and, with a touch of inexperience, I wore no protection, which she had insisted on. When we finished, I just held her. It was the most beautiful and memorable experience I'd had up to that point in my life.

In fact, the girlfriend in question was just nine years old, but this did not prevent Ken sarcastically adding that she was not his steady girlfriend. 'We coupled for a week or so,' he claimed, 'but her heart belonged to several other guys in the neighbourhood. She and I had sexual relations twice more before ending our relationship.' Warming to his theme Bianchi admitted that he had 'scholastic problems' because his real interest was always with the female sex: 'I was crazy about girls . . . I dated different women on a regular basis. Romance is wonderful, life was my opiate and women were my fix. I could easily be distracted from my studies by the right woman.'

With equal clarity, Kenneth Bianchi also remembered Sue Davis, a young girl from his school who was junior to him, it seems, who invited him to her home where there was a swimming pool. And, at this point in his writing, Bianchi launches into a more complete quasi-erotic account of a problem that occurred during that very same swimming session, and it still bothers him decades later:

> She was a little chubby. She had a spinal problem, and was bubbly and full-figured. We were in the pool, and I reached out to hug her. She turned and my hand brushed against her breast. I wasn't disappointed, but it was unintentional. We broke up after that. She thought I had touched her breast without her permission. That allegation upset me.

According to Bianchi's rambling, somewhat unsubstantiated account, Sue Davis was just eleven, and Bianchi did more than touch her breast, he touched about everything else, and she told her parents who, in turn, contacted the police. Bianchi was pulled in for questioning and denied everything, so, with one account conflicting the other, the police were unable to bring charges. Ken was, however, listed on the police computer as a possible child sex offender. So, it is clear from the pen of the killer himself that, by the age of 18, the oldest girl he had had sex with was 14, and the youngest – three of them – were aged nine.

In 1970, Ken resumed his studies and set his sights on joining a police academy. He enrolled at college, and, now aged 19, he was living with his adoptive mother at 105 Glenda Park, Rochester.

With only a decent showing in Geography, in all other subjects Ken, with his well-established attention–deficit disorder, failed dismally, so it is not surprising to learn that he not only flunked his degree, but he was also deemed to be totally unsuitable for work in law enforcement. As a sort of low-grade consolation prize, he was, however, offered the more menial job of jail deputy, a position he promptly turned down while all of his fellow students were joining the police academy left, right and centre. Ken was now a laughing stock and he didn't like it one bit. But Kenneth's narcissistic obsessions were to have further, far wider-reaching and more dangerous implications than anyone could have predicted around this low point in his life, as we will soon see.

Ken's failure at college had been a severe blow to his over-inflated self-esteem, for he had convinced himself and had promised his mother that he would become a cop. When this dream was shattered, so was his ego, so he took to petty-thieving and was soon dismissed from every part-time job he took.

Ken did, however, have something in common with one small group of people – that sub-culture of society called 'emerging serial killers' – for he was a pathological liar. Telling lies was his way of making himself seem cleverer than he actually was. Kenneth could not allow himself to be seen as inferior in the eyes of his peers, and looking back at him, as he was then, it is patently clear that this 'Billy Liar' suffered from the psychological condition of grandiosity – and he still does to this day. Here we find a man who is never wrong and always brighter than anyone else. And, as a personal example of this, he boasted to me in correspondence that because of his trustee status within the penitentiary he had been allocated a double-bed cell – a privilege afforded to only the most respected inmates. Cue, Christopher Berry-Dee appearing, without a formal invitation, at Kenneth's front door, with, 'Nice house you have here, Ken.' And, to give an idea of the dimensions of Ken's single-bunk cell – as I have said, you could not swing a cat in it by its tail. A 'trustee' he is not, for as a child-killer he is one of the most hated individuals within the entire Washington penal system.

* * *

Upon leaving school in 1971, Bianchi married an attractive lass and high-school friend called Brenda Beck. Tall, leggy, with a mane of long auburn hair, she was a super catch for any hot-blooded male. He took a part-time job at the 'Two-Guy's' store, and he furthered his education at the Rochester Community College where he reviewed plays and films for the college newspaper, *The Monroe Discipline*. Ken's enthusiasm then faltered; consequently, he failed to complete many of the classes, which included Psychology, in which he drew an 'incomplete'. However, Psychology, and indeed Law Enforcement, were subjects he would return to under somewhat less than honest circumstances eight years later.

At the same time as Ken's academic efforts were tottering on the edge of a cliff, his personal life suddenly collapsed around him when his wife Brenda – who Bianchi would later call one of the only two true loves of his life – caught him in bed with another woman, Janice Tuschong – who was, it seems, the second true love of his life. Completely the polar opposite in looks and morality to the woman now soiling her bed, Brenda threw him out on to the street where, once again, he became the subject of much ridicule amongst the few casual friends he had left.

In 1994, Frances Bianchi broke her silence for the first time. In a taped interview with me she said, 'Ken was a blatant liar.

You'd catch him doing something . . . ask him why he did it, he'd tell you, "I didn't do it." I'd catch him in lies, and he would deny everything. And, in the end, you felt like you were the crazy one, and not him. Christopher, he is such a smooth liar. He tells such lies that you believe him. You really believe what he says until you prove it for yourself.'

So Bianchi needed to be admired for something he was not. This was his way of compensating for his shortcomings. He *had* to excel in everything he undertook; after all, this was what his mother had drummed into him, expected of him, demanded of him and, like all people who suffer from grandiosity, it is a catastrophe if something fails them. When that happens, a bout of severe depression is imminent and, in Ken's case, the crisis was immediate and lethal.

The collapse of Bianchi's self-esteem during this period of his life proved just how precariously his self-esteem had been hanging by a thread, for nothing genuine that could have ever given him strength, or support, had been allowed to develop inside his mind. As Dr Alice Miller says, 'The grandiose person is never really free. First because he is so excessively dependent on admiration from others; and second, because his self-respect is dependent on qualities, functions and achievements that can suddenly fail.'

With Bianchi they did fail, and looking back through his history we can see that his relationships, and his efforts to succeed, hung in the air on a very fine thread indeed. His self-esteem and grandiosity – his entire psychopathological infrastructure – were crumbling away like weathered cement. Morally, Bianchi was corroding. Then, when his unstable support mechanism eventually failed, it required just one more adverse influence to knock his house down.

* * *

Bianchi was now aged twenty. At the very time his desperate attempts at becoming a police officer were foundering like a ship in a hurricane, his marriage lay in tatters, too. And, as soon as he became involved with Janice Tuschong, he messed that relationship up as well. Then, out of the blue, three horrific child murders shook his hometown of Rochester. These killings took place within a mile radius of Ken's front door, and he soon found himself being interviewed as a suspect in the killings. The media dubbed the cases 'The Alphabet Murders' or 'Double Initial Murders', because each victim's Christian name began with the same letter as the surname; what is more, their bodies were found in towns bearing the same initials.

THE ALPHABET MURDERS

The first murder was that of ten-year-old Carmen Colon, on Tuesday, 16 November 1971. Her body was found at Churchville County Park, and this event took place within days of Bianchi learning of his third set of failed exam results, and we remember Bianchi's own words: 'I was crazy about girls . . . I dated different women on a regular basis. Romance is wonderful, life was my opiate and women were my fix. I could easily be distracted from my studies by the right woman.'

There was a gap of 17 months before the murderer struck again. The murder of 11-year-old Wanda Walkowitz (whose body was found in Webster) coincided almost to the day with Bianchi being thrown out of Janice Tuschong's apartment in April because she had caught him sleeping with one Donna Duranso. The bed-hopping Bianchi would later tell author Christine Hart during an interview: 'I loved my wife, Brenda and I loved Janice and Donna.'

Bianchi's relationship with Donna Duranso collapsed in November 1973 and, a day later, the Monday after the Thanksgiving break, 11-year-old Michelle Maenza went missing. Two days later, her body was found fully clothed along a lonely road in Macedon, Wayne County.

All three girls had been raped and then strangled to death. There were other links between the murders as well: all lived in rundown neighbourhoods; all were walking alone when they were taken from the streets; all were from broken homes – their fathers gone, the mothers on welfare; all had eaten a small meal and a milkshake just before they met their deaths; all had white cat hair attached to their clothing, and each girl was last seen alive in the company of a young, white male, aged late teens/early twenties, who was driving a white compact saloon car. The description of the car and the man matched Bianchi precisely.

All three girls were streetwise. They had been warned by their mothers not to speak to strangers, therefore, investigators reasoned that whoever abducted them might have used the ruse of being a police officer, or even a clergyman.

Of course, there were other suspects in the frame, and one man committed suicide before the police arrived to interview him. Post-mortem blood tests, though, proved that this man – Miguel Colon, Carmen's uncle, whom FBI profiler Robert Hazelwood thought fitted the bill – could not have been the killer because the culprit was a non-secretor, an individual of blood group A, B or AB whose secreted bodily fluids (such as saliva, semen etc.) do not contain their blood-group antigens. Bianchi is a non-secretor, a group making up just 20 per cent of the US population.

During his interview with Rochester homicide cops, Bianchi was as plausible as ever. A natural-born liar, well able to sell ice cream to Eskimos (in fact, at the time of the murders he was working in a milkshake bar) or spectacles to the blind, he convinced officers that he had watertight alibis for the three murders in question. However, he refused, as was his legal right in those days, to give body fluid samples, which would have confirmed that he was a non-secretor. Then, amazingly, even more so as Frances Bianchi owned a white cat, and he drove a white car, suspicion fell away, and no one checked the veracity of his alibis.

When I questioned him at the Washington State Penitentiary, Bianchi agreed that his mother had owned a white cat at the time of the murders. Frances was able to confirm this. And he concurred that he did, indeed, drive a white car, but went on to say that it had not been in his interests to give bodily fluids, arguing that he was a secretor – which he is not – and insisting he had been telling the truth about his alibis.

Ken also asserts that he has been ruled out as a suspect in the 'Double Initial Murders', when this is not the case. When I visited the Rochester PD, Captain Lynde Johnson claimed that Bianchi has always been in the frame, while other observers claim he is not.

★　★　★

'It seemed that whenever Ken had a fight with a girlfriend, or had a problem,' Frances told me in 1992, 'he went out and killed someone. I even told police the same thing.' And she was to repeat this when speaking to the author Christine Hart, who recalls in her book *In For the Kill:*

> His mother, Frances, a very sharp, intelligent and plain-speaking woman whom I had got to know over the phone, had said to the cops that she blamed his girlfriend Kelli Boyd for making her son Kenny into a murderer. Frances said, 'Every time Kelli threw Kenny out or ended it there would be a murder.' During my visit, I had asked Ken about his mother's comments and he replied, 'Sure, you could find a trigger here or there and say me and Kelli argued here or there, but I'm not the killer, so it's irrelevant. Anyway, how would Mom know when we argued?' Ken had usually rung her is why. I checked his mother's version of events.

Bianchi's early life shows that he is atypical of the emerging serial murderer type in psychological make-up. He was superficially attractive to women, although, when his partners looked deeper, they found that he was transparent, immature, unfaithful and a pathological liar. Such men might seem to have many female friends, but they are unable to form or sustain any meaningful, lasting relationships. Deep down, they have formed a growing dislike, even a hatred, of the female sex in general. In Bianchi's case, he treated women and children like so much trash – to be used, abused and thrown away.

We also know that Bianchi was a paedophile who preyed on very young girls. Indeed, just four years after the final 'Double Initial Murder' Bianchi would be involved in the abduction, rape, torture and murder of 14-year-old Sonja Johnson and 12-year-old Dolores 'Dolly' Cepeda, in Los Angeles.

There is no doubt that Ken felt that the world was stacked against him. He sat brooding for hours, asking himself why, as he was so clever, he had failed, when all around him were enjoying success. And, like so many of his breed, it is not what Kenneth says or does that is so important, but what he will *not* say, or patently avoids saying, or conveniently forgets, so vital when trying to find the reason why he turned into such an abhorrent killer.

For instance, Bianchi has always claimed that he is a secretor; therefore he could have never been involved in other murders including the 'Double Initial' killings. Indeed, he went further by stating in correspondence to me that he could produce his medical notes to support this claim. However, when pressed to supply these documents, Bianchi ducked the issue by saying, 'Actually, I seem to have lost the notes but I am 99 per cent positive I am a secretor. It is in my notes. But without the notes I cannot be completely sure.'

In a search for the facts about this claim, I contacted the FBI, who released a document dated Wednesday, 2 June 1982. In it, Agent Robert Beams, a specialist in blood grouping and body fluids, confirmed that, after taking samples from Bianchi, he was able to say that Bianchi was a non-secretor. More to the point, a later discovery made in Bianchi's cell (a search instigated by me) proved that he had had a copy of the FBI report in his possession for well over a decade. Ken seems to have believed that everyone in the world is a mug, except himself.

However, no account of Kenneth Bianchi's life and crimes would be complete without mention of his adoptive cousin and accomplice in murder, Angelo Buono, who lived in Glendale, Los Angeles.

THE ITALIAN STALLION

'SATAN'S OWN M.C.'

Tattoo on Bianchi's upper left arm allegedly
acquired when he joined a motorcycle club . . .

. . . Although having been through Buono's history with a fine-toothed comb, and after consulting with police, there is nothing to support the claim that he had ever joined any motorcycle club. Indeed, the only bikers he ever came into contact with were the local chapter of the Hell's Angels, and on one occasion they threatened to blow his head off with a 12-gauge shotgun!

★ ★ ★

With a population in the region of 3.8 million, Los Angeles is the third largest city in the USA. Although the homicide numbers are significantly dropping (in 2012 down to circa 5.72 per 100,000), in 1975 the homicide rate was circa 21.1 per 100,000 making LA one of the highest, per capita, in the western world.

Ten miles north of LA is the sprawling suburb of Glendale

where, in 1975, Kenneth Bianchi alighted from a coach at the Eagle Rock Plaza terminal minus his worldly possessions; his two suitcases had been lost during the gruelling 2,600-mile trip from Rochester and he wouldn't retrieve them for several days. And meeting Ken was his adoptive cousin (his adoptive mother's nephew), Angelo 'Tony' Buono, known variously by his cronies as 'The Italian Stallion' or 'The Buzzard'.

Scrawny, lank-haired, skinny-legged and ugly, Buono's background is of interest to us because it offers some clues to his subsequent dysfunctional, violent and sadistic adult life: his mother and father had violent rows and split up when he was very young. While Buono Sr. was away in the military, his mother found it almost impossible to make ends meet so she struck up a relationship with a butcher exchanging sex for meat and young Angelo was sucked into petty crime. His childhood idol was a rapist and killer called Caryl Chessman, who lulled his victims into trusting him by impersonating a cop.

Angelo, with an incessant stutter had spent several stints in prison, had six kids by several mothers, all of whom ended up on the receiving end of his violent temper, and he bragged of abusing a 14-year-old girl 'to break her in'. Interestingly, his business, an auto-upholstery workshop at 703 E. Colorado Street, Glendale, lent him an air of respectability, as he was a skilled technician, numbering Frank Sinatra and other stars among his clients.

One of Bianchi's first priorities upon arriving in Los Angeles was to find a job to help him pay his way with Angelo, and he managed to find employment as a real-estate customer services clerk with California Land Title (Cal Land). Kenneth had learned of the vacancy through Buono's female bank manager who put in a good word for him when he applied for the position. Then, at the firm's 1977 New Year's Eve party, he met Kelli Kae Boyd who worked at the company's head office in Studio City. In her book *Women Who Love Men who Kill*, Shelia Isenberg quotes Detective Frank Salerno who described Kelli Boyd as an 'overweight, short and plain young woman', who Bianchi would later say gave him gonorrhoea after falsely telling him that she had been raped. Whatever, the case, she fell for Bianchi's smooth chatter, and they dated for a month before she decided to end the relationship because of Ken's immaturity and insecurity. 'He was very possessive, and he always wanted to know where I was going and whom I was doing it with, and I didn't really like that very well,' she later told Detective McNeill of the Bellingham Police Department.

With enough cash now to find a place of his own, Ken left Buono's place and rented rooms at Tamarind Apartments, 1950 Tamarind Avenue, and no sooner had he shut the door than he picked up the telephone and started wooing Kelli again. As was his practice with previous girlfriends, he sent her bunches of flowers and, before long, he was treating her at the most expensive restaurants he could afford. They moved in under the same roof and, at the beginning of May 1977 she announced that she was pregnant with his child. She was to give birth to their son Ryan on 23 February 1978.

Life with Bianchi was always going to be a rough ride. Perhaps Kelli had imagined that she had found her 'Mr Right', however the couple argued frequently, and more than once Kelli turned him out. Each time, he returned to Angelo's place where he slept on the floor, or he would call his mother who mediated reconciliation.

Throughout all this, and to her credit, Kelli still worked at Cal Land, although heavily pregnant. She was frugal with her money, while Ken Bianchi, who earned considerably less than Kelli, would fritter his wages away. Even when he was promoted to Assistant Title Officer, he still needed more cash, so he decided to earn more on the side. He would reinvent himself as Dr Bianchi with a doctorate in Psychology, and here, in a letter to me, is Bianchi's account of why he formed this bogus service. This was first published in my book *Talking With Serial Killers 2* (John Blake, London, 2005):

People in California are big on window dressing. Joining the *Psychology Today* book club, I took in books to decorate my shelves, I was introduced to Dr Weingarten, and I asked him if I could rent part of his offices at night. I sounded literate, and he accepted me on the reference of a mutual friend. There was no extraordinary effort to fool the doctor, and if he had asked just some basic questions about psychology, he would have seen right through me. Placing ads in *The Los Angeles Times*, I received credentials from other psychologists and students applying for a job with me. A diploma replacement service supplied more decorations for my walls and shelves. Also, I had several basic psychology books from back east. I knew I was doing wrong, but I took every precaution to not harm anyone.

So, now we find our 'Dr Bianchi' obtaining genuine diplomas by sleight of hand from students who applied for a post with him, and as soon as the documents dropped through his mailbox, he substituted his own name. To add further authenticity to the phoney venture, he forged letters from well-known institutions, who thanked Dr Bianchi for his 'generosity', and for the 'small cash donations, and his valuable time in giving such enlightening lectures'. Of course, all of this was a figment of his over-active and crooked imagination. He then told Kelli that he had earned his Psychology degree way back in Rochester, and that he was helping two 'colleagues', one of whom was the unwitting and trusting Dr Weingarten, with their 'overload of patients'. But then, like all of Bianchi's schemes, it fell apart as quickly as a new Buick.

Several times Kelli had asked Ken for further details of his Psychology degree, the details of which seemed vague, so she phoned Frances for corroboration – and Mom was in the dark, too. So, during an unannounced visit to Los Angeles to see her son, who was now a 'doctor', Frances called at his home and then his office. She was not impressed. She berated Ken, threatening to expose him as a cheat and a liar. But it was like water off a duck's back to the ever-buoyant Ken and her warnings went unheeded. Ken continued to pour what little spare money he had into advertising for patients until his funds dried up. Patients failed to materialise, and he dumped the prefabricated sideshow when Kelli threatened to expose him, too.

But Bianchi had another card up his sleeve. He told Kelli that he had lung cancer and begged her to take him back. In a statement to the police, she claimed: 'Those days were very fretful for me. I took time off work to be with him. He had appointments at the hospital, and I drove him there to make sure he was OK. But he made me wait in the car. He had many, many bad ways, and some very good ways. He was bad at paying the bills, and he was always skipping off work. On balance I loved him and I didn't want him to die without seeing our child. Yet, all the time he was lying to me about the cancer. Then he got dismissed for having drugs in his officer desk drawer. That's when I kicked him out for good.' No doubt with his phoney diplomas, books and a string of colourful expletives following him. This time Kelli had had enough; having finally realised that Kenny was living in 'La-La Land'.

Poor old Ken. The guy who was so bent he couldn't lie straight in bed had lost his job with Cal Land, his bogus counselling service had flopped for lack of clients, and I can tell you that in LA this takes some beating: it seems that for every citizen there are two shrinks in the City of Angels! For her part, Kelli was pregnant, they had no home and the bills were mounting daily.

So, apart from wrecking his own life, he was flushing Kelli's down the drain too, so, she made the wise to move in with her brother at 200 East Palmer, the day after Thanksgiving 1977. Although the exact date is unknown, within a week or so she relocated again, this time to Adelaide Avenue, and shortly thereafter she travelled north to Bellingham, Washington State, where her parents put a secure roof over her head. Sadly, however, a sado-sexual serial killer would follow in her tracks.

THE OUT-CALL SERVICE

About a week after Kelli left him, Ken, who was never one to allow grass to grow under his feet, bounced back when he was introduced to a drop-dead gorgeous *Baywatch* type at a party. Blonde, attractive 'Hot Totty' just turned 16, Sabra Hannan was an aspiring model with all the physical attributes to match her ambitions. For his part, Bianchi was loveless and penniless, and Angelo was sick and tired of handing out cash to his immature cousin, so, within minutes of meeting Sabra, the quick-thinking Ken came up with another scam, one which would raise money, and also please Angelo into the bargain.

After placing a drink in her hand, Ken slipped his arm around Sabra's waist and gently eased her into another room where he explained that she was the most beautiful woman he had ever seen. He told her that he had friends in the movie business, and that she could easily earn $500 a week from the outset, and this figure would rise when she became better known.

That night, Sabra, now a little worse for drink, was lured to the Buzzard's nest, and Buono's eyes lit up when he saw the slim-figured, busty teenager. As the hours drifted by, Sabra fell asleep, totally unaware of the scheming cousins who were whispering quietly in another room.

This time, Ken had come up with a great idea: the two men would force Sabra into prostitution. Before the week was out, she was under no illusion that they would kill if she attempted to leave. By then, she was already their sex slave and soon-to-be hooker.

Fearful for her life, Sabra was now coerced into introducing her friend, 15-year-old Becky Spears, to the cousins. She, too, was forced into prostitution, and every night both men sodomised the girls to the degree that they had to wear tampons in their rectums to stop the bleeding.

After a fortnight of living hell, Becky was summoned to a wealthy lawyer's office for late-evening sex. Upon her arrival, she looked so downhearted her client asked her how she had become involved in prostitution. With tears flooding down her face, she explained that Buono and Bianchi subjected her and Sabra to degrading sex acts and sadistic cruelty. She said that the two men had threatened to track them down and kill them if they ran away.

To his credit, the lawyer acted immediately. He drove Becky to the airport where he bought her a ticket to her home in Arizona and, just before she boarded the aircraft, he stuffed a large wad of notes into her pocket. Then, he kissed her on the cheek and said goodbye.

As might be expected, Angelo went ballistic when his youngest hooker failed to return home, so he made several threatening phone calls to the lawyer, stammering, 'Give me her fuckin' address, or I'll f–f–f–f–fuckin' shoot you.' Through his real-estate contacts, Bianchi obtained the lawyer's home address then spitefully placed an ad in a local newspaper, advertising the luxurious property and its entire contents for sale. However, these were the types of threats which the attorney could easily deal with, for among his clientele was the local Chapter of the Hell's Angels, and he asked them to pay Mr Buono a visit.

Fitting new mats into a customer's car, Angelo was still fuming with rage when he was tapped smartly on the shoulder. At first, he ignored the leather-clad bikers, which was not exactly the diplomatic thing to do. Then, as one biker produced a sawn-off, pump-action 12-gauge shotgun, the largest of the group, six-four-inch, 350-pound 'Tiny', reached through the car window and extracted the struggling Buono by his throat. 'Do we have your attention, Mr Buono?' he asked.

Unfortunately, there is no record of the discussion that followed; however, we might assume that Buono received a damn good thumping. Unsurprisingly, the cousins didn't bother the attorney again, and Sabra Hannan was allowed to go free.

This incident was certainly the crucial turning point that led to the perverted Buono becoming a serial murderer. Word of his humiliation flashed around the neighbourhood like a bush fire. He lost face with his gap-toothed cronies, and the intensely macho crook was outraged that he had been exposed as a weakling in front of Bianchi and the passing public. At 'Henrys' – Buono's favourite eaterie – regular customers and staff alike sniggered behind his back. It was rumoured out loud that 'The Italian Stallion' could no longer control his women.

When I questioned Bianchi about his role in the stable of hookers, he denied that he ever touched Becky or Sabra. He added that a man called 'JJ' was a partner with Buono, and that he was merely the driver and responsible for collecting the cash of which he might receive a small percentage.

After his arrest several years later, Bianchi was interviewed by LAPD Sergeant Frank Salerno about the call-girl service. The following transcript was published in 2005:

Salerno: What was the financial arrangement for the call-out service? You guys obviously were going to get something out of what the girls made?

Bianchi: The girls would be working for JJ, completely, and the girls would have to pay Angelo . . . I can't remember the exact percentage because it varied.

Salerno: So, it was coming out of the girls' take?

Bianchi: Right, and it would go to Angelo.

Salerno: Strictly to Angelo?

Bianchi: Yeah, and then Angelo would, you know, give me what I . . .

Salerno: What? What would he give you?

Bianchi: It varied. It just depended on what the girls got. Sometimes if the girls got only – came home with only $20, there would be no take or very little take and I wouldn't get anything, you know, it would just be a pass situation. Sometimes the girls would come home with like $100–$200.

Salerno: What would you get out of that?

Bianchi: I would probably end up with about $20–$30 out of that.

Salerno: Out of $100 or out of $200?

Bianchi: Out of about $200.

Salerno: What would the girls end up with?

Bianchi: The remainder, probably about $140.

Salerno: And Angelo would get $20 or $30?

Bianchi: Right, about the same.

Salerno: So, in essence, you and Angelo were still partners in . . . an out-call service or something along that line?

Bianchi: Right.

POLICE MAKE A KILLING

With the slave girls gone, Bianchi's and Buono's pimping income dried up so the two men had to find more teenage girls. They tried to abduct one lass, then realised that she was the daughter of the famous actor, Peter Lorre. Snatching her from the sidewalk was far too risky. Eventually, they found a young woman and installed her in a room at Buono's home adjacent to his workshop, in Glendale. They also bought a 'trick list' from a prostitute calling herself Deborah Noble with names of men who frequented hookers. However, the truth was quite the opposite, because it was a list of men who wanted to visit one particular good-time girl in her own apartment. To make matters worse, this prostitute already had a pimp, and she had no intention of going into business with the likes of Bianchi and Buono. The list was useless; the dirty duo had slipped up yet again and, to explain the effect this rip-off had upon these two clowns, Bianchi wrote in a letter, 'We went in search of the vendor [of the list], madder than hell.'

The police have always maintained that Bianchi and Buono never found the seller of this list, and that an acquaintance of the seller, Yolanda Washington, was the first victim of the Hillside Strangling series. However, Bianchi told me that this was not the case. Ken argued that Laura Collins had sold them the phoney list, and that is why she was the first to die.

Also, of some interest is the fact that when the Hillside Strangler task force was assembled in December 1977, Laura Collins's name was erased from the victims' list, and it was not until January 1978 that the then Assistant Chief of Police, Darryl gates, publicly confirmed that Laura was, indeed, the first victim.

LAURA COLLINS

Born 15 June 1951, 26-year-old Laura was last seen alive just after noon at Ventura Freeway and Lankershim Boulevard, on Sunday, 4 September 1977. Her partially clothed body was found near the Forest Lawn off-ramp off the Ventura Freeway, Burbank, at 10.30 a.m., Friday, 9 September. The very pretty black girl had been strangled, and this homicide became the blueprint for all of the subsequent killings.

YOLANDA WASHINGTON

At 1.34 p.m. on Monday, 18 October 1977, a naked body was found perversely sprawled on its stomach alongside Forest Lawn Drive; close to the famous cemetery of the same name, and just south of the Ventura Freeway. A photograph shows her face down, arms outstretched, right hand bent at the wrist, the legs spread-eagled. It appeared that she had been dragged from a vehicle and deposited near a pile of broken road-surfacing concrete a few feet from her head. Behind the body was a yellow 'No Trespassing or Loitering' sign.

The tall and leggy black woman was immediately identified by Vice Squad officers as Yolanda Washington; an attractive 19-year-old with almond-shaped eyes and medium-length black hair. She was a part-time waitress and hooker known to have touted for business with Laura Collins.

Enquiries soon established that Yolanda had last been seen alive just before midnight the previous day as she solicited for business at Vista Del Mar Avenue and West Sunset Boulevard. On a good night, she could earn over $300, which helped her support her 30-month-old daughter, Tameika.

The autopsy showed that she'd had sex with two men shortly before meeting her death – one of whom a non-secretor. With her killer/s kneeling over her, she had been strangled with a piece of cloth while she was lying down. There were marks of restraint around her wrists. She had been anally raped.

Bianchi confirmed this to me, saying that he had killed her in the back seat of his car and had removed a turquoise ring from her finger, an item that he later gave to Kelli Boyd.

JUDITH 'JUDY' ANN MILLER

Just after midnight on Monday, 31 October 1977, a white female was abducted from the West Hollywood area of Howard and Wilcox Avenue. Small and thin, with medium-length reddish-brown hair, 15-year-old Judy Miller lived in a ramshackle hotel, her base as a part-time streetwalker. From trailer-park stock, her mother was wanted in connection with a welfare fraud, and her father had jumped bail for a similar offence.

It was a pretty grim sight that Halloween morning at Alta Terrace and La Crescenta Avenue. The naked body lay close to the kerb in a middle-class residential area, covered by a tarpaulin by a property owner to screen the corpse from the children in the neighbourhood. The bruises on Judy's neck showed that she had been strangled. She had ligature marks encircling both wrists and ankles. Insects feasted on her pale skin. On one eyelid was a small piece of light-coloured fluff that Sergeant Frank Salerno saved for forensic examination, and it did not appear that she had been murdered at this location. (The fluff was later matched, in every respect, to material found in Buono's workshop.)

The medical examiner determined that Judy had died around

midnight, some six hours before she was found. It was also clear that she had been raped and sodomised.

Bianchi would tell me that Judy had been taken back to Buono's house where she had been raped. Bianchi sodomised her, and then he strangled her. He admitted to finishing her off by suffocating his tragic victim with a plastic supermarket bag. 'She involuntarily urinated after death, just as Washington had done,' Bianchi claimed, with an evil grin playing around his mouth. 'We made her go into the washroom before we killed her to stop her peeing, but it didn't work. She was tied by the arms, legs and neck to our special chair in Angelo's bedroom. She didn't like dying one bit.'

ELISSA TERESA 'LISSA' KASTIN

Born 10 December 1955, Lissa Teresa Kastin was a white dancer/ waitress at the Healthfair Restaurant near Hollywood Boulevard and Vine Street. The 21-year-old was a cabaret performer with the LA Knockers, a popular dance ensemble, and she became the stranglers' fourth victim. Presentably attractive, with a Roman nose and bushy dark hair, she was stopped by Bianchi and Buono, who were posing as police officers, at 9.15 p.m. on Saturday, 5 November 1977. They ordered her into their black-over-white sedan and, like Judy Miller, she was taken back to Buono's home for what Bianchi called 'questioning'. There, she was tied down in the special chair, and her striped sweater and short skirt were cut off with scissors. The two men were repelled because she had hairy legs, and Bianchi was reduced to raping her with a root-beer bottle as he throttled her. When she kicked out in her death throes, Buono sat on her legs, shouting, 'Die, you cunt, die.' The poor young woman was allowed to suck in lungfuls of air many times before she lost consciousness for the last time.

At 1.15 a.m. the next day, Lissa's body was found at upscale East Chevy Chase Drive and Linda Vista Drive. Identification was made swiftly after a TV broadcast reported the murder and her father telephoned the police and reported his daughter as missing.

At the autopsy, no semen was found to be present in the vagina or anus, which supported Bianchi's declaration to me that neither of the two men had physically raped this victim.

JILL BARCOMBE

Jill was an 18-year-old white hooker who had moved to Hollywood following a string of prostitution convictions in New York. She was last seen alive at West Pico Boulevard and Ocean Avenue at around 7.00 p.m. on Wednesday, 9 November 1977. Jill was found naked and strangled at 5.50 am the following morning at Franklin Canyon Drive and Mulholland Drive. The young woman had clearly put up a fierce fight for her life, as severe head trauma was present.

JANE EVELYN KING

A 28-year-old aspiring actress and part-time model with real 'wow' factor, Jane King was rated by the 'Hollywood Set' as a stunning blonde bombshell who had exploded on the scene when she was just 16. Over the years, Jane had raised the eyebrows of every hot-blooded male and film producer who saw her. She was also a Scientology student and a follower of L. Ron Hubbard's work on Dianetics – the eradication of negative thought and energy in order to lead a more fulfilled life. Police claimed that she was a part-time hooker, but this was entirely incorrect.

Jane was last seen alive outside 9500 Lemona Avenue, at 10.10 p.m. on Wednesday, 9 November 1977. Again posing as police officers, Buono and Bianchi cruised up, arrested her on suspicion of prostitution and drove her back to Buono's house where she was dragged screaming through the living/dining area into the east bedroom where she was stripped naked. Bianchi confessed that they were 'delighted to find her pubis was shaven'. However, because she struggled while she was being raped, the two men decided to teach her a lesson. A plastic bag was placed over her head while Bianchi sodomised her. Jane pleaded desperately for her life during a four-hour period of terror before she was allowed to suffocate to death as Bianchi climaxed.

Jane's decomposing naked body was found on a bed of dead leaves in undergrowth at the Los Felix Boulevard off-ramp of the Golden State Freeway on Wednesday, 23 November. She lay on her back, legs open, with the right knee drawn up.

SONJA MARIE JOHNSON AND DOLORES ANN 'DOLLY' CEPEDA

The murders of Sonja and Dolores, and the violence and brutality they suffered, shocked everyone involved in the case and the entire city of Los Angeles. Sonja (14) and Dolores (12) were two innocent little girls who happened to be in the wrong place at the wrong time.

Judge Roger Boren – former prosecutor at Bianchi and Buono's trial in LA – told me, 'Angelo Buono and Kenneth Bianchi followed the girls riding on a bus as they travelled from a shopping mall, and apparently used some police ruse that they were being arrested. They took these two children to Buono's house – tortured them and strangled them to death.' As Roger, later a Supreme Court Judge, handed me the photos of the dead girls in situ, he was white and shaking all over. It was still clearly affecting him twenty years later. 'They took the girls to a hillside overlooking one of the largest freeways in Los Angeles and discarded their bodies. That particular part of the hillside was used by many people to discard trash. There were couches, mattresses . . . things of that sort had been thrown down that hillside. And these two bodies had been discarded in a like manner. In fact, they were not discovered for two weeks.'

Sonja and Dolores, both pupils at the Saint Ignatius School, 6025 Monte Vista Street, were last seen alive on Sunday, 13 November 1977, boarding a bus at the Eagle Plaza stop at Colorado Boulevard, which was just a mile from Buono's premises. The two men followed the bus and, when the children alighted near their own home, again posing as a police officer, Bianchi approached the girls and accused them of shoplifting. They were taken 'downtown' and interviewed in Angelo's place. Sonja was raped and murdered in a bedroom by Buono, while the terrified, compliant Dolores, sat outside with Bianchi.

'Where's my friend?' asked Dolly when Buono came out alone.

'Oh, don't worry,' said Bianchi, 'you'll be seeing her in a minute.'

The last thing Dolly saw was the dead face of Sonja on the bed beside her as Bianchi raped and sodomised her, before throttling her to death.

Children playing on a rubbish tip at Stadium Way found the girls' naked bodies at 4.00 p.m. on Sunday, 20 November.

The crime scene photographs show Dolly and Sonja sprawled out among discarded beer bottles and tin cans. There is a 'No Dumping' sign just a few feet away. Sonja rests almost on her right side, her left arm tucked up under breasts, the hand nudging her chin. The right arm, hand gripped tight in a death spasm, was outstretched and underneath her right side. The legs are almost straight, the left foot draped over the neck of Dolly who was on her stomach; her torso slightly crooked and leaning to the right of her legs, which are parted. Dolly's left arm is also tucked underneath her body, her hand covering her mouth as if to stifle a scream. The right arm, bent at the elbow, is outstretched. There are human bite marks on her left buttock. These marks were later found to match Bianchi's teeth.

I have visited all of the crime scenes involved with Bianchi and Buono, but nothing could have prepared me for the drive with my film crew, through teeming rain, along Stadium Way with homicide detective, Leroy Orozco, one of the lead investigators in the case, to this dreadful place. We all stood silently with a grey mist now enveloping the hillside. Down there, to the east, is the Golden State Freeway, the traffic is knotted into a jam as hundreds of cars, their taillights glowing ruby red as they slither to a standstill along the highway. A little further is one of LA's massive flood canals. Just four miles due south is downtown central LA.

We said a prayer for those girls, and when one sees such terrible things as those photographs, and such god-awful places where women and little children are dumped like garbage, their precious lives snuffed out, *only* then can one even begin to understand the true, evil nature of men like Kenneth Bianchi and Angelo Buono.

KATHLEEN 'KATHY' ROBINSON

'The public were just outraged that we, as law-enforcement officers, could not do anything to stop these brutal murders,' Detective Richard Crotsley, LAPD, told me in an interview. 'Especially the single women in this city who went to work at nights, going to markets, going to see their families. They were petrified.'

* * *

Like Jane King, 17-year-old Kathy was an attractive blonde who was well known around the hotspots of Hollywood. Her flowing hair caught the attention of the Hillside Stranglers at 9.30 p.m. on Wednesday, 16 November 1977. She was walking towards her car, parked near West Pico Boulevard and Ocean Avenue (where Jill Barcombe had last been seen alive), when Buono and Bianchi drew up alongside her. Flashing a phoney police badge they had bought at a swap meet, they ordered her into their car. She was found fully clothed, strangled, with her throat cut, at Burnside and Curson Avenue, at 8.30 a.m. the next day.

KRISTINA WECKLER

A quiet young woman, 20-year-old Kristina Weckler was an honours student at the Pasadena Art Centre of Design. She lived at Tamarind Apartments, Tamarind Avenue, Glendale. This was the same apartment complex where Bianchi had once resided, and he knew the young woman and had pestered her for a date. Kristina, who knew that Ken was living with the pregnant Kelli Boyd, had rejected his advances.

Kristina's naked body was found at Ranons Avenue and Wawona Street on Sunday, 20 November. Detective Sergeant Bob Grogan immediately noticed the ligature marks on her wrists, ankles and neck. When he turned her over, blood oozed from her rectum. The two bruises on her breasts were obvious. Oddly enough, there were two puncture marks on her right arm, but no signs of the needle tracks that indicate a drug addict.

Bianchi told me that, at around 6.00 p.m. on Saturday, 19 November, he knocked on Kristina's door. Flashing his phoney badge, he told her that he was now a police officer, and that someone had crashed into her car parked outside. Once in the parking lot, she was unceremoniously bundled into his car and driven to Buono's home where they tried to kill her using a new method. They had intended to inject Kristina with caustic cleaning fluid; however, when this barbaric method of murder failed, they covered her head with a plastic bag and piped coal gas into her lungs. Bianchi raped Kristina, ejaculating into her during the moment she convulsed in death. She died as the result of strangulation by ligature.

Bianchi, however, told police something different. He said that he had knocked on Kristina's door and had asked her if she wanted to go to a party. At first, Kristina said that she was tired. But Bianchi was insistent and she took up the offer, slipping on a pair of brown loafers, a beige long-sleeved blouse and a skirt (she was wearing slacks), and followed Bianchi to his car, in which Buono was sitting.

They arrived at the murder house at about 12.30 a.m. It was obviously deserted and the men said that the other guests would soon arrive. Within minutes they were killing her. Using the method described above, the terrified and totally submissive Kristina took over an hour to die.

Describing how Buono injected the poor girl, Bianchi told police:

He [Buono] suggested that . . . he said, 'How about just injecting air into her? The air bubble would probably kill her.' I said, 'Oh, you want to try something different. Whatever.'

We both walked into the dining room, put the chair back at the dining-room table. He grabbed her underwear and her socks and went back into the bedroom and set the needle down on the bed . . . at one end of the bed and he said to her, 'Come on, now, we're going to stand up,' and he sat on the edge of the bed and he helped her get her clothes on, her underwear and socks, he said, 'OK, now, come on. Stand up.' And he helped her stand up and we walked her to the open part of the room at the bottom of the bed and set her down on the floor, face up. He took the needle, took the cap off of it, he pulled back the plunger and he told me, he said, 'Hold her legs.' I held her legs. He crouched down. He's on her left side. He stuck the needle in her neck [left side] and pushed the plunger in and pulled it out.

He did it a couple of times. She flinched and made a

murmuring sound and he stood up and he said, 'Let go of her legs,' and he walked towards me and pushed me lightly back towards the doorway and he says, 'Just stand here and see what happens.' So I stood there for about five to ten minutes. Nothing happened. He says, 'What I should do is put something in the needle. Stay here. I'll be right back.' He went into the kitchen area. When he came back there was a blue solution, some kind of blue solution in the needle.

He injected her and said, 'Help me to get her up.' We helped her to her feet and she was still shaking. Walked her into the kitchen and walked her to the front where his stove was being put in, or the connection was, and lied here down on the floor. He stood up and started to walk away from her and he indicated me to walk with him. He had to talk to me. We walked into the dining room, and in the dining room he said, 'What I'll do is put a bag over her head,' he says. 'I'll use the twine; I'll cut off a piece of twine, so we can make a seal on the bag,' he says, 'and the pipe, the bendable pipe is long enough,' he says. 'Stick that under the bag and when I tell you, turn on the gas and when I tell you, turn the gas off.'

After we'd had a little discussion in the dining room, we walked back into the kitchen. Kristina Weckler's lying on the floor in his direction, in front of the fixture. Angelo is standing here to one side. She's still shaking really bad, probably from that blue stuff that was injected into her. He put the bag over her head and there was no unusual movement when he did that. He told me to get the pipe and stick the pipe under the bag, which I did. He then wrapped the twine a couple of times around her neck and pulled it tight and said, 'OK, go ahead. Turn it on.' I turned on the gas, the bag inflated. He said, Turn off the gas.' I turned off the gas, and he waited until it deflated. Turned it on again. We repeated this probably about four or five times.

Finally, it was obvious that she had stopped breathing, so he said to take the tubing out, which I did ... put the tubing back and made sure the valve was turned off all the way. He took the twine off of her and the bag off her head. He took out his keys and rolled her over and unlocked the handcuffs. I took off the tape and gag from her mouth and took the blindfold off and he removed her pants and underwear. We both walked into the dining room and put everything into a paper bag. He then got the roll of tape and taped up the bag. I walked to the back door. He walked to the dumpster. Moved a few things around and tossed the bag in there. Put the things on top of the bag. He came in, asked me for the keys to my car. He said, 'I'll open the trunk.' When he got through opening the trunk, he walked to the street, looked around and came back again ... then we dumped her off.

LAUREN RAE WAGNER

A promising lead in the hunt for the killers came on Monday, 28 November 1977, the day after a student and trainee secretary disappeared from 9500 Lemona Avenue, Sepulveda, in the San Fernando Valley. The father of 18-year-old Lauren found her car parked, with the driver's door open and the interior light on, near his house and directly in front of the home of an elderly woman called Beulah Stofer.

Mrs Stofer would tell police how she had seen the slim, young redhead abducted by two men. They were driving a black-over-white sedan, and first thought that it had been a police car.

At 7.30 a.m. the following day, a driver on his way to work found a naked body at 1200 Cliff Drive in the Mount Washington area; about 20-miles southeast of Lauren's home and approximately four miles from Buono's killing house. Lauren was lying on her back, her left arm outstretched, her left lower leg just touching the road. Her mass of rich, red hair framed her pretty face, and her eyes were peacefully closed. It looked as though she had burns on her palms. Like the unusual puncture marks on Kristina Weckler's arms, it seemed as though the killers were experimenting – possibly with methods of torture. There was also something else that was different – a shiny track of some sticky liquid, which had attracted a convoy of ants. If this substance was semen or saliva, there was a possibility that the killer, or killers' blood type, could be determined. Tests on semen found on earlier victims had revealed nothing.

Bianchi told me that, back at Buono's house, Lauren pretended to enjoy being raped in the desperate hope that her attackers would allow her to live. However, they tried to electrocute the young woman by attaching live electrical wires to the palms of her hands, but this only caused extreme pain and superficial burns. Bianchi then raped her, and Buono strangled Lauren to death with a ligature.

The two killers soon realised they had been seen by the inquisitive Mrs Stofer, so they obtained her telephone number, and called her from a kiosk in the Francis Howard Goldwyn Hollywood Regional Branch Library, at 1623 Ivar Avenue, where they subjected the lady to death threats. Undeterred, though, she was able to furnish police with an excellent description – one that matched Bianchi and Buono in every respect. She also added that the men's car had pulled up directly behind Lauren's when she stopped outside. That, there were the sounds of voices, a scuffle . . . then she watched as Lauren was forced into her abductors' vehicle, which reversed into Plummer Street and roared away.

KIMBERLY 'KIM' AKA 'DONNA' DIANE MARTIN

On Monday, 14 December 1977, police were called to a vacant lot on a steep slope at 2006 N. Alvarado Street, where they arrived at 7.03 a.m. The sun had just come up, and it was a clear day with very few clouds in the sky. Rampart Divisional Patrol Unit 2-A-47, consisting of officers Lewis and Akeson, had responded to a radio call alerting them to a dead female body lying by the roadside, which ran through the floor of the canyon splitting Lakeshore Avenue and Alvarado Street.

When homicide detectives Oakes and Richard Crotsley arrived, they noticed that the tall, blonde victim was lying on her back in the now familiar spread-eagle position, and that post-mortem lividity had started to form in her toes. The young woman was Caucasian, and in her twenties. There were ligature marks circling her wrists, ankles and her neck. On her left forearm she had a tattoo – a square 'cross' with four dots within its border. On the right ankle was a second tattoo of faint design bearing the name 'Kim'. With no identification to be found, she was tagged as 'Jane Doe # 112', and the stranglers' penultimate victim was on her way to the morgue.

Using documents furnished by the LAPD, and confirming this with Bianchi himself, it is now possible to plot Kimberly's last hours in some detail. And we can see the cunning of the Hillside Stranglers as they entrap their victim.

At precisely 8.30 p.m., on Tuesday, 13 December 1977, the phone of 'Climax Nude Modeling', 1815 Serrano Avenue, rang, and Michelle Elaine Rodriguez answered it. The call came from a man who gave the name 'Mike Ryan' (Kenneth Bianchi using his son's Christian name), and below is the transcript of that recorded conversation:

Rodriguez: Hello. Modelling service.

Bianchi: Hello. Yes. Can you get me a girl?

Rodriguez: That depends where you are located, sir.

Bianchi: I'm in Hollywood.

Rodriguez: That will be no problem. I can have a girl with you in about 15 minutes.

Bianchi: How much does it cost?

Rodriguez: $40 for a modelling service.

Bianchi: Okay. My wife has left town for the first time in two years, so I would like you to send me a pretty blonde model if you could. Possibly wearing black stockings and a dress.

Rodriguez: That will be no problem, sir. May I have your name?

Bianchi: Michael Ryan.

Rodriguez: And could you spell your last name, please?

Bianchi: R–Y–A–N.

Rodriguez: May I have your telephone number?

Bianchi: 462-9794.

Rodriguez: Sir, that is a payphone. [Once again, Bianchi was using the kiosk in the Hollywood Library.]

Bianchi: Ha, hah, hah. You know it's funny. A lot of people seem to think that this is a payphone. It must be a digit in the number or something.

Rodriguez: That must be what it is. The reason I thought it was a payphone is that the fourth digit of the number is a '9'. It's a payphone.

Bianchi: That must be it, or the fact that you hear my TV in the background. Would you like me to turn it off? [The 'television noise' was the sound of people talking in the library.]

Rodriguez: Oh, no. I'll verify it.

Bianchi: All right.

Rodriguez: And, what is your address, sir?

Bianchi: 1950 Tamarind.

Rodriguez: Sir, could you spell that for me?

Bianchi: T-A-M-A-R-I-N-D.

Rodriguez: Is this a house, or an apartment?

Bianchi: This is an apartment. Number 114.

Rodriguez: Sir, how are you going to pay?

Bianchi: Cash.

Rodriguez: May I ask where you found our advertisement?

Bianchi: *The Freep*. [A local free paper.]

Rodriguez: Okay, sir. I'll have a girl out to you shortly.

This was the end of the first conversation, and Michelle then rang the operator to verify the number. She always followed this practice to ensure she didn't send a girl out to a prank call. First she would ask the operator if the number was a payphone. If it was, under normal circumstances the operator would confirm it; however, if it was a private number, the operator would advise the caller that she could not give out that information. But, on this rare occasion, Bianchi had luck on his side, for the operator spoke to her supervisor, and came back to Michelle, saying, 'No, my supervisor will not allow me to give out that information.' Of course, Michelle understood this to mean that the client had booked one of the girls from a private address – which it wasn't – and therefore the call was good. She phoned 'Mr Ryan' back, and he picked up the handset immediately 'as if he was waiting for the call', said Michelle later to the police. Unwittingly, Michelle had now sealed the fate of Kimberly Martin.

Bianchi:	Hello.
Rodriguez:	Hello. Michael?
Bianchi:	Yes.
Rodriguez:	This is the modelling agency calling to verify your call.
Bianchi:	Okay. Thank you. How much longer will it take before the girl will call me?
Rodriguez:	Very shortly.
Bianchi:	Okay. Thank you. Goodbye.

Michelle then phoned Kimberly Martin, who worked under the name of 'Donna'.

Rodriguez: I have a call. It's a cash call-out in Hollywood in an apartment. Do you want it?

Kimberly: Yeah. Give me the information.

Rodriguez: Michael Ryan. Phone number 46209794. 1950 Tamarind, Hollywood. Cash. Apartment 114. Sounds like a good call to me. It's an apartment. It's near your location, but always be careful and make sure he's not a cop.

Kimberly: Sounds good to me. I'll give him a call.

Rodriguez: Okay. Goodbye.

Kimberly Martin called her prospective client before ringing the agency back.

Kimberly: Sounds good to me. I am going right on it.

Rodriguez: Call me when you get there. Goodbye.

Bianchi had been seen sitting on the library steps at around 9.00 p.m., before he suddenly stood up and walked off. Buono was picking him up.

The distance from the library on Ivar Avenue to 1950 North Tamarind Avenue is almost a mile, taking an average of five minutes to drive. Bianchi and Buono drove south to Hollywood Boulevard, then Vine Street, and turned east along West Sunset Boulevard to the junction of Tamarind.

At around 9.05 p.m., Kimberly left her apartment. It would take her 15 minutes to drive the 3.8 miles to Tamarind, where she parked up and walked into the lobby, where several people saw her at 9.25 p.m. Shortly thereafter, residents heard a woman screaming, 'Please don't kill me!' but all of them thought that this was a domestic dispute. Minutes later, though, they found the contents of a woman's handbag strewn along a hallway.

Bianchi claims that he and Buono dragged Kimberly out through a rear entrance and into the underground car park where they had left their car. They drove six miles to Buono's killing house, where she was tortured, raped and murdered. 'We killed her because she was fuckin' useless in bed,' Bianchi explained to me.

CINDY LEE HUDSPETH

Even though 84 officers were assigned to the Hillside Strangler's investigation, the general public now thought that the police were helpless. They were not wrong. With some 10,000 leads to follow up, thousands of fingerprints to be processed and a reward for $140,000 posted for information that would lead to the killer/s' arrest, the task force were no nearer catching the stranglers than they were on day one.

After press headlines suggested that the killers were posing as police officers, Joe Public trusted no one. It was even suggested that two renegade law officers might be running amok on some kind of sick vendetta. Indeed, it got to the point where nobody could be certain of the true identity of a man wearing a uniform, or flashing a silver shield, and citizens were simply not stopping when requested by any cop, uniformed or not. So the police implemented a new policy; one that allowed motorists to drive to a police station with a police cruiser, its red, white and blue flashing strobes, following them, and this prompt action partially put people's minds at rest.

★ ★ ★

'Nothing happened on the murders during the month of January, possibly because Angelo Buono's mother was in the hospital with a terminal illness,' Judge Roger Boren, who was prosecutor at Bianchi and Buono's trial in LA said to me in an interview. 'But in February of 1978, the last of the Hillside Strangling murders in Los Angeles occurred when Cindy Hudspeth's body was found up in the mountains above Glendale on the Angeles Crest Highway.'

On Friday, 17 February 1978, an Angeles National Forest Rangers helicopter clattered over a ravine along the Angeles Crest Highway. The observer spotted an orange Datsun car caught up in shrubs on a steep hillside, precariously close to a drop of several hundred feet. The pilot made a low pass, and while his aircraft hovered overhead, he summoned police, who arrived at the scene to discover 20-year-old Cindy Lee Hudspeth in the car's boot. She had been strangled and her body bore the same ligature marks as the previous victims.

The police soon learned that the brunette who worked as a telephonist was also employed as a part-time waitress at the Robin Hood Inn, a restaurant frequented by Angelo Buono. In his statement to police, Bianchi claimed that he had arrived at Buono's auto-upholstery shop where he saw Cindy's car parked outside. 'She had called to enquire if Angelo could make new mats for her,' he said. The two men spread-eagled Cindy on a bed, hog-tied her, then raped and strangled her over a period of two hours. Then, with the dead body in the boot, Bianchi drove her car, closely followed by Buono in another vehicle, to the ravine where they tried to push the Datsun over the edge. It rolled 50 feet then stopped, but by then the killers had fled.

The murder of Cindy proved to be the last of the Hillside Stranglings, for after a heated argument with Bianchi, during which Buono pointed a loaded revolver at Ken's head and told him to 'F-f-f-ff off', Bianchi packed his bags and left 'The City of Angels'. The reason for the argument was twofold. First, Bianchi was becoming a financial liability, secondly he wanted to join the LAPD, and had told Buono that he had taken a ride-along in a squad car while making his application. Buono blew his top and went back to refurbishing cars. He kept his head down and did not commit murder again, while Ken drove all of 1,220 miles north to Bellingham, Washington State, leaving thirteen dead bodies, countless broken lives and a mountain of debt in his wake. A new hunting ground awaited him.

KAREN LAURETTA MANDIC AND DIANE A. WILDER

The most straightforward route from Los Angeles to Washington State is along Interstate 5; however, having time on my hands, I drove through San Francisco, and took the more scenic drive along Route 101, passing through the lush orange groves to Eureka, Arcata, on to Crescent City, where I enjoyed a brief visit to the Pelican Bay State Prison. With the rolling surf of the Pacific Ocean beneath a precipitous drop on one side, I moved on into Oregon redwood country, passing through small towns and picturesque villages – Coos Bay, Florence, Newport, then Lincoln City – before a right turn took me to Portland, Oregon, where I joined Interstate 5 for the long haul through Washington State up to Bellingham.

The small, seaport city of Bellingham – named in 1792 after Sir William Bellingham, the Controller of the Storekeeper's Account of the Royal Navy – has a population of about 82,000, and sits 20 miles due south of the Canadian border, on the northwest seaboard of 'The Evergreen State'. Bellingham, in Whatcom County, is the gateway to the Mount Baker recreational area, which looks over one of the most magnificent vistas in the area – the pine-clad slopes of San Juan, the Vancouver Islands and the Strait of Juan de Fuca.

When I visited Bellingham in 1996, the place was wrapped in an icy coat, a typical winter in those parts, and my thoughts travelled back in time to January 1979, when the weather was similar, but laced with the cold chill of murder. Violent crime in this neck of the woods was such a rarity in the 70s that, when Chief of Police Terry Mangan was informed one Friday morning that two co-eds from the Western Washington University (WWU) had been reported by friends as 'missing under suspicious circumstances', his first thought was that they had left town for an early vacation without telling anyone.

Born on 28 October 1956, Karen Lauretta Mandic, from Bellevue, was a junior, majoring in business administration while 27-year-old Diana A. Wilder, from Bremerton, was a transfer student, majoring in dance at WWU's Fairhaven College. They shared a rented house at 1246 Ellis Street, directly opposite St Joseph Hospital.

Chief Mangan was a former Roman Catholic priest whose close friend Sister Carmel Marie once ran the Saint Ignatius School in Los Angeles. She had introduced Terry Mangan to the bookkeeper of her diocese, one Tony Johnson and his wife

Mary, of Eagle Rock. In November 1977, when the Hillside Stranglings were at their peak, Mangan had read in newspaper that Johnson's 14-year-old adopted daughter, Sonja, had been one of the victims. Now, in January 1979, following an amazing string of tragic circumstances, Mangan would secure the arrest of one of Tinsel Town's serial killers in his own backyard.

Karen Mandic was a beautiful 22-year-old with long, blonde hair. She had last been seen alive at 7.00 p.m. on Thursday, 11 January, when leaving the Fred Myer Super Shopping Center, at 800 Lakeway Drive on Interstate 5, where she worked as a part-time cashier. Ken, who by now was back living with Kelli and his baby son Ryan, at 401E North Street, had previously worked at Fred Myer as a security guard. He was now employed as a security officer with the Whatcom Security Agency (WSA), a local company that provided mobile and static security patrols through a 50-mile radius of Bellingham. Bianchi had pledged Karen to secrecy; nevertheless, she was thrilled with the opportunity to earn some extra cash, and earlier in the week, had told two friends, Steve Hardwick and Bill Bryant, that a man who had recently asked her for a date (in fact, he had asked her for a date several times) had offered her a house-sitting job for the Thursday evening, and it paid $100 an hour.

Upon learning of this offer Steve Hardwick was suspicious from the outset. Karen, however, would have none of it, insisting that everything was okay. She explained that the house, owned by a Dr Catlow, was in an upscale area, that the doctor was going on vacation in Europe with his wife Cleora, that the alarm was not working, and that she had invited along a friend called Diane Wilder for company.

Dr William V. Catlow was a recently retired Georgia-Pacific Corporation executive who lived in the beautiful, sprawling ranch-style property overlooking Chuckanut Bay, and it was easy money, she told Hardwick. All they had to do was wait until the burglar alarm technician turned up later in the evening, and then she would return to Fred Myer and cash up. Besides, Bianchi worked for WSA, which was a highly regarded firm, and even Hardwick knew that.

Nevertheless, Hardwick, who could smell a latrine rat from miles away, was still highly suspicious, so he pressed Karen further. 'Don't worry,' she snapped back, 'it's only for two hours, and I'll be back to finish up at the store by 9 p.m. Everything will be okay. I am taking Diane with me. Ken has given my name to the insurance company who are paying the bill. I can't change anything now.'

When Karen failed to return to Fred Myer later in the evening, the store manager telephoned Hardwick, who immediately drove to Dr Catlow's house at 334 Bayside, where the split-level property appeared deserted. Although he could not recall Bianchi's name, Hardwick did remember WSA, so he telephoned the night dispatcher, Wendy Whitton, and requested any information held on the Bayside account. Wendy, who was not authorised to reveal details of her employers' business, promised the anxious Hardwick that she would call the company's co-owner, Randall 'Randy' W. Moa, and, as soon as she did, alarm bells began to ring.

Moa and his partner, Joe Parker, had just completed a somewhat belated security background check on Bianchi's CV, and, in doing so, they had spoken to one Susan Bird, an attractive woman who lived locally. Susan was shocked to hear that Bianchi had obtained work in the security business because he had recently suggested to her that, because of her stunning figure, she would make a good prostitute, and he could become her pimp. She was even more concerned as she knew that Ken had applied to the Bellingham Police Department for a job as a cop.

At first, Moa and Parker didn't believe Susan Bird, so she put them in touch with a girlfriend called Annie Kinneberg. Annie and her pal, Margie Lager, confirmed what Susan had said, relating that Bianchi had also wanted to photograph lesbian models for clients that he said he had back in LA. 'He's a kinky bastard,' Annie explained. 'He's living with a woman called Kelli, and they have a little boy. That guy is real weird, you know.'

Upon receiving the call from Wendy Whitton, Moa sprang into action. First, he radioed Steve Adams, and ordered the night patrol officer to check out the Bayside address himself. Unfortunately, Steve went to the wrong address, 302 Bayside, where he knocked up the bleary-eyed owners who knew nothing at all. Then, having realised his mistake, he called the office, and waited in his truck for further instructions.

In the meantime, and in another effort to solve the problem, Moa telephoned Bianchi at home. Ken denied all knowledge of the house sitting job. He also denied knowing anyone called Diane Wilder or Karen Mandic, adding to his protestations of innocence by claiming that he had been to a Sheriff's Reserve first-aid meeting that evening.

Then Moa contacted Gordon Scott, the instructor of the Sheriff's Reserve for confirmation of what Bianchi had told them, and learned that Bianchi was lying. Ken had failed to turn up for the class, with the excuse that he had to teach a class for his employer. Moa then rang the Bellingham Police Department, who phoned Bianchi at 2.30 a.m., asking him to come to WSA's office, where officers asked Bianchi if he knew the two young women. Initially Ken flatly denied the suggestion, then realising that he was painting himself into a corner, he backtracked, saying, 'Maybe Karen.' A gut feeling told the cops that Bianchi was not telling the truth because he wouldn't look them straight in the eye. When questioned about not attending the Sheriff's Reserve meeting, he appeared even more shifty and nervous, explaining that he had gone out driving alone. However, with little evidence to take him into custody, Bianchi was allowed to return home.

THE CUL-DE-SAC

There were told to lay face down and then they were separated, tied up and, individually, one by one, untied, undressed and I had sex with them. Then they were both dressed again. Then I killed them separately. I believe, ah, Diane Wilder was the first and Karen Mandic second. Then they were carried out and put in the back of their car and driven to the cul-de-sac.

Kenneth Bianchi confessing to the author at interview

At 6 o'clock that morning, Bill Bryant, who was a university-campus police officer, obtained a key to Karen's apartment. By the telephone, written in red ink, was a message dated 9 January in Diane's handwriting. It read: *'Karen. Ken B called. Phone 733-*

2884.' Picking up the scrap of paper, Bill decided to call the number. It turned out to be WSA, and, lo and behold, it was Bianchi who answered the phone. 'I know your voice,' said Bryant. 'You called Karen's apartment on Tuesday, and I told you that she wasn't in.' Once again, Ken denied knowing Karen Mandic, adding that anyone could be using his name.

Bryant then called his father, who was also a police officer, and he, in turn, called the Bellingham Police Department who re-interviewed Bianchi later in the morning. Officers Geddes and Page confronted him with the note, and Ken reacted angrily. 'I'd sure like to know who has been using my name,' he snapped. 'I'm well known. I was in the newspaper when I left Fred Myer to come here in charge of operations.'

Nevertheless, even though Bianchi was now the chief suspect in the girls' abduction, the officers could do little more than allow him to carry on with his work, despite the evidence mounting against him.

That night, according to the HistoryLink website (www. historylink.org), detectives obtained permission from Catlow's family to search the house on Bayside Road. Nothing appeared out of the ordinary, but they discovered wet footprints on the kitchen floor. (The prints would later be found to match the soles of Bianchi's cowboy boots.) The WWU security office reported that neither Mandic nor Wilder had attended their morning classes. A frantic search for answers continued throughout the day, as Detective Knudsen explained to me.

At 4.30 p.m. the same day, Shirlee Schlemmer, who lived in Willow Road, spotted a green Mercury Bobcat parked at the end of Willow Court North – a heavily wooded, then undeveloped cul-de-sac of Willow Road, and just a mile from Dr Catlow's house. She phoned the police.

Detectives rushed to the spot and observed two bodies stuffed into the car's back seat. The Bellingham Fire Department arrived with a basket crane and floodlights to illuminate the area. Bellingham Police evidence technician Robert Knudsen skilfully managed the crime scene. The bodies were carefully removed from the car, wrapped in clean white sheets, to prevent the loss of any shred of evidence, and taken to Saint Luke General Hospital, 809 E Chestnut Street. Medical Examiner Dr Robert P. Gibb conducted the autopsies and determined that both girls had been raped and death was due to strangulation by ligature. The Mercury 'Bobcat' was transported to the Bellingham Police garage for forensic analysis and the cul-de-sac cordoned off to search for evidence. A search of the vehicle turned up a piece of paper with the notation '334 Bayside 7 p.m. Ken.'

* * *

'The car was locked,' Scenes of Crime officer Robert Knudsen, of Bellingham PD, told me during an interview, 'however, the passenger door was only on the first catch and so I had no trouble getting into the vehicle that way. I opened both doors, and took a closer look, and the bodies of two young ladies had been tossed in like two sacks of potatoes, one thrown on top of the other.'

With this grim discovery, an order went out for Bianchi's immediate arrest, but first the police needed the help of Randy Moa. Knowing that Bianchi might be armed, and considered dangerous, Moa radioed Ken in his truck, instructing his unwitting employee to check out a disused guard shack at the Port of Bellingham South Terminal, a remote area of the docks. Moments after he arrived, Detective Terry Wight arrested him. Detective Page recalled: 'I saw Terry's gun barrel get screwed into Bianchi's right ear, then another officer shoves a muzzle into the guy's left ear. Terry says, "You wanna die, then you can die in stereo."'

Both of Bianchi's motor vehicles had now been impounded at Bellingham Police Station, where Detective Knudsen waited for Kelli Boyd to arrive before he could search them. At 2.00 am on Saturday, 13 January, though, he started looking for clues on Karen's Ford Mercury Bobcat. Crawling underneath the car, Knudsen noted that the fuel tank had a fresh dent on the driver's side. It appeared from the angle of the damage that this was a 'back-up' dent and, later that day, the investigator found paint exactly matching that on the gas tank on a dislodged rock in the driveway of 334 Bayside. This evidence was solid proof that, at some time, the Bobcat had been on Dr Catlow's property.

Moving inside Dr Catlow's home, Detective Knudsen and colleagues went through the premises with a toothcomb. Physical evidence collected from the crime scenes, the bodies and the car, was sent to the Federal Bureau of Investigations laboratory in Washington, DC for analysis. Carpet fibres found on the clothing worn by Mandic and Wilder, as well as those found on clothing Bianchi wore that night, matched samples taken from the carpets at the Catlow residence. A meticulous search of the basement bedrooms revealed head hairs that matched Wilder's. A single pubic hair, found in the basement stairwell, along with other pubic hairs found on Wilder's body, matched Bianchi's, while traces of her menstrual blood were later found to be present on his underwear.

When Kelli eventually arrived at the police pound, Knudsen went through Ken's beaten-up VW and, in the front passenger footwell, a brown leather attaché case was discovered. Tipping the contents onto a table, Detective Nolte found that every document tied a 'Dr Bianchi' to a psychiatric counselling service in Los Angeles. Taken together, these were unusual items to say the least, so Nolte and Knudsen took stock. It seemed that they might have captured a double murderer, sex pervert, thief, bent security guard-cum-pseudo cop and psychiatrist all in one hit.

The investigation now intensified. Detective Nolte, noting Bianchi's California driver's licence, contacted the Los Angeles County Sheriff's Department to check on his background. By happenstance, the call was referred to Detective Sergeant Frank Salerno, a member of the Hillside Strangler Task Force that had been investigating the murders of thirteen women since October 1977. Once he heard the address on Bianchi's licence, Salerno immediately made the connection and made plans to fly to Bellingham.

With Bianchi now in custody, the investigation moved up a gear. While police broke the tragic news to the girls' parents, Detectives Nolte and McNeill, Field Investigator Moore, along with LAPD detectives Frank Salerno and Dudley Varney, conducted a thorough search of Bianchi's home, where in the bedroom they picked up a pair of blue uniform trousers. The crotch had been ripped and Kelli confirmed that they were the trousers that her common-law husband had been wearing the previous evening. She also pointed to a red, plaid shirt, and there was an identical one lying underneath it. Kelli said that Ken had been wearing one of those shirts the night before, and fibres, identical in every respect to those of these shirts, were later found in Dr Catlow's home. The officers also took possession of a pair of cowboy boots, and they soon matched the sole-tread pattern with imprints found both at Willow Drive and Bayside.

Hanging on a hook in the bedroom closet was a .357 calibre, Highway Patrolman's revolver, complete with a standard Sam Browne belt and holster. Again, in the same closet, Nolte discovered a shoulder holster and several cameras. The firearm was licensed and in extremely good condition. The cameras and photographic equipment were of professional quality, and this added veracity to the claims of Susan Bird, Annie Kinneberg and Margie Lager that Bianchi wanted to photograph them.

The officers now turned their attention to Kelli's dressing table, where they found a quantity of jewellery and seven watches. Kelli explained that Ken had given her most of these items as presents – in fact, these had been taken from former Hillside Strangler victims. They were Bianchi's trophies of the crimes.

Bianchi's home was now searched from top to bottom. In the basement, cops found several thousand dollars' worth of brand-new tools, all in their original boxes without price tags or sales receipts. It was soon discovered that this treasure trove had been stolen from Fred Myer when light-fingered Ken worked there as a security guard.

However, the stash of stolen goods didn't end with the tools, for on one shelf there was a large quantity of medical supplies, enough to supply a doctor's surgery. Ken had stolen it all from the Verdugo Hills Hospital in Los Angeles. And when Detective

Moore made the mistake of prising open a cupboard, he was literally buried under scores of tins of crabmeat that tumbled out. Ken had taken the horde from a cold storage company where WSA had assigned him as a guard. Finally, a box full of brand-new jackets and touch-tone telephones was opened. These had been stolen from the Uniflite Corporation, whose offices were at the dock's South Terminal.

But this merely proved that Bianchi was a thief, not a murderer, and at this stage there wasn't a merest hint that he had been involved in the Hillside Stranglings.

At the time of his arrest, Ken had been in possession of a large bunch of keys, which were now in a police property box. Detective Nolte had overheard Randy Moa saying that a ring of keys, along with several client account cards for the southside district of Bellingham, were missing from the office, so he went to the property box and retrieved them. Moa identified them as belonging to those accounts for which Bianchi was solely responsible. One of the keys fitted Dr Catlow's front door, and indeed, the account card was tied to this key. They now had proof that Bianchi had had access to the Bayside address.

With the very real prospect of them having arrested a cold-blooded serial killer dawning upon them, the police then searched Ken's WSA pickup, call sign '5'. However, the only item of note recovered from the truck was a striped towel. Tests later showed that it was stained with the semen of a non-secretor and, as we now know, this fitted Bianchi exactly.

On Saturday, 13 January, a vital witness came forward in the form of Raymond Spees, who claimed that, during the late evening of the murders, he had been to church. Between 10 and

10.30 p.m., he said, he was returning to his home past the cul-de-sac where the bodies were found in Karen's car. As he passed the entrance to the cul-de-sac, a vehicle came out rapidly, and he had to swerve to avoid it. Spees described the vehicle as a yellow WSA pickup truck with a flashing light bar on the driver's cab. Spees was positive about this identification because he knew the firm, and noted its emblem on the cab door. Spees also noticed that the driver was shielding his face with his hand.

On Monday, 15 January 1979, Nolte and his colleagues searched Karen Mandic's apartment for the second time. In a drawer, Nolte found a business card in the name of 'Captain A. Bianchi' of the Whatcom Security Agency. Nolte spoke to Randy Moa who reported that no such 'Captain' title had been authorised by his company. Later in the day, Bianchi appeared in Whatcom County Superior Court before Judge Jack Kurtz and was charged with possession of stolen property. Prosecutor David McEachran informed the court that Bianchi was also the prime suspect in the recent double homicide, a capital crime carrying the death penalty, and asked for a high bail. Judge Kurtz agreed Bianchi was a potential threat to the community and a flight risk, and set bail at $150,000. He appointed Bellingham lawyer Dean Brett to represent the defendant during future court proceedings.

A few days later, police carried out a thorough search of the South Terminal area where Bianchi had been arrested. Behind discarded pipework, just 20 feet from where Bianchi had stopped his pickup, they found a coat belonging to Diane Wilder and, in one of the pockets, were the keys to Karen's car. Obviously, as the two young women couldn't have dropped the coat off at the

South Terminal, their killer must have done so. The noose was tightening around Bianchi's neck.

It was now crucial for the police to establish Bianchi's movements for the times in question as, if he produced a solid alibi to show that he couldn't have committed the murders, the police would be back at square one.

In her statement to police, Kelli was positive that Ken had arrived home on the Thursday evening at about 10.30 p.m. She told the cops that she noticed that had ripped the seat of his denim trousers, which she thought was 'kinda comical', but she was surprised when he threw the garment into a trash bin. She had retrieved the trousers because she thought that the cloth might come in useful as her mother was making a rug, and she needed all the denim she could lay her hands on. Kelli also recalled that Ken had been sweating profusely when he walked through the door, and this was unusual. 'He smelled kinda strange,' she said.

When Kelli was asked about a little gold Italian 'Good Luck' horn on a chain, which had been found on her dressing table, she explained that it had been a gift from Kenneth way back in Los Angeles. Later, this item of jewellery proved to be identical with one known to have belonged to the murdered Yolanda Washington.

With Kelli placing Bianchi at home around 10.30 p.m. on the night of the murders, the police looked elsewhere for witnesses who might have seen him out and about, and they first spoke to a Mrs McNeill who lived at 327 Bayside, and almost opposite Dr Catlow's residence. She recalled that, at around 9.30 a.m. on Thursday, 11 January, she had seen a yellow WSA pickup truck enter Dr Catlow's drive. At noon, she saw an identical vehicle enter and leave the property and, at around 7.00 p.m., or shortly thereafter, she heard a vehicle enter the drive but she did not see it. When questioned about the sound of the engine, Mrs McNeill said that it had sounded like the vehicle that had made the earlier visits.

With overwhelming evidence mounting against him, Bianchi consistently refused to admit guilt, and then he asked for legal representation. Attorney Dean Brett advised his client not to talk to the officers again without him present and, initially, Ken found Brett 'a shining example of an energetic champion of justice'. This flowery accolade was withdrawn a week later after he started to sum up his predicament. Ken was furious that Kelli had held a yard sale to dispose of his property, and then he accused her of having an affair with Dean Brett. Ken was also worried about the lies he had told police officers about his movements during the time of the murders. He had told police that he had attended a Sheriff's Reserve meeting, and this was blatantly false. In the years to follow, he wrote to me with a pathetic excuse for telling the lie:

I hate confrontations. People only have their whereabouts checked when they are suspected of doing something wrong. So, knowing I hadn't done anything wrong, and nothing to hide, I had given the original, short answer, about going to the Sheriff's Reserve class. That was simpler than the longer, true explanation. Besides, if I had killed the girls, I would have remembered it. I didn't, and that's what I kept telling the police.

Poor old Ken! This is yet another example of deep-seated, psychopathological denial, and it is illustrative of Bianchi's thinking process around the time of the murders and, indeed, his warped thought processes today. Of course the 'true explanation' to which he refers is that he had just raped and strangled two innocent young women. Now, that would have taken some explaining away.

ACTING UP

On Friday, 26 January 1979, Bianchi was formally charged with two counts of first-degree murder. Although the FBI had yet to analyse some of the physical evidence, there was enough to proceed with the murder case, and the possession-of-stolen-property charge was dismissed. In order to ensure Bianchi a fair trial, Judge Kurtz issued a gag order prohibiting anyone involved with the investigation, including witnesses, from releasing information about the defendant or his connection to the murders. In addition, the judge sealed McEachran's affidavit-of-probable-cause, which detailed evidence supporting the murder charges.

Bianchi was arraigned on Monday, 29 January 1979, and pleaded not guilty to two charges of first-degree murder. Judge Kurtz ordered he be held without bail and also be handcuffed during all future court appearances. Under state law, the prosecution was given 30 days to decide the issue of seeking the death penalty. The judge also denied a motion by *The Bellingham Herald* to lift the order sealing the affidavit-of-probable-cause, stating that the defendant's Sixth Amendment right to a fair trial superseded the First Amendment right to free press.

(The issue was ultimately decided by the Washington State Supreme Court on April 30, 1979, which ruled that the newspaper should have pursued another legal avenue to push for First Amendment rights.) The 'Affidavit of Probable Cause' set out the allegations in detail, and this was the first opportunity for Bianchi and his legal team to study the case presented by the state. It was also the chance for Ken to embark on the first of his many 'fly-specking' exercises, where he examines everything in minute detail, for which he has become notorious ever since. The main thrust of the prosecution was to file for the death penalty, but there was a plea bargain offer on the table; if Bianchi pleaded guilty, the state wouldn't press for a death sentence, and Bianchi would live. This somewhat rocked Bianchi's boat, for he had no intention of throwing his hands in the air and admitting anything. Dean Brett, however, was quick to point out that protestations of innocence would no longer wash; besides, the lie-detector test to which he had submitted had failed him. Nevertheless, Bianchi tore up the plea-bargain offer, and he returned to his cell to sulk.

In the United States, the 1972 moratorium on capital punishment had been lifted in 1976, and Dean Brett was anxious that his client should not become the first killer to be hanged in Washington State, so he attempted to mitigate Ken's culpability for the Bellingham murders by suggesting that he should plead 'Not Guilty by Reason of Insanity' (NGI). This was a risky call because by no stretch of the imagination could Bianchi be classified as legally insane. But, to this end Brett felt obliged to inform Ken of the horrors of death by hanging, going on to paint a morbid and terrifying picture of this form of execution. 'Most go to the gallows screaming,' he told the white-faced Bianchi. 'Some collapse and have to be strapped to a board. An' hanging is goddamn painful if it don't work out right.'

'That meeting scared me straight,' Bianchi wrote in a letter to me. 'I was in a corner not of my own making, and I had nowhere to run or hide.'

So now confronted with the stark choice between death or life behind bars, Bianchi reluctantly agreed to plead NGI.

With their client's signed agreement in their pocket, Ken's legal team employed the services of John Johnson, an investigative social worker, who started to probe Bianchi's history right back to day one. Johnson was a methodical and tidy man; so tidy in fact that it was rumoured that he had trained his dog to crap in someone else's yard. He was an excellent researcher, too, and before much time had passed he reported back to Bianchi and Brett. It was good news, for it was suggested to Ken that he might have been abused as a child and this would have unhinged his mind. In fact, the defence team went even further. Kenneth's failure in remembering killing the co-eds could be due to some form of amnesia. Therefore, with this information now at hand, there was the possibility of Ken receiving a reduced custodial sentence with a specific period before parole, or better still, his time could be served in a psychiatric institution where the silver-tongued killer could work his ticket to freedom, as so many of his ilk do.

When talking to me, Dean Brett denied any such attorney/client manipulation, although it is certain that he advised his client to undergo a series of hypnosis sessions, which Bianchi called the 'modern version of the rubber cosh'. And then Ken seized on what he thought was a great idea. He would invent a multiple personality disorder!

Although the medical profession had been aware of the enigmas of multiple personality disorder (MPD) since the early 19th century, the general public learned of the condition largely through the 1957 movie *The Three Faces of Eve*, which was based on the book of the same name written by two psychiatrists.

MPD seems to be caused by severe psychological traumas in childhood, such as sexual abuse or extreme cruelty, and these experiences can be so painful that the victim literally blots them out. In later life, a violent shock can reactivate the trauma, causing the 'everyday' personality to blank out.

The most remarkable case of MPD in recent years was that of Billy Milligan. In 1977, he was arrested in Columbus, Ohio, for rape. Billy later declared to a social worker that he was not Billy but 'David', and subsequent examinations by psychiatrists made it clear that Milligan was a genuine MPD case.

Sexually abused in childhood by his stepfather, Billy had become another personality to escape the misery. Eventually, he split into 23 separate personalities, including a lesbian, a suave Englishman who also spoke Arabic, an electronics expert and a Serbo-Croat. (It has been never been explained how Milligan came to speak Serbo-Croat.) Nevertheless, all these personalities were so distinctive that only a remarkable actor could have simulated them. It was later discovered that the lesbian personality committed the rape, and another of the personalities had turned Billy in to the police. And it is now thought that the Milligan case – much publicised in the late 1970s – may have given Bianchi the idea of pretending to be a 'multiple'.

Bianchi had indeed watched *The Three Faces of Eve* while he was in custody. He had even read the book, and it is known from his custody records that he also saw the film *Sybil*, which concerned another multiple-personality disorder. So the whole idea of MPD was a gift from the gods, and Bianchi rubbed his hands with glee.

Kenneth Bianchi was sitting in his cell beaming with delight as his attorney arranged the first of many hypnosis sessions. Once again, the killer was playing centre stage and the immediate follow-up came about when forensic psychiatrist Dr Donald T. Lunde recommended that Ken accept a course of hypnosis under the expert supervision of a Dr John Watkins. Dr Lunde reasoned that, if anyone could find a genuine MPD, then it had to be Watkins.

On Wednesday, 23 March 1979, Dr Watkins, a specialist in multiple personalities and hypnosis from the University of Montana, was brought in to carry out the first of many sessions with Ken. By now, Bianchi was more than eager to co-operate and, within minutes, it appeared that he was in a trance. He started speaking in a strange, low voice, introducing himself as 'Steve Walker'. This 'Steve' came across as a highly unpleasant character with a sneering laugh. He told those present that he hated Ken. 'Ken doesn't know how to handle women,' he said. 'You gotta treat 'em rough. Boy, did I fix that turkey. I got him in so much trouble, he'll never get out.'

Dr Watkins believed that what he was witnessing was indeed a genuine multiple personality, and he bought Ken's performance hook, line and sinker. With a little prompting, 'Steve' turned to the Los Angeles murders, describing how Ken had walked in on Angelo Buono while he was murdering a girl. At this point,

'Steve' admitted he had taken over Ken's personality, and had turned Ken into Angelo's willing accomplice for all the Hillside Stranglings.

'Are you Ken?' asked Dr Watkins.

'Do I look like Ken? Killing a broad doesn't make any difference to me. Killing any fuckin' body doesn't make any difference to me. Angelo is my kind of man. There should be more people like Angelo in the world. I hate Ken,' snarled 'Steve'.

To Dr Watkins, at least, it seemed perfectly clear that Kenneth Bianchi was made up of two opposing personalities – the loving father, kind friend and hard worker who made up Ken, and the vicious rapist, sadist-cum-serial murderer who made up 'Steve Walker'.

Watkins firmly believed that Ken had subconsciously invented 'Steve' as a repository for all his hateful feelings towards his adoptive mother, Frances. And, in this way, Ken could remain a loving, devoted son, the affectionate guy that almost everyone knew and liked, while 'Steve', who was apparently unknown to Ken, would periodically emerge to wreak terrible revenge on young women.

Word soon leaked out that Bianchi was 'coughing' to the LA murders, and that he had implicated his accomplice, Angelo Buono, so the LA task force detectives rushed to Bellingham and sat outside Ken's cell door in anticipation of what might happen next. However, dissatisfied with this not quite Oscar-winning performance, Bianchi expanded on his scheme and, knowing that the inquisitive police would read his diary, on Wednesday, 18 April 1979, he wrote a diary entry for them to read:

If this person is more real than just a dream, and if this is the same person who has been haunting me, which is more likely, this person could have been responsible for the uncontrollable violence in my life, the instigator of the lies I've done. The blank spots, amnesia, I can't account for, and the deaths of the girls, all the ones in California, and the two here. But if he is in me, then he killed them using me – why can't I remember for sure? I want to know if this is so – what if?

To be absolutely sure of his multiple personal diagnosis, Dr Watkins also administered the Rorschach inkblot test to check out both Ken and 'Steve', the results of which appeared to support his overall hypothesis – both tests differed and were consistent with two personalities – so he reported back to Dean Brett, saying, 'It is one of the clearest cases of Dissociative Reaction and Multiple Personality I have diagnosed in over 40 years.'

Somewhat condescendingly, Bianchi would later write, while shooting himself in the foot, 'Dr Watkins is a kind, soft-spoken, honest behavioral expert who was caught up in the excitement of the moment. When all the hypnosis sessions stopped, the MPD never appeared again.' But, then how would Bianchi know?

The damage, however, had been done and a leak prompted *Time* Magazine to pronounce: 'BIANCHI – A MULTIPLE PERSONALITY'. These headlines so outraged Judge Kurtz that he decided to appoint a panel of experts to evaluate Bianchi, and summoned Dr Watkins and Professor Donald T. Lunde to act for the defence. Doctors Ralph Allison and Charles Moffett represented the court, and Doctors Martin Orne and Saul Faerstein acted for the prosecution, in an effort to sort, as the police suggested, 'the bullshit from the bullshit'.

Fortunately for Dr Watkins, he had an ally in the judge's camp in Ralph Allison, who was also the author of a famous book called *Minds in Many Pieces*. Dr Allison's credentials were impeccable and, under apparent hypnosis, Ken, through 'Steve', claimed, 'I fuckin' killed those broads . . . those fuckin' cunts. That blonde-haired cunt, and the brunette cunt.'

'Here in Bellingham?' asked Allison incredulously, gripping the arms of his chair.

'That's right.'

'Why?'

''Cos I hate fuckin' cunts.'

After that short exchange, Dr Allison pressed his subject about the murder of Yolanda Washington in Los Angeles, and 'Steve' piped up again. 'She was a hooker. Angelo went out and picked her up. I was waiting on the street. He drove round to where I was. I got in the car. We got on the freeway. I fucked her and killed her. We dumped the body off and that was it. Nothin' to it.'

In apparently regressing Ken back to his childhood at around the age of nine, Dr Allison found an environment filled with pain and suffering, which, he thought, had spawned Ken's alter ego 'Steve'. Under the so-called hypnosis, Ken claimed to have met 'Steve' while he was hiding under his bed. 'Mommy was hitting me so bad, I met Stevie,' he whimpered in a childlike voice.

Dr Allison was now in his professional element, and probed a little deeper. 'How did you first meet Stevie?' he asked quietly.

'I closed my eyes. I was crying so hard,' Bianchi whined. 'All of a sudden he was there. He said "Hi" to me. He told me that

I was his friend. I felt really good that I had a friend I could talk to.'

Outside in the corridor, police officers sniggered, rolled their eyes towards the heavens, while others stuck their fingers down their throats. Detective Nolte looked as if he was chewing glass, and soon wandered off saying that he was going to buy a couple of gallons of holy water and some garlic. Detective Terry Wight popped a mint into his mouth and remarked, 'That fucker is blowin' smoke in our yard. He's either fuckin' innocent or he's a damn good actor.' And Terry Wight was right on the money. This was going to be a red-ball case, weeks of unpaid overtime and little sleep, just to get Bianchi into court. With a bit of luck, they might get a judge who suffered from insomnia, and a jury with at least one brain between them, but the cops also reasoned that, even if the judicial train did manage to haul itself into the right station, the shrinks would say that Bianchi was nuts, and he would end up doing a merry-go-round of psychiatric interviews for decades to come.

Of all the experts who were summoned to evaluate Bianchi, Professor Donald T. Lunde, MA, MD, was perhaps the most qualified. A Clinical Associate Professor of Psychiatry and Behavioural Science, and Lecturer at Stanford University, he is the author of two books, *The Die Song*, and *Murder and Madness and Fundamentals of Human Sexuality*. He is also a member of the American Academy of Psychiatry and the Law. Therefore, it might not seem unreasonable to infer that Professor Lunde would provide a correct assessment of Kenneth Bianchi's state of mind. Unfortunately, he did not.

Professor Lunde began his report, dated Monday, 23 July 1979, by explaining how he had formed his evaluation of Bianchi, and on what sources he had based his findings. His four-month study included three short sessions with the subject, which took place on 11, 12 and 13 July. He had read some 3,000 pages of police documents, witness statements and psychiatric reports and school records. He also gained access to the information compiled by Dean Brett, John Johnson and the DA's office. He reviewed the audiotape and videotape interviews, and read transcripts of examinations performed by his colleagues. Donald Lunde even interviewed Kelli Boyd, along with dozens of other people who knew Bianchi, although Frances Bianchi refused to speak to him.

Lunde started by making a glaring error when he reported that Ken had been fostered for the initial 11 months of his life, when it had only been three months.

Mistake number two came when he misread the DePaul Clinic evaluations by stating that Mrs Bianchi had blamed her late husband for being unable to have children, when, until the time of her death in 2011 she had claimed no such thing. And he compounded this error by saying that Nicolas Bianchi was 'overshadowed and overpowered' by his wife, when this was not so.

Professor Lunde also gave the wrong dates for Kenneth's schooling, and he was fundamentally inaccurate when he claimed that Ken's enuresis (bed-wetting) problems were psychosomatic in origin when they were physiological.

The professor suggested that Bianchi's mental condition was of a 'dissociative reaction, with extreme stress bordering on psychosis', and in his report, he wrote:

This condition (Dissociative Reaction) has been present since at least the age of nine years, and is manifested by periods during which the defendant acts without awareness of his actions, and for which he subsequently has amnesia. During some of these periods, the incredible amount of unconscious (repressed) hostility towards women present in this man surfaces. The best demonstration of what I have just described is seen in some of the videotapes, which were made while Bianchi was under hypnosis, and emerged as quite a different personality calling himself 'Steve Walker'.

To be fair to Professor Lunde, he said that it was debatable whether Bianchi represented a true case of multiple personality, as he felt that Bianchi could have been capable of faking his symptoms given the wealth of literature – to include the book *Sybil* – in his possession and the fact that Bianchi had previously unsuccessfully tried to pass himself off in Los Angeles as a medical expert. But Professor Lunde went on to conclude that 'Bianchi is not psychologically sophisticated enough, nor is he intelligent enough to have constructed such an elaborate history which gives him the mental defence if he were subsequently charged with a crime.'

Professor Lunde added: 'Furthermore, one would have to assume that Bianchi began plotting his strategy for these crimes and his defence at about age nine, since this is when the first documented symptoms of his mental disturbance occurred.'

However this a major problem here, for there were no 'first documented symptoms' of Bianchi's alleged 'mental disturbance' in existence, other than Bianchi's claim under alleged hypnosis that he first met 'Stevie' while hiding under a table. Indeed, the doctors at the DePaul Clinic had made no such reference to this, nor had anyone else.

Professor Lunde could not contemplate for a moment that Ken had literally coached himself on MPD simply by reading a book in his cell, by watching the movies, *The Three Faces of Eve* and *Sybil*, or that the crooked idea had only entered his head as he contemplated a fate at the end of a hangman's rope. The professor considered Bianchi unsophisticated and not educated enough to concoct such a defence, seriously underestimating the cunning of Bianchi, who is the greatest cock-and-bull storyteller since the beginning of time – but Professor Lunde did!

But this was not quite the end of the matter as far as Professor Lunde was concerned, because, while stating that Bianchi was mentally competent to stand his trial, he reported that, in his opinion, Ken was indeed suffering from Dissociative Reaction:

It [Dissociative Reaction] has affected him in such a manner that he would have been unable to perceive the nature and quality of his acts with which he has been charged, it is my opinion that the defendant did not have a moral sense of right and wrong, but was aware that what he was doing was against the law, and for this reason, precautions were taken to avoid incriminating evidence.

So, Professor Lunde believed that Bianchi was only taken over by 'Steve' when he needed to rape and murder, and at no other time, all of which, if taken literally, and in the belief that Bianchi was a multiple, would entail trying 'Steve' if he could be found, and place him in the dock instead of Ken. But, according to Lunde, although Ken had no moral sense of right and wrong, conversely, Bianchi knew that, when he was committing his heinous crimes, and undertaking the careful pre-planning, the murders themselves and the elaborate cover-ups, that he was in fact breaking the law.

Having studied the case file, and having interviewed Bianchi for some eight hours, Dr Moffett felt it wiser to sit on the fence, believing Bianchi to be 'psychotic and probably schizophrenic', which did nothing to endear him to Dr Allison who was effectively on the same team. However, Dr Moffett still plunged into the same trap as Watkins, Allison and Lunde, in believing that Bianchi had genuinely been hypnotised.

Having now sown the seeds of a multiple personality in the minds of three eminent psychiatrists, with a fourth leaning towards a different diagnosis altogether, Ken had only to sit back and watch with amusement as the experts argued the toss about the state of his mind, for each psychiatrist who examined him was predisposed to stake a claim on being correct.

By co-operating with the psychiatrists, Ken pleased them, and they are the first to agree on this point. When Ken tried to ram normality down the throats, it was a successful and calculated attempt to prop up their beliefs that he really had been hypnotised; therefore, any words that fell from his lips had to be the truth. Dr Moffett, like Lunde and Watkins, firmly believed that Ken had been hypnotised, which led him to conclude that 'Steve' was the result of an 'ego, or an identity split' rather than the 'different personality' which his colleagues and now agreed upon. Moffett added, 'is this so different from a patient hearing the voice of Satan and struggle against alien control?'

In believing that 'Steve' existed as a 'split' rather than an entirely 'separate' personality, Dr Moffatt missed another vital observation which would have proved Bianchi to be a bare-faced liar, for Ken was delighting in reliving his wicked crimes in all their gory detail, safe in the knowledge that this was coming from 'Steve'. Safe, too, in the knowledge that he could confess without blame being apportioned to him personally. He was suckering the doctors; he was playing the starring role to a well-established and well-intentioned audience who could make him internationally famous. Kenneth had struggled all his life to be someone and, at last, he had almost achieved his goal.

Dr Moffett's diagnosis, actually, wasn't wildly off the mark, as he claimed that Ken was suffering from 'delusional grandiosity', but added, 'Ken lives on the brink of regressed and infantile terror. He literally wakens in his cell at night, hiding under his bed in nameless terror.'

Bianchi did wake from his sleep, and he did hide under his cell bed. However, not unlike the phoney notes he penned in his jail diary that were sure to find their way to the authorities, these nocturnal activities were feigned sideshows to arouse the attention of the guards, to further bolster his act, and to substantiate the façade of his vulnerability.

Dr Moffatt eventually concluded in his summary to Judge Kurtz, 'He [Bianchi] intellectually knows right from wrong. The combination of his grandiose alter ego, and his dissociation, and his lack of awareness of the violent aspects of his own being, would not permit him to effectively control and govern his actions.'

When Dr Orne from the Department of Psychiatry at the Pennsylvania Medical School arrived in Bellingham, he fired a single salvo, and blew not only his colleagues, but also Bianchi, out of the water in a flash of brilliance. Aware of the benefits to the killer if he succeeded in faking a multiple personality disorder, Dr Orne decided to analyse, not so much Ken's personality, but the assumption of multiple personality itself. This was a unique move, a lateral test to see whether Bianchi had really been hypnotised at all, for Dr Orne figured that, if this man could fake a multiple personality disorder, then he could easily fake hypnosis. In Dr Orne Bianchi was about to meet his nemesis.

Before attempting to hypnotise Bianchi, Dr Orne mentioned in passing, and deliberately almost out of Ken's hearing, that it was rare in the case of multiple personalities for there to be just two personalities. Bianchi overhead the doctor, and, shortly after he entered a phoney trance, out came 'Billy', who amounted to personality number three. Minutes later, Dr Orne asked 'Billy' to sit back and talk to his lawyer who wasn't present in the room, but, on this occasion, Ken overplayed his part. Of course, 'Billy' had no lawyer at all, but this did not stop Ken from leaning across the table and shaking the invisible attorney's hand. Then Dr Orne had Dean Brett walk into the room. Bianchi, or 'Billy', immediately shifted his attention to the visible lawyer, asking, 'How can I see him in two places?' This behaviour proved beyond a shadow of doubt that Bianchi was faking hypnosis and, following a few other tests, it was shown that Bianchi was faking MPD, too.

So, at long last, Ken had come unstuck and he was now exposed as the faker he really was. And the entire fabrication completely collapsed when a detective recalled seeing the name of 'Steve Walker' among the documents found in Ken's attaché case. Steve Walker, it transpired, was the real psychology student who had unwittingly furnished Bianchi with his own diploma – the very same item that Ken had altered to suit his own ends – back in Los Angeles. It was checkmate!

While psychiatrists were examining Bianchi, Bellingham detectives continued putting the finishing touches on their homicide investigation. On 23 April 1979, Los Angeles Police Chief Daryl F. Gates increased the pressure on Bianchi by announcing the task force had enough hard evidence to charge him with ten 'Hillside Strangler' slayings. On 9 May, Los Angeles County District Attorney John Van de Kamp filed a complaint in Superior Court, initially charging him with five murders, those with the best evidence. But they would be more than enough to send Bianchi to the gas chamber, if convicted.

After pleading guilty to seven murders, which included the Bellingham slayings, and agreeing to testify against Angelo Buono, on Friday, 19 October 1979, Bianchi was sentenced to two life terms to run consecutively without the possibility of parole. In Los Angeles County Superior Court, just 30 minutes later, Buono was taken into custody without a struggle and charged with 24 felonies, which included 10 murders, extortion, conspiracy, sodomy, and pimping and pandering. Although the Los Angeles District Attorney's Office had evidence linking Buono to the crimes they believed his fate rested on Bianchi's credibility as a witness. The acceptance of his guilty plea by Judge Kurtz in Bellingham had rendered him a competent witness in the eyes of the law.

On Saturday morning, 20 October 1979, Bianchi was flown

from Bellingham to Los Angeles in a leased Continental Airlines jet. He appeared before Superior Court Judge William B. Keen on the morning of Monday, 22 October 1979, and pleaded guilty to five of the 'Hillside Strangler' killings, one count of conspiracy to commit murder and one count of sodomy. The judge immediately sentenced Bianchi to five life terms for the murders, one life term for the conspiracy and an additional five-year sentence for sodomy, to run concurrently. After imposing sentence, Judge Keen said: 'I wish I had the power to have the sentences run consecutively, but in this state (California) they must be merged as a matter of law.' Although Bianchi would be eligible for parole in California in just seven years, officials estimated he would serve 20 to 35 years before being returned to Washington to serve his two consecutive life sentences.

★ ★ ★

Bianchi began violating the terms of his plea agreement almost as soon as he arrived in Los Angeles. In what became the longest preliminary hearing in the history of Los Angeles County, 10 months, he attempted to influence judicial proceedings by making contradictory statements to destroy his credibility and have the case against Buono dismissed. But, on 16 March 1981, Municipal Court Judge H. Randolph Moore ruled there was sufficient probable cause to believe Buono had committed murder and ordered him to stand trial. The case was assigned to Superior Court Judge Ronald M. George (later Chief Justice of the California Supreme Court) and scheduled to begin on 2 November 1981.

Of course, 'Steve' and 'Billy' never surfaced again, but someone else did – a beautiful, part-time actress and writer. Her name is Veronica Compton aka 'VerLyn'.

FEMME FATALE

> Let's deal with our mutual friend, Bianchi. Ken's not stupid. Ken is the slickest criminal I've ever met in all of my years, and I've met a few criminals. But, without doubt, Ken is the master of them all. He is very circumspect . . . that's where his brilliance lies, in his ability to premeditate things, and to protect himself. He is very good at that.
>
> *Veronica Compton to me at the Western*
> *Washington Correctional Center for Women*

While held in custody at the LA County Jail during Buono's trial, Ken almost engineered his freedom when a 24-year-old actress and budding screenplay writer fell in love with him. She had a figure that made most men – and many women – drool and, as one woman observed, 'VerLyn has a figure that most women would die for.' Indeed, even after serving 15 years in prison – she has since been released – when I interviewed her she was still an extremely beautiful woman.

Veronica was, and still is, highly intelligent, too, but it would be fair to add that she never fully applied her many abilities to any studies or goals and, around the time of the Hillside Stranglings, the she was deeply hooked into a downward spiral of cocaine and sexual perversion, the latter of which would become her downfall.

In the waning days of 1979–80, Veronica was into sadomasochism, practising as a dominatrix. She was partying every night, heavily dependent on the cocaine high that fuelled her fantasies and fed her enormous sexual appetite for whipping the flesh of LA's movers and shakers.

When I met Veronica at the Western Washington Correctional Center for Women (WWCCW) close to Gig Harbor, she explained, 'In those days, I was inexorably slipping deeper and deeper into the nether world of the leather and the lash scene. The more lurid, the more wickedly cruel the fantasy, the better.'

She also explained that she had had aspirations to be an actress and a screenplay writer. In fact, she had penned a number of frantic, blood-dripping fiction pieces, which were far too extreme for any mainstream publisher to commission. One of those stories was called *The Mutilated Cutter*, concerning a female serial killer who injected semen into her victims' vaginas to make police believe that a man was the murderer.

The Los Angeles trial of Bianchi and Buono was in full swing at this time, so Veronica wrote to Ken asking him to help her in her research for *The Mutilated Cutter*. Within a short space of time, they were meeting frequently in the county jail, and Veronica fell in love with Bianchi, who had allegedly convinced her that he was an innocent man. Whether he was innocent or not, this was a thrill ride VerLyn could not miss.

Week after week, they shared fantasies and intimate love letters – correspondence which would make the Devil blush (I have read much of it). Ken being quick on the uptake, and ready to take any advantage that came his way, found the plot of *The Mutilated Cutter* of particular interest. He persuaded VerLyn to carry out her literary plot in real life – in Bellingham, which, he suggested, would prove that the Hillside Stranger and killer of Karen Mandic and Diane Wilder was still at large. 'If you can do this, I will be let out of prison and be free to marry you,' he told her.

At this time, VerLyn was also enjoying a sordid pen-pal love affair with the notorious 'Sunset Slayer' Douglas Daniel Clark – another death row inmate who I interviewed on camera – during which they discussed that if he were ever to be released they could open up a morgue and have sex with the dead. However, the first and most important part of Ken's scheme was to smuggle his semen out of jail. The problem was soon solved when he cut the finger from a stolen kitchen rubber glove, masturbated into it and then tied the open end with the cord from a string of rosary beads, which he had acquired from a visiting Roman Catholic priest. He then stuffed the small package into the spine of a law book, which Veronica had lent him, and, when she called to visit him on Thursday, 16 September, she walked out of the jail with the book tucked under her arm.

With the first part of the plot completed, they now had to establish alibis for the times of the Los Angeles murders, for even Bianchi could not be in two places at the same time and, if he could prove that he was elsewhere when the killings took place, he reasoned – past confessions through 'Steve' or not – that he would be home and dry.

To establish this difficult feat of establishing alibis, Veronica travelled out of state, staying at hotels, where she granted sexual favours to the staff in return for blank bar tabs and backdated receipts for rooms Ken had never used. This proved easy for she forged Ken's signature on those documents, and, to add even further credence to the plan, she stole fuel-station receipt books and filled them in. Of course, for the obvious reasons the plan wasn't watertight, but the idea was that, in the weeks to follow, she would miraculously uncover this 'new evidence', have it forwarded to the police and hope that this would eventually ensure her lover's release from prison.

On 19 September 1980, and now completely under Ken's hypnotic spell, thrill-seeking VerLyn flew to Seattle then drove to Bellingham. Here she befriended a young woman called Kim Breed in a bar. Veronica sent me an audiotape detailing the scheme:

The task would be settled in mere hours. The victim would fit the needed requisites. I would arrive in Bellingham, Washington, on a fall afternoon. Another woman's body would be discovered shortly afterwards. The method of killing would be familiar to the Whatcom County Homicide team. Their worst nightmare would be relived: a serial killer had apparently returned to the city to continue the reign of terror he had enjoyed only 20 months previously. What they were not to know was that this individual was not a serial killer, neither was it a man.

The peculiar murder tools remained undisturbed in the luggage I retrieved from the airport conveyor. There were no suspicious glances; and, with a small pillow under my clothes, I was just another pregnant woman, dressed perhaps a bit too 'California', with my long, blonde hair held back with a silk scarf, a muslin dress and designer sunglasses, more suited to a beach-side patio than gloomy Washington.

Still, even with the clothes, I could hardly qualify as anyone noteworthy.

My purse contained plenty of money and a cache of narcotics; both would be essential in my work ahead. A taxi took me to a small motel off the town's main boulevard. I signed the register with a fabricated name, the same one I had used for my plane tickets, to keep my real identity a secret. Without taking off my gloves, I picked up the room key, and said, "Thank you," in my best-affected Southern drawl. It, like everything about me, was a performance. A creation. A fiction.

The motel room was standard, but it held everything necessary for my purpose. There was a queen-size bed, a mirrored vanity area and a small bathroom. Still keeping my gloves on, I unpacked the one suitcase, and arranged the items in a vanity drawer. I carefully laid out two pieces of rope, one with a pre-tied noose, the other loose, to be used to tie the victim's wrists.

Satisfied with my organisation of the items, I started the ritual of medications – tranquillisers, cocaine and alcohol, to be taken as he [Ken] had directed. Finishing with them, and with my addictions sated for the moment, I felt hopeful that the hallucinations would be kept at bay, so I settled into tending the blonde wig and adjusting the padding that made my flat stomach give the appearance of pregnancy under my dress. All part of the fictitious creature partly of my making and partly of Ken's.

During her first evening in Bellingham, VerLyn befriended

26-year-old Kim Breed, a Bellingham Parks and Recreation employee, while drinking at the Coconut Grove Tavern at 710 Marine Drive. After spending several hours together, Compton lured Breed to Room 10 at the Shangri-La Downtown Motel, 611 E. Holly Street, with the promise of some cocaine. Once there, Compton managed to tie Breed's hands and twice strangled her almost to the point of unconsciousness. Although intoxicated, Breed was a martial arts expert, bigger than VerLynn, and unusually strong, she managed to struggle free and escape.

Veronica fled back to Los Angeles but she was easy to trace. On Thursday, 2 October 1980, she was arrested at her trailer park home in Carson, California, on a Whatcom County warrant charging first-degree attempted murder, and held on $500,000 bail. The media, delighted at this turn of events, dubbed her the 'Copycat Strangler'.

When she was arrested and returned to Bellingham, she knew that she was in a serious predicament. In this conservative city, where wearing a garter belt was considered 'kinky', and drug addicts thought to be the curse of the nation, VerLyn was about to stand her trial with the odds a million-to-one in favour of a guilty verdict. Her trial began on Monday, 9 March1981, before Whatcom County Superior Court Judge Byron L. Swedberg. To guarantee a fair trial, a jury of four men and eight women was selected from Pierce County, bussed to Bellingham, and sequestered in a hotel for the duration. The case was basically a question of credibility. Breed testified that Compton set her up and tried to kill her, while Compton claimed the incident had been a charade to gain publicity for her screenplay *The Mutilated Cutter* and that Breed was in on it.

The case was concluded on Friday, 20 March 1981. After deliberating for just three hours, the jury found Veronica guilty of first-degree attempted murder with a special finding of being armed with a deadly weapon (a ligature), which carried a mandatory minimum sentence of five years. On 22 May 1981, Judge Swedberg sentenced her to life with possibility of parole, due to the calculated viciousness of the attack on Breed. (Indeterminate life sentences in Washington usually run about 13½ years, although the state parole board may review the prisoner's sentence after seven and a half years.)

After sentencing in May 1981, Veronica was sent to the Washington Corrections Institute for Women at Gig Harbor. Using bolt cutters she went through the perimeter fence and escaped on 26 July 1988, but was recaptured in a suburb of Tucson, Arizona, nine days later. The Washington State Board of Prison Terms and Paroles added two years to her parole eligibility for escape and possession of a firearm. On 27 August 1989, while in prison, VerLyn, now aged 33, married James P. Wallace, aged 60, a retired Eastern Washington University (EWU) professor. Their paths crossed in 1987 when she attended a lecture on crime and punishment delivered by Wallace, a legal affairs expert who sometimes taught at state prisons. Shortly thereafter, Compton sent him a letter asking about some information in his lecture. The pair began a two-year correspondence that eventually turned into romance and marriage. Compton and Wallace were granted conjugal visits and in 1993, she gave birth to a daughter at St Joseph Medical Center in Tacoma. She returned to prison while Wallace and Compton's mother cared for the baby. On 14 March 1996 she was released on parole and went to live at Wallace's home in Cheney. But two weeks later, she was sent back to prison for parole violations. While in prison, she wrote *Eating the Ashes* (New York: Algora Publishing, 2003), a book about rehabilitation in the US penal system. She was again released on parole in 2003, after being incarcerated for 22 years.

BUONO'S TRIAL

According to HistoryLink and other sources, which include court documents, while in Los Angeles, Bianchi again tried to influence judicial proceedings by recanting his pre-trial testimony against Buono and then disavowing his recantations, undermining his value as a creditable witness. Los Angeles County District Attorney Van de Kamp, who was eyeing the job of California Attorney General, was afraid of losing the case based, in his view, almost entirely on Bianchi's testimony. In July 1981, he allowed the trial prosecutor, Roger Kelly, to move to dismiss all of the ten murder charges against Buono and release him. But, after deliberation, Judge George ruled that there was enough evidence to warrant a trial and ordered the case to proceed. Van de Kamp then declared a conflict of interest as his office had already come to the conclusion that they could not convict Buono. Judge George accepted the conflict and reassigned the case to the California Attorney General's office under George Deukmejian. It was then assigned to deputy attorneys general Michael Nash and Roger Boren to prosecute. They believed that the evidence linking Buono to the murders was overwhelming, even without Bianchi's testimony, and began vigorously preparing for trial.

Pre-trial hearings began on Monday, 2 November 1981, with

numerous motions, testimony, and lengthy oral arguments. On a motion by defence to exclude all hypnosis–induced testimony, Judge George ruled that Bianchi had feigned hypnosis and his multiple personalities, and his testimony was admissible.

Buono's trial began on Monday, November 16, with jury selection a drawn-out process that took three months to complete. The number of victims and mountains of forensic evidence to introduce slowed the proceedings, causing the case to drag on. Bianchi, the 200th witness to testify, spent 80 days on the stand. He continued to slow the trial's progress, proving a reluctant witness and making deliberately contradictory statements. At one point he claimed he had completely lost his memory. Another time he denied committing any murders, including those in Bellingham.

Jury deliberations finally began on Friday, 21 October 1983. On 18 November 1983, after being sequestered for 28 days, the jury of seven women and five men found Buono guilty of nine of the ten murders and voted to impose life sentences without possibility of parole, rather than the death penalty. With aduration of two years and two days, it remains the longest criminal trial in American history and cost Los Angeles County taxpayers $2 million.

On Monday, 9 January 1984, Judge George formally sentenced Buono to nine concurrent terms of life without the possibility of parole, a penalty set by the jury. 'In view of the jury's mercy, I am, of course, without authority to impose greater punishment,' he said. 'I would not have the slightest reluctance to impose the death penalty. If ever there was a case where the death penalty was appropriate, it is this case.' Judge George placed much of the blame for the length of the trial on Bianchi, charging that he did everything possible to sabotage the case. He ruled that Bianchi did not testify 'truthfully and completely' and ordered him remanded to the State of Washington to serve his sentence. 'It is my firm belief that Mr Buono and Mr Bianchi should never see the outside of prison walls,' Judge George said. 'They should never be paroled.' On 1 February 1984, the California Department of Corrections filed a detainer with the Department of Corrections in Washington to ensure that if Bianchi is ever released from their custody, he will be turned over to California to serve his life sentences there. Both states would have to grant parole or clemency in order for Bianchi to ever be released from custody.

INCARCERATION

Angelo Buono would serve out his natural life sentence at the notorious Folsom Prison. In 1986, he married for the fourth time – his bride being a somewhat misguided Christine Kizuka, the mother of three and a supervisor at the California State Department of Employment Development in Los Angeles. As might have been expected, this marriage was short-lived, too and, because Buono was not eligible for parole, conjugal visits were denied them.

Kenneth Alessio Bianchi arrived at the Shelton Reception Center in January 1985, and was furious that his file had 'SEXUAL PSYCHOPATH' emblazoned over the cover, with the words 'Child Killer' underneath. This file was supposed to remain out of the sight of other inmates, but, by the time Ken arrived at his cell, the prison grapevine had ensured that his true identity was known throughout the Pen. Now he had a price on his head, as everyone wanted the kudos of having killed one of the infamous Hillside Stranglers.

In February 1985, Bianchi was taken to the Washington State Penitentiary (WSP) at Walla Walla, where he was immediately placed in 'Punitive Segregation', known as 'The Hole' in prison parlance. Ken was confined here for almost two years, living in terror of his life. During this period, he had the gall to apply for parole, while reasoning that, if this failed, he would turn to God to see if 'The Almighty' could help him out.

The well-meaning and naive William B. Mathews, a 63-year-old communications technician who doubled as a Christian visitor, recalls meeting Bianchi shortly after his arrival at Walla Walla, saying: 'I remember it was a time of duress for Ken. He told me that urine had been thrown over him several times, and faeces thrown at him once by other inmates. I might explain that Ken gave his life to Christ during the first week of his stay at WSP. I wish that it was possible to convey what it was like when I walked through that filthy tier called "The Hole", to see this man, Ken, with so much joy and peace within himself.'

So, wily Kenneth was up to his old tricks yet again, this time by flicking a switch and becoming a devoted servant of God almost overnight. And delighted he would have been, for with the threat of murder around every corner, it goes without saying that he would have been very pleased to see the friendly face of William B. Matthews peering at him through the bars.

In support of Bianchi's somewhat premature parole application, which was scheduled for 17 December 1985, residents of Walla Walla, Gordon and Dorothy Otter, wrote to the Board of Prison Terms and Paroles on 16 August, stating: 'From our observations of Mr Bianchi, we feel that he is sincere and a dedicated Christian man, who has a very positive attitude. He is always pleasant, takes an active part in the religious services, and he is concerned about the welfare of others.'

The Otters had good intentions, but it seems that they failed to grasp the fact that the main reason inmates attend religious services is to get out of their cells for a short while, grab a decent biscuit, enjoy a cup of coffee – with sugar – and suck up to any do-gooders who just might be inclined to influence parole hearings in their favour. Kenneth was no exception, and the Otters fell for it. Unfortunately, the Otters had also failed to appreciate the true extent of Ken's concern for the 'welfare of others', which did not extend to the many women and children that he had raped and slaughtered. The more obvious fact that Ken hadn't been within a mile of a church in his life, and probably didn't know what a Bible looked like, didn't concern the Otters at all.

On the very same day that the Otters' letter arrived at the parole office, a reference in favour of Bianchi's reformed character sent by Pastor Dick Jewett, of the Stateline Seventh-Day Adventist Church in Milton-Freewater, Oregon, dropped through the parole board's letterbox. It read:

I am filing this reference on behalf of Ken. He is a member in good standing of my church. I have baptised Ken myself and, after extensive interviews, I have satisfied myself as to his sincerity. He is an active member and regular attendee at our services on the prison campus. His attitude and conduct at the present time is exemplary.

It was obvious that Ken had been very busy indeed, especially when parole officials opened yet another letter which had been sent by a Mr and Mrs Black:

> We had the privilege of witnessing Ken Bianchi make a commitment to the Lord in Baptism. Ken appears to be very sincere, devoted and earnest. His views are conservative, but he never fails to look at both sides. He has always been polite and sensitive concerning this. He wants to attend college, which shows he has many goals. My husband and I have been involved in the Prison Ministry just over two years. We have written and talked to many prisoners. From these experiences we have learned to be fair judges of character. It is obvious to us that Kenneth Bianchi truly loves the Lord and his behaviour and attitude strongly proves it.

Another letter of recommendation was received from Father Frederick Ellsworth, a good-natured priest from the Christ the Healer Orthodox Mission, saying, 'Ken is open, willing to share and quite responsive. I have two young daughters, and I would even welcome him into my home. He would fit in well with my family and his writing has been a highlight.'

Or there was the support of Bruce Zicari, a tax consultant from Penfield, New York, who declared, 'I would certainly like to reiterate my confidence and high regard for Kenneth Bianchi, and I am certain that he has the capabilities to be successful at whatever filed of endeavour he might choose.' Of course, Bianchi's endeavours in the field of sado-sexual serial homicide had been highly successful.

Fortunately, however, none of these recommendations impressed the parole panel and it rejected Bianchi's application out of hand. So Ken settled down to his studies and he starting by attending a Saturday-morning computer class. In doing so he was paving his way to participating in regular college programmes. For the time being, Bianchi put God on the back burner, but not before offering some theological enlightenment to me in a letter:

I have academically completed a Ministerial training programme given by the Evangelical Theological Seminary, and I am blessed to have been ordained by a Full Gospel Church back in 1986. My faith has taken an exploratory course with independent studies in Eastern religions, Earth religions, Judaism and Biblical archaeology. I even mailed out, free of charge, a written homily entitled 'Word on the Word'. I ceased doing it because it became too expensive. I would not, and cannot, accept donation.

As might be expected, Ken is being a little economical with the truth here, for, having spoken with prison officials, I learned that he raked in as much cash as he could before the Washington Department of Corrections stopped him from running his own 'Save Ken Bianchi' campaign. It also transpired that, for years, Bianchi's church had sent him quarterly newsletters detailing forthcoming religious events. They addressed the correspondence to none other than 'Reverend K. Bianchi'. This, however, did not last long, for, when James Blodgett, a newly appointed, tough, no-nonsense warden took over, Bianchi's ordination certificate and letters were confiscated.

But to give Ken credit where credit is due, he keeps on trying – or trying, at least, to pull the wool over everyone's eyes. In June 1988, he received his 'Associate in Arts Degree'. In truth, he cannot draw a straight line, paying more artistically inclined inmates to do moderate pencil work for him, which then he signs as his own and selling them to anyone daft enough to pay for them.

Then there was his pen pal website, where he was once again scrounging for cash. And he was not shy, either, modestly describing himself as a 'God-fearing Man.':

Hi, my name is Kenneth. I have been wrongly incarcerated for many years. My desire to develop friendship beyond this edifice of political smoke and mirrors is, in part, because I need to dispel the myth that I am void of humanity and, in part, because most of my family and friends are either deceased or have faded away.

Wrestling clumsily with his vocabulary and losing the battle, Ken continued:

My basic interests are Law, philosophy, and spirituality. My desire is to meet people who are objectively cogitative on which they can develop a mutually inspiring relationship through some engaging mental intercourse. I welcome women of all races. I weigh 210lbs. Solid as a rock 'smile', healthy, compassionate, sincere, loving, honest and good-looking.

And here's the punch line: 'In order to try and raise money for my day-to-day items and additional art materials, I would be prepared to sell a small number of my prints of any of my featured drawings. Thank you for your attention and I look forward to hearing from you.'

To convince me how artistically talented he was, Ken sent me gratis a cardboard tube containing half-a-dozen of his pencil drawings, all signed 'Ken Bianchi', of course. However, even a cursory glance showed that each drawing had been 'knocked up' by different hands. So, here was yet again; trying to con people just like the psychiatrists, the police, the judiciary, his mother and Kelli, the Church and everyone else he came into contact with.

Were Bianchi to reside in the UK, he would be guilty of contravening the Trades Description Act, or, at best, of being extremely economical with the truth, for 'The Hillside Strangler' made no mention of his homicidal CV anywhere. However, his lack of success in gaining pen pals would be a source of unhappiness for him, perhaps due to the prospective applicants having read the small print on this particular wrapper or, indeed, having failed to understand what he was talking about. But someone did, and her name was 36-year-old Shirlee Joyce Brook.

Little is known about Shirlee, but we may safely assume that she was just another individual who had a genuine intention of finding a soul mate who would pay his debt to society, be released, and eventually get married. And, of course Shirlee is not unique for there are thousands of women, and men, of all ages who spend their lonely hours writing and pledging their love to scum such as Bianchi or, more recently in the UK a man who has proposed to convicted serial killer Joanne Dennehy [*see* my book

Love of Blood, John Blake Publishing, London, 2015]. Even Rose West gets around two offers of marriage each year.

The subject of the previous chapter, Michael Ross, received hundreds of similar letters, while another of my subjects, the late serial killer Arthur John Shawcross, actually married Clara Neal. The mother of several children and grandmother to at least 11 more, she told me during an interview: 'I will keep 'Art' on tablets so he won't murder again. I really love him. He is such a wonderfully gentle man.' Then she and Arthur had to gall to invite me to their wedding.

You could make this up if one tried, but at least Shirlee was not a quitter after being 'blown out' by none other than the monster, Theodore 'Ted' Robert Bundy. Before he sat down in 'Ole Sparky', Ted had been inundated with correspondence from potential lovers who sent in photos showing all of their charms, so perhaps he was too preoccupied to reply to 'Sexy Shirlee'?

Attractive in a mousy sort of way, she breathlessly explained, 'Ken just hit me as a fun person and I wrote back. I told him that I'd received his answer much quicker than I expected and we started writing daily.'

They had corresponded and had chatted on the phone since 1986 – she paid for all of his stamps and the calls. Then on Thursday, 21 September 1989, they exchanged rings – paid for by her – in the prison chapel. She had met him for the first time just the day before the ceremony with the killer wearing an immaculate tuxedo, paid for by the bride who wore a white wedding dress and veil. The guests included several members of Shirlee's family and several of Bianchi's friends.

The following day, prison records show that Ken refused to

work, claiming, 'You must be joking. It's the day after my fuckin' wedding.' This caused Officer Estes to write up Bianchi for an infraction. Shortly afterwards, Officer Grudzinski overhead Bianchi threatening to 'fuckin' get Estes' at the first opportunity. This loose remark, although probably made in the heat of the moment, resulted in Bianchi being disciplined and thrown again into 'The Hole'. He lost his job in the law library – a rare privilege amongst the several thousand inmates – and the opportunity to consummate his marriage during a 23-hour session with Shirlee in the Combo Area of the penitentiary. When prison officials denied Bianchi any conjugal visits, he sued, but Walla Walla County Superior Court Judge Donald W. Schacht declared that they had acted within their authority. The visits had been denied for security reasons and because of his record of extreme violence towards women, as reported on the HistoryLink website.

Surprise, surprise, Shirlee divorced Ken in 1993 after she learned that he was writing to a number of other women, to all of them pledging his love.

Meanwhile, in 1989, our man received a 'Bachelor of Science in Law Degree', and since then he has earned a 'Juris Doctor Degree' and he is now a Member of the National Bar Association. It could be argued that Bianchi knows as much about the law as anyone, and he does, for, in 1992, he sued a playing-card manufacturer for $8.5 million.

Eclipse Enterprises Inc., of Forestville, California, had launched 10 million of its 'True Crime' collector cards in July the same year. This incurred the wrath of Bianchi, who argued that in the 110 card line-up, number 106 showed his face, which was causing him irreparable harm, and affecting his appeal process.

'They appropriated my face to make money. They breached my copyright,' he griped in a letter. It was obviously a spiteful action, and a claim that had no basis in law, for Bianchi's photograph – which is today plastered all over the internet – is a matter of public record, and free to be used by anyone. Nevertheless, while Bianchi had free access to the legal system, Eclipse did not. Although the defendants' fought the action and won, the costs involved brought Eclipse to bankruptcy. A former partner in the firm, Katherine Yronwode, explained to me, 'Bianchi was part and parcel of my company's collapse. The cost of defending the case caused the breakup of my marriage, and everything I had worked for 20 years to achieve came to nothing. I cannot say what I think of Bianchi.'

SUMMING UP BIANCHI

After my impromptu visit to see Bianchi in his cell, he threatened to sue the Department of Corrections for allowing me to violate his civil rights. This threat was not hot air. For a start, it brought down a mountain of paperwork for the DOC to deal with and, with his appeal against the Bellingham convictions – Petition C95-0934 – filed on 11 June 1995, in the pipeline, we were not to hear the last of Kenneth Bianchi. As the notorious serial killer, Keith Hunter Jesperson, pointed out to me, 'Bianchi is unable to murder again so prison has now become his killing fields.' However, the threat of legal action came to nothing, and when I passed over to the DOC all of Bianchi's correspondence to me – in which he clearly puts his head in the noose for the Bellingham killings – his appeal against the sentence was thrown out of the window.

Over the years of cumulative experience, professionals know that the majority of psychopaths – or 'sociopaths' or 'antisocial personalities', as they are also called – lie, manipulate, deny and deceive to avoid taking responsibility for their crimes. Dr Richard Kraus is quoted in the late Jack Olsen's book *The Misbegotten Son*, as saying in reference to psychopaths: 'Their robotic cruelty reflected dehumanisation, stunted conscience, and inability to empathise. They are usually smooth, verbose, glossy, neat, and artificial – both controlled and controlling. Behind a 'mask of sanity', they live superficial and often destructive lives.'

Kenneth Bianchi is all of these things and more, so one might categorise him as an exploitative, displaced, sadist serial killer.

He is exploitative in that his sexual behaviour was that of a man always on the prowl for women to exploit sexually, to force women to submit sexually with no care about the victim's welfare.

He is displaced in that his sexual behaviour was an expression of anger and rage, the cumulative backlog of experienced and imagined insults from the many people he had met over the years, all of which continually chipped away at his self-esteem and fragile ego. It was his mother, Frances, who told me, 'It seems that, whenever Ken had a fight with a girlfriend, or had problems, he went out and killed someone.'

And, of course, Bianchi was a sexual sadist. With Angelo Buono, another perverted individual cast from a similar mould, both men were able to enjoy their sadistic tendencies to the full and this made them extremely dangerous creatures indeed.

It goes without saying that Bianchi did suffer a form of psychological child abuse during his formative years, and there can be no doubt that this damaged him in some way. But, as professor Elliot Leyton succinctly points out, 'So, what? Millions of children suffer far worse child abuse than Ken ever did, and 99.99 per cent of them don't commit the crimes that he did.' So, there is no mitigation here at all.

By his own admission, he was having sex with young girls before his teenage years, whom he refers today as 'women'. It is also known from correctional staff that he frequently masturbates at the thought of having sex with pre-teen girls and his murder victims even today.

Throughout his life, Ken suffered the social stigma of being a bastard, and perhaps there is some truth in the fact that he really wanted to be someone special, to be able to prove his worth, not only to himself, but also to his adoptive mother who had all but drained him of emotion for some 16 years. But therein lies the rub, for everything he set his hand to – much as with Michael Ross whom we met in the first chapter – with the exception of rape and serial murder, he failed at dismally. Whether it was love or work, he was a born loser.

As for Ken's multiple personality disorder, the invention of 'Steve' and 'Billy', these were really only two in a long list of alter ego – Dr Bianchi, WSA Captain Bianchi, the fake cop, the terminal cancer patient, the phoney film producer – all of which he put in place to compensate for his secret but self-acknowledged inadequacies. And without these phoney alter egos propping up his low self-esteem, he would have crumbled mentally.

But has he learned from all of this? Unfortunately not, for his fascination for alternative identities continues to this day. He has legally adopted a couple of squeaky clean, new names, with a good old-fashioned Italian ring about them: 'Anthony D'Amato', meaning 'of the beloved', and then 'Nicolas Fontana'. Of course, we shouldn't forget the 'Reverend Kenneth Bianchi'. Yet the debate as to whether, or not Bianchi is a multiple personality continues to rage today, even though he has been exposed as having invented 'Steve' and 'Billy', to which he agrees.

When interviewed by police, Frances Bianchi claimed that Kenneth had four distinct personalities. She claimed that she knew three of them well, but that the fourth had always remained a mystery to her.

Detective Frank Salerno is clear that he never has bought into the MPD theory, and nor have any of the other police officers I interviewed for the purpose of this book. Indeed, if I could have lined up all of the cops in a row and asked them to sum up Bianchi in a short sentence, the answer would have been: 'He's a fuckin' bullshitter. Period!'

At the time of writing, for his part, Dr Ralph Allison is no longer convinced that Ken is a multiple, but, rather, is someone with an 'Internalised Imaginary Companion (IIC)'. Completely ignoring the obvious – that Bianchi adopted the name 'Steve Walker' after stealing a genuine psychology student's certificate back in Los Angeles, and admitting as much – the doctor prevails in his view that: 'Steve' was 'made by Ken's personality as a way to get back at his mother when she was yelling at him at home, during his youth . . . it was then that Ken imagined "Steve" into being, and he became Ken's hit man in expressing his hatred of women who were like his mother.'

Were any of Bianchi's victims like his mother? Of course not! Were little schoolgirls, Dolores Cepeda and Sonja Johnson, like his mother? Of course not!

When the author Christine Joanna Hart pressed Dr Allison on what is an ICC, he replied:

> An ICC is what is called a 'Thoughtform' in para-psychological literature, or an imaginary playmate or companion in pediatric psychology. However, the pediatric doctors assumed that all imaginary companions exist outside the bodies of the children who created them. That is false, as the child can place it anywhere he wants it to be, outside sitting in a chair, inside a doll, or inside his body taking over his body to do its deeds. It is designed by the child to take care of the child's emotional needs, whether that be to combat loneliness or to avenge some insult to the child by a hostile adult. It is made voluntarily by the child with a vivid imagination and can, therefore, be destroyed by that same child as an adult.

Dr Allison went to explain to Christine Hart that 'ICC is a term I invented to describe these "other selves" which were not alter-personalities. Initially, I called them IMPs, for Internal Malignant Personalities, which seemed to be a good acronym, as an IMP is a playful spirit. But I realised that only some were malignant, and others were benign, so I changed the label to something that was morally neutral, Internalized Imaginary Companion, or ICC.'

Having long ago dumped the diagnosis that Bianchi had a 'MPD', then to an 'IMP', more recently adopting an 'ICC', Christine Hart then asked Dr Allison to explain who Doctor Martin Orne was, and why was Orne diagnostically against him? After a preamble, Allison pulled no punches. Completely ignoring the fact that he, and Dr Moffett, had been hired by the court, he said: '. . . he [Dr Orne] was well known to the prosecutor to be a sceptic of MPD, so he was hired to disprove the diagnosis of MPD initially offered by Dr Watkins. We were aware that Dr Orne was not likely to diagnose anyone with MPD, so we were not surprised when he maintained that Ken was just a liar. In Buono's preliminary hearing, Dr Orne also stated that Ken had never been hypnotised by any of us, something I greatly dispute . . . I was caught in the middle of a "battle of the experts", with Dr Orne on one side saying that Ken was only a liar, and Dr Watkins saying Ken was a bona fide multiple. I knew he wasn't a multiple, but I didn't then know just what he was.' [Source: *In For the Kill* – Christine Hart]

This was rather unfair. Dr Orne had not been hired by the prosecution to disprove a MPD diagnosis, he'd been hired to confirm whether or not Bianchi was capable of faking hypnosis, and prove that Ken was faking he most certainly did!

★ ★ ★

When Christine Hart asked Bianchi if he had ever been in love, he replied:

I've had lovers but never been in love . . . I've only truly loved women I knew back east . . . east–coast women [referring to Rochester, New York, which almost 400 miles from any part of the east coast]. I loved Donna and a girl called Janice and my wife Brenda Beck. Here, in Washington, I lived with a girl, Kelli. I stayed with her for my baby. I fooled around on the side, hoping to meet 'the one'. Kelli wanted me to move out, so she got her way when I got arrested. She then went and slept with cops who were working on my case, and my social worker; which I think prejudiced my case, and my attorney, Dean Brett . . . Kelli was very sneaky, and I never got to see my son ever again. That cold bitch with ice flowing through her veins to a cold stone heart robbed me of my own fucking son. In LA she gave me fuckin' gonorrhoea. She told she'd been raped but never reported it.

Bianchi had nothing good to say about Veronica Wallace Compton, either:

Compton was a hooker, coke-head and housewife, and she met me once and it was through a glass screen. All that bullshit about how I gave her my semen – sorry to sound crude – how could I when there was a guard there and a glass screen? Yet year after year, whenever my parole comes up, she is brought up and it screws up my chances and keeps me in the joint. I fuckin' hate Compton, I can tell you.

Bianchi then went on to say that although VerLynn was a beauty: ' . . . beauty is only skin deep, an' I've turned down some beauties in my time, as I think they can be trouble. I had a model in tears once in the reception of the visitors' room. She was just amazing to look at, tall as hell, long blonde hair, great long legs, she visited me and they [the guards] said, "No, you can't see him again," and she was on her knees in the foyer, screaming and crying.'

Christine Hart then asked Ken why he'd denied knowing the attractive Karen Mandic when the police first interviewed him, and, as usual, he came up with an imaginative answer: 'There were loads of women in the store that looked hot, Chris. Ones that came into the store and ones that worked there. I knew Karen to say good morning to, that was it.'

'You don't remember asking this Amazonian princess to house-sit at Bayside where she ended up strangled in the basement?' asked Hart.

'No, I didn't,' replied Bianchi, looking miffed.

Christine Hart then turned to Shirlee, the woman Ken had married in prison. 'What happened to Shirlee?'

'Shirlee? That was a bit of a pretence,' he started with another pack of lies. 'It wasn't anything romantic or sensual at all. It was to help her with money. She was a pen pal and very poor. Many reporters found out she was writing to me. She asked to marry me so that she could sell her story to them. I said, "Okay, and then you can give them an interview and feed yourself." I haven't spoken to her since her mother died about 20 years ago. I don't bother with people on the outside – pen pals or otherwise. When I get a letter from a person who tells me they're a psychology student or interested in my case, or that they like me or some shit, I go to my toilet and shred it to bits,' conveniently forgetting that he had rapidly responded to Christine Hart's first letter, and will reply to anyone who shows any interest in him in the hope of conning them out of money.

Dr Ralph Allison came in for criticism too: 'Allison is a fuckin' idiot,' Bianchi railed. 'The hypnosis made me say all that stuff about "Steve". Allison is a nut-bag. "Steve" wasn't a demon, Chris. He wasn't real. It was an aberration brought on by hypnosis.'

'How would you know?' Christine asked.

'Why would "Steve" be a demon?'

'All those evil things he said to the cops – "I killed the blonde cunt and the brunette cunt and that one fucks really badly." Those women who died had nothing to do with me.'

Bianchi was now looking straight into Christine's head. A vein pulsed in his neck.

'I listened to those tapes of me confessing, Chris, and I couldn't believe it. The hypnosis produced a chicken clucking on a stage. I was confessing to terrible crimes of an evil monster who committed horrendous murders. Those bent cops used to say, "What colour is the inside of the murder victim's car?" and push me over a photo of Cindy Hudspeth's car and I could see it was brown. I'd say, "Brown," and they'd say, "Yes, it was brown." "You must have raped her, strangled her and then pushed her over the cliff in her car while she was in the back," but I did not kill Cindy Hudspeth.'

'You and Angelo gassed a girl?' suggested Christine Hart.

'I did not gas a girl. I told the cops what they forced me to confess to from the files they made me read day in, day out. No one saw me with Angelo at the time of the Hillside murders.'

'Did you ever speak to him after you were both sent to prison?'

'I sent Ange a card just before he died in prison, Chris. It was a normal Hallmark greetings card. I wrote on it, "Hey there, Ange, I'm sorry for everything!" I signed it "No hard feelings."'

★ ★ ★

One of the most interesting and delusional characters Christine Hart interviewed for her book, *In For the Kill*, is Ted Ponticelli, an advisor and close friend of Bianchi's, who is an alleged former cop, who says he served with Internal Affairs for five years and claims that he advises 'British media outlets on serial killers,' and has been asked for 'advice on cases where victims were still missing – profiling for the BBC News – I do know my stuff, you know,' he boasts.

Well, God help us all if he does!

Ted Ponticelli is convinced that Bianchi is innocent of all of the Los Angeles murders because he says: 'I have interviewed the man who did it [*sic*]. He's a convicted killer called William Suff. He's on Death Row for a string of rapes and killings and he has already admitted to killing six of the Hillside Strangling victims but that's all been hushed up.'

But you see, Ted, we are not as dumb as you'd imagine us to be.

The William Suff to whom Ponticelli refers is one William Lester 'The Molester' Suff, who, at the time of the Hillside Stranglings was in a Texas prison, along with his wife, Teryl, for the battering to death of their two-month-old daughter. In 1974, he received 70 years behind bars but was released, after serving ten years, in 1984. Clearly, this serial killer expert hadn't the savvy to check out Texas Court of Criminal Appeals, or, Texas Department of Corrections records, for they clearly document that Suff was locked up when the Hillside Stranglings were committed between September 1977 and February 1978.

Mr Ponticelli also has a bee in his bonnet with regard to the Bellingham homicides, when he argues: 'There was absolutely no physical evidence connecting Bianchi to the crimes. There was one single pubic hair from the victim Karen Mandic found on the stairs of the basement where she was strangled. How could Knudsen have found one of Bianchi's public hairs, when the crime scene was hoovered over by the first lot of cops found nothing?'

Unfortunately, Ponticelli has got himself somewhat confused – the police didn't hoover anything up in Dr Catlow's home before the crime scene was released almost a week after the murders. Besides, principal investigator, Robert Knudsen, found the hairs early morning on 12 January – and I have seen the signed and witnessed scene-of-crime logs that prove it.

But Mr Ponticelli completely shoots himself in the foot when he states:'None of Bianchi's DNA was found on the body [Karen Mandic]. In truth Ted Ponticelli is correct, but he ought to have known, being the man who claims he 'knows his stuff', that DNA fingerprinting *was not invented until 1984* – five years *after* the Bellingham murders – and that the first killer ever to be arrested and convicted using DNA profiling was Colin Pitchfork, from Leicestershire, England, in 1987. Additionally, what Ponticelli fails to realise is that non-secretor semen was found on Karen and Diane, and this matched the non-secretor semen found on a striped towel discovered in Bianchi's WSA pickup truck. Furthermore, pubic hairs from both girls were discovered on Bianchi's torn work jeans, saved by Kelli Boyd after Ken threw them into a trash bin.

* * *

Like most serial murderers, Bianchi is an excellent example of the antisocial personality. He is a liar and manipulator through and through. He will deny guilt to suit himself and, when the cards are stacked against him, he will lie again and again at the drop of a hat to suit the circumstances. Indeed, one gets the impression that Ken does not know the meaning of the word 'truth'.

As he appeals his convictions for the murders of Karen Mandic and Diane Wilder, oblivious to the fact that he hasn't got a snowball's chance in hell of getting parole, he also appears to have forgotten that he gave Bellingham police details of the murders that only the killer would know, explaining, under the guise of 'Steve', that, 'The rope was tied so tightly my knuckles went white. I was so full of anger as I strangled Karen Mandic but I had no idea why I was so angry.' More recently he has concocted a risible scenario whereby a former employee at the Whatcom Security Agency conspired with university cops, Hardwick and Bryant, not only to murder the two co-eds, but also to shift the blame onto him. Yes, it is true that Kenneth Alessio Bianchi does actually exist in a world where elephants fly, lead balls bounce and fairies reign supreme.

Angelo Buono, aged 64, died from a heart condition at the Calipatria State Prison, Imperial County, California, on Saturday, 21 September 2002. His body was cremated and the ashes scattered at an unknown location.

★ ★ ★

While all of the other Hillside Strangler's victims rest in unknown graves, Dolores Ann 'Dolly' Cepeda (12) is buried at the Forest Lawn Memorial Park, Glendale.

Her headstone reads: 'Our Princess – Age Twelve – Who Loved and gave so Much'.

Sonja Marie Johnson (14) is buried at the Resurrection Cemetery, Montebello, Los Angeles. Her headstone reads: 'Beloved Daughter and Granddaughter'.

Cindy Lee Hudspeth (21) is buried at Pierce Brothers Valhalla Memorial Park, North Hollywood, beneath the inscription: 'The Light of Our Life'.

Karen Lauretta Mandic (22 is buried at the Sunset Hills Memorial Park, Bellevue, King County, Washington State.

NOTE: This chapter is based upon two years' continual correspondence and an interview with Kenneth Bianchi, his adoptive mother Frances and Veronica Wallace Compton; unrestricted interview access to Bianchi at WSP Walla Walla by the WDC and the assistance of police and the judiciary in Los Angeles, CA, Rochester, NY, and Bellingham, WA.

Other reference material is drawn from HistoryLink.org, Christine Hart's book *In For the Kill*, my previous book *Talking With Serial Killers 2*, and other sources acknowledged throughout the text.

JOHN MARTIN SCRIPPS

'THE TOURIST FROM HELL'

'They won't hang me. I'm British.'

> *John Scripps four days before his execution at Changi Prison,*
> *Singapore, 19 April 1996, to the author*

I had freelanced for the *Mail on Sunday* several times previously before the telephone call from then editor Jonathan Holborrow came one Thursday morning. 'Christopher, how are you?' then without waiting for a reply confirming that I was indeed dead or alive, he asked: 'You know about John Scripps. The English serial killer waiting to be hanged in Singapore. Chris, you were in Singas for over a year. Would you cover the case for us?'

CBD: Um, well I . . .

JH: Will £17k cover it? Keep some for yourself and bring back receipts.

CBD: I've never heard of the man.

JH: You'll find a reference to him on the Internet. I'll have the cash biked down to you this afternoon. Leave tomorrow and take no more than two weeks. Bye.

I was to visit Singapore and Thailand twice in my investigation, which would take me from my quiet Wickham country home, opposite the twelfth fairway of a golf course, to the gallows at Changi Prison and a hanging quite foul.

Dubbed by the media 'the Tourist from Hell', John Scripps became the first Westerner to be hanged in Singapore for murder, and only the second Westerner for any offence. Dutch citizen Johannes van Damme was 'topped' by the Singapore authorities for drug trafficking in 1994. He was arrested on 27 September 1989, when he was found to be carrying 4 kg of heroin, and sentenced to death on 26 April 1993.

This was to be Singapore's most sensational murder case since that of Adrian Lim, who with his wife and girlfriend, were convicted in May 1983 of the murder of two children in 1981. Lim, 46 years old and a self-styled spirit medium, and the two women, Hoe Kah Hong and Tan Mui Choo who were both in their early 30s, were hanged together in Changi Prison in November 1988.

Although there are a number of British citizens on death rows around the world, Scripps would become the last British murderer to be hanged since the abolition of capital punishment in Great Britain in 1964. On 13 August that year, Peter Anthony Allen, aged 21, was hanged at Walton prison, Liverpool. On the same day, John Robson Walby, alias Gwynne

Owen Evans, aged 24, was hanged at Strangeways Prison, Manchester. They had been jointly convicted of the murder of John West, a van driver from Workington, Cumberland, in furtherance of a robbery.

★ ★ ★

John Martin Scripps was born in Hertford on 9 December 1959. The family moved to London when he was a small boy and he remembered a happy early childhood, in which he was close to his sister Janet. When he was nine years old, he experienced the loss of his father, who committed suicide after he learned that his wife was leaving him for another man. John told me that he had discovered his father at home with his head in the gas oven. At about the same time, his mother was diagnosed with throat cancer and, although she recovered, John's world fell apart.

According to the FBI, 70 per cent of multiple murderers have undergone trauma at some point in their childhood. 'The trauma festers away and becomes a fantasy of getting revenge,' says Ian Stephen, a forensic psychologist who works for the police and prison service in Strathclyde. 'In Scripps's case the anger might have been directed against the fact that he has been deprived of a father, deserted.'

John became increasingly introverted. He cut himself off from his friends and found it impossible to concentrate on learning to read and write. He acquired these basic skills later on, in prison, although his handwriting always remained very childish.

At the age of 14, he disappeared while at a training camp in

France organised by the Finchley unit of the Army Cadet Force. A year later, he was in juvenile court for burglary and theft.

According to his 'rap sheet', John's first adult conviction was for indecent assault in 1978, when he was fined £40 at Hendon Magistrates' Court. Thereafter, it was grim catalogue of offences, including burglaries in London, followed by jail time in Israel for stealing from a fellow kibbutz worker. In 1982, he was jailed again for burglary and assault in Surrey.

He managed to abscond from the prison system and embarked on a crime journey through South East Asia and America. In Mexico, he met and married 16-year-old Maria Arellanos, but, by 1985, he was back in Britain once again, facing a prison sentence for committing burglary. Prison could not hold John Scripps and he absconded, yet again, to return to crime.

Justice caught up with Scripps in 1987, when he was jailed for seven years in London for heroin offences. The following year, his young Mexican wife divorced him. However, while on home leave from prison in June 1990, he disappeared for the third time and flew to Bangkok. He was now aged 31.

When later interviewed by HM Customs & Excise officers, Scripps said that he had flown out of Bangkok to meet a girl he had been writing to. On arrival in the Thai capital, he booked into the Liberty Hotel for three days, taking a cheap room, costing about £10 a night. Accompanied by his girlfriend, he frequented a few bars and visited the local tourist attractions. Romance seemed to be in the air and they made a trip to Ayutthaya, the historic former capital, where they stayed for a few days. The couple then moved on to Pattaya, known as 'Sin City', and from there, to Phuket, where they roomed at Nilly's

Marina Inn, at Patong Beach. Scripps spent ten days in Thailand before deciding to fly back to London. He had spent £1,000 during his sojourn in the East, including £270 on clothes and just over £100 buying 48 phoney watches. He'd also bought a quantity of heroin.

BUSTED AT HEATHROW

At 1.20 a.m. local time on Saturday, 25 August 1990, Scripps boarded Gulf Air Flight GF 153, destination Muscat in the Sultanate of Oman. On arrival he proceeded to the transit area of Seeb International Airport to await his connecting flight to Heathrow, London. He was travelling on a British passport issued in the name of 'Jesse Robert Bolah'. This travel document, No. 248572V, had been stolen.

As Scripps prepared to board Flight GF 011 to London, he was subjected to a routine security check, which included a body frisk. Police Corporal Saeed Mubarak of the Royal Oman Police found two packages wrapped in red tape in his pockets. Thinking that the packages might contain explosives, he summoned assistance from Inspector Saeed Sobait. The two police officers went through Scripps's hand baggage where they discovered a larger packet of white powder. The dilemma for the authorities was that the white powder could not be tested without detaining the passenger. It was therefore decided to give one of the packets, which, as it later turned out, contained 50 grams of diamorphine, and the passport to the aircraft's captain. Scripps was then allowed to proceed to London, effectively under detention and the responsibility of the Gulf Air flight crew.

Scripps nervously boarded the TriStar and settled into seat

39H. Midway through the flight schoolteacher Gareth Russell, sitting in 39K, noticed his fellow passenger drop something on the floor and kick it under his seat.

As soon as the aircraft entered British airspace, the pilot contacted HM Customs & Excise and, moments after the plane had taxied to a stop, a rummage team headed by David Clark boarded. The packet, which Scripps had kicked under his seat, was found. After a field test for opiates had proved positive, he was charged under Section 3(1) of the Misuse of Drugs Act 1971, contrary to Section 170(2) of the Customs & Excise Management Act 1979.

John Scripps was held in custody that night to allow Customs and police officers to search 6 Gordon Road, Farnborough, where he was staying with his uncle, Ronald White. A folder of documents was found, containing a West German passport in the name of 'Robert Alfred Wagner' and a Belgian identity card in the name of 'Benjamin Georges Edmond Stanislas Balthier', with Scripps's photograph attached to it. The men named in these documents had been reported missing many years previously, and there has been no trace of them since.

Later that day, Scripps was interviewed again. He was asked how he earned his money, how he could afford to travel all over the world, and how he could afford a very expensive Samsonite suitcase. He cockily replied, 'It may be very expensive to you, but it isn't to me. If you can't afford a suitcase like this, it's because you're working as minor subservients of the State for a standard wage, and you're not willing to go out and work all hours.'

At 10 p.m. on 31 August, Scripps was released in the name of 'John Martin', and instructed to answer bail on 29 October 1990.

He failed to report and, on 28 November, he was arrested by Detective Constable Malone at his mother's home at 11 Grove Road, Sandown, Isle of Wight. Police found more drugs and he was charged with possession of 50 grams of diamorphine at 80 per cent purity. At the time, the street value of this amount was estimated at around £9,473, while the remaining 191.5 grams of heroin he had tried to smuggle through Heathrow Airport was valued at £38,551. Given the knowledge that Scripps possessed drugs valued in excess of £48,000, the police now understood how he could afford his jet-set lifestyle.

Because John had absconded from a previous seven-year custodial sentence for drugs offences, he was held on remand in HMP Winchester until his trial. He instructed his solicitors that he would plead 'Not Guilty'. His defence was simple enough. His case would stand or fall by his claim that he had found the red-taped package containing the heroin and had handed it to the police. He categorically denied that any drugs were found on his person at Seeb Airport. Further, he argued that the traces of heroin discovered in the pockets of the jeans he was wearing at the time resulted directly in him being asked to open the package he had found containing drugs. He denied any knowledge whatsoever of the traces alleged to have been found in the pocket of his shirt. If he managed to wriggle out of all of this, he was still not completely out of the woods, for the police had found heroin on him during his arrest in Sandown, and his wallet had been stuffed with £2,000 in notes. The implication was that this amount of drugs went way beyond 'for personal use', and that Scripps was dealing smuggled drugs on the Isle of Wight, yet another allegation he denied.

Inmate V48468 Scripps was granted legal aid, and case No. T910602 was held at Winchester Crown Court on 6 January 1991. Represented by the enigmatic barrister Bruce Maddick, Scripps suddenly changed his plea to 'Guilty' in an effort to gain leniency. Despite this ploy, he was sentenced to 13 years' imprisonment. He spent just three years and ten months in jail before contriving another escape.

John started his sentence at HMP Albany on the Isle of Wight and, during a six-week period, between March and April 1993, Prison Officer James Quigley instructed him in butchery. The authorities could never have guessed that while they were training an inmate in butchery skills, they were also equipping him to slaughter and dismember humans, the gruesome calling to which he subsequently set his hand.

'He was shown how to bone out forequarters and hindquarters of beef, sides of bacon, carcasses of pork, and how to portion chicken,' James Quigley would later tell a Singapore judge, adding, 'He was a quick learner, and very fast on picking up on how to slaughter, dismember and debone animals.'

Scripps's ultimate odyssey began on 28 October 1994, when he failed to return to the semi-open The Mount Prison, Bovingdon, Hertfordshire, after four days' compassionate leave because a member of his family was ill. Throughout the week before he walked out of the open prison gate, he had been openly selling his possessions to finance his escape. He even bragged to fellow prisoners that he was going on the 'trot', and he had acquired the birth certificate of another inmate to obtain another passport. Whether Scripps had stolen the document or had traded it for some of his property is unknown. Nevertheless, although some of this intelligence was picked up by the prison security staff they failed to act on it.

'John Scripps was no longer considered a flight risk,' the Governor Margaret Donnelly explained after he had fled. 'He had no history of violence. He was quiet and reserved.' It would appear that she did not know that Scripps had absconded from every home leave he had ever been granted. And, far from being quiet, reserved and allegedly no longer a risk, the smooth-talking drug dealer was about to become a vicious serial killer. Indeed, had he served out his entire sentence, even with parole, his victims would be alive today, or would certainly have lived a lot longer than they did.

TIMOTHY MCDOWELL

Scripps now embarked on a globetrotting, three-nation rampage. His first port of call, before the killing started, was Holland, where he met a former drug dealer whom he had encountered while on remand in Winchester Prison. He travelled next to Belgium and Spain, and reached Mexico in late November. Here, he attempted reconciliation with Maria Arellanos, telling her that he had been released from prison on a technicality. He explained that he was returning to Thailand to buy silk clothes and wanted them both to set up a boutique in Cancún. He told her that he was now a deeply religious man and, to convince her, became a devotee of the Virgin of Guadeloupe, Mexico's patron saint. For her part, Maria would have none of it. She had since married a police officer, and after Scripps had made himself a complete nuisance he was told, in no uncertain terms, to bugger off.

To finance this boutique venture, Scripps befriended Timothy

McDowell, an amiable British backpacker who was holidaying in Belize and had travelled to Mexico in 1994. It is now known that Scripps beat the 28-year-old Cambridge University graduate and management consultant to death. He dismembered the body and dumped it into an alligator-infested river. Shortly after the murder, the victim's bank account was milked dry, the not inconsiderable sum of £21,000 being transferred to Scripps's bank account in London. This exact sum of money was later wired to another account, in San Francisco, under the name of 'Simon Davis', one of John's many aliases.

GERARD GEORGE LOWE

Thirty-three-year-old Gerard George Lowe had arrived at Singapore's Changi Airport on the morning of 8 March 1995. Dressed casually in khaki Bermuda shorts and an orange T-shirt, he was indistinguishable from all the other international travellers as they stumbled wearily off the plane and on to the moving walkway. Gerard was just another tourist, and that was the point. Travelling alone in a strange country, he noticed a friendly face, and, as people do in airports when they are trying to establish their bearings, he found himself talking to a complete stranger. The tall, soft-spoken Englishman, in his thirties, politely introduced himself as 'Simon Davis'. As they chatted, Lowe explained that he was a South African brewery design engineer who was on a shopping spree to Singapore to take advantage of the low cost of video recorders and cameras. When Scripps caught sight of Gerard's gold credit card, he knew he had found another victim.

It was immediately apparent to Scripps that his new acquaintance was thrifty, so he suggested they share a room.

Scripps proposed the River View Hotel, because he had stayed there before. This is a middle-class businessman's stopover, with a grey, marble reception area and a tacky boutique selling plastic orchids and 'Hong Kong Girl' perfume. The place was fully booked, however, and the two men had to wait several hours before they were given a room. 'They seemed very normal,' as Robert Pregarz, the hotel's manager, later testified at Scripps's trial. 'They were smiling and laughing together. There was nothing strange.'

Within minutes of booking in, the new guests made their way to Room 1511. After they had unpacked their cases, Lowe settled down at a small, round table, from which he could admire the panoramic view of Singapore and, picking up a pen, started to compile his shopping list, while John Scripps picked up something else.

Scripps chose this moment to steal up behind Lowe and brought down a 3lb camping hammer on his victim's head in a single, crushing blow. After his capture and subsequent detainment in Changi prison, he told me during an interview:

I think he was a bit surprised when I hit him. At first he thought I was mucking about. That made me mad with him because I thought he was a homosexual. I threw him against the wall and he started to fall down. He was shaking and then he pissed himself. I knocked him about a bit, and got him to tell me his bank card PIN. When he was in the bathroom, he was conscious. There was water dribbling from his mouth. He gurgled, or something like that.

Without a trace of emotion, Scripps added, 'Well, I cut his throat an' left him to bleed to death like a pig.'

The following exchange between us then took place at interview:

CBD: So, let's get this right, John. You slam this innocent man against the wall of the room, then beat him half-senseless. Then you drag him into the bathroom, lift him into the bath, forcing his head down to his knees. You turn on the taps, and cut through the back of his neck to paralyse him. Then, you stab him in the neck, or whatever, and let him bleed to death. Did he know what was going on by then?

JS: Do you want the fucking truth?

CBD: Yes.

JS: Yes.

CBD: Yes what?

JS: Do you want blood out of a fuckin' stone?

CBD: Did Mr Lowe know what was going on?

JS: Yes! He pissed and shit himself. It made a stink. He was shitting himself. Yeah. Right. Oh, fuck it. Yeah. I can't say about it. It wasn't good and I spewed up. He really shit himself, but he couldn't do much about it, could he?'

CBD: I suppose not, John. What did you do after you'd killed him?

JS: I cut him into parts so's I could dump the body.

CBD: Is it true that you used the little saw that went with your Swiss Army knife?

JS: That's bollocks. I have a knife like that for camping. But anyone will tell you that you can't use a little saw like that for cutting carcasses.'

CBD: Okay. What did you use?

JS: A six-inch boning knife. I was taught how to look after knives, you know.

CBD: Now, I know you're telling the truth. Go on.

JS: Well, after the blood had been washed away, I took his head off. Just like a pig. It's almost the same. You cut through the throat and twist the knife through the back of the neck. There ain't much mess if you do it properly . . . I cut off his arms at the elbows. You just cut through the ball and socket joints. You don't saw anything.

CBD: And?

JS: Well, the legs. Um, on a pig you have the legs, and you have to use a saw to make . . . I think it's called a 'square cut', But, honest . . . I just stuck the knife in and twisted and cut until the legs came away at the hip joint, I suppose. When I got to the knees, I just cut through and they snapped back so's I could fold them. Fuckin' heavy stuff, right?'

After packaging the body parts in the black bin-liners Gerard Lowe had brought with him to wrap up his duty-free purchases, Scripps deposited the bundles in the only wardrobe. He liberally sprayed Lynx deodorant around the room in an attempt to mask the smell of his own vomit. It proved inadequate, for a couple who stayed in Room 1511, in the days that followed, reported a lingering, strange fishy odour. Finally, Scripps showered and cleaned up the bathroom. Again, he was not absolutely thorough and missed a few tiny blood spots on the shower curtain and toilet bowl. These traces were to provide crucial evidence when he was eventually brought to court to answer the charge of murder.

★　★　★

Murder, committed in this almost meticulous fashion, can rarely be a crime of passion. It is an eminently practical business, carried out with the studied objectivity of a professional. It requires thought, planning and an ability to attend to every detail with cold-blooded efficiency. And, giving macabre credit where credit is due, while Scripps did miss a few minute traces of his butchery in the bathroom, there is no doubt that he was an extremely efficient killing machine; one who thought on his feet and maximised his one opportunity when it presented itself, demonstrating a clinical, unhurried persistence after the event. He would dispose of the corpse and start practising the forging of his victim's signature on tracing paper.

John's next move was to visit a store, where he told the sales assistant that he was Gerard George Lowe and that he wanted to buy a few laptop computers. By 9 p.m., he was back in the hotel's River Garden Restaurant; sitting down to a prawn cocktail, followed by fillet steak and fresh salad, all washed down with a bottle of chilled white wine. It was a balmy evening. The string of multi-coloured lights strung around the patio reflected in the Singapore River just yards away. John Scripps was at peace with himself, and the world, while the duty waiter remembers that Scripps left a substantial tip when the restaurant closed around 10.30 p.m.

The next morning, Scripps informed the hotel receptionist that his companion – Lowe – had already left and that he would settle the bill when he booked out later. He then went on a spending spree in the city's glittering shopping malls. He threaded his way from one air-conditioned shop to another, using Lowe's gold credit card again and again. His first purchase was a pair of Aiwa speakers. Then came a pair of Nike trainers and socks, as well as a video recorder, which he arranged to be sent to his sister Janet in England.

On the morning of 9 March, Scripps used the credit card for another shopping bonanza. He also drew S$8,400 in cash from a local bank and made a telegraphic transfer of US$11,000, to an account he held in San Francisco under the name of 'John Martin'. He used the card to buy a S$30 ticket to attend the Singapore Symphony Orchestra, where he heard a programme of Brahms and Tchaikovsky. Finally, in an extraordinary whimsical but callous bid to maximise his gains, he bought five 'Big Sweep' lottery tickets.

Later that night, he packed the dismembered body parts into a large suitcase, slipped out of the hotel and took a taxi to Singapore Harbour. Here, under the cover of darkness, he dumped the gruesome contents into the waters swirling around Clifford Pier.

Scripps spent his last night at the hotel, and ate at the same restaurant. The next day, flush with cash, he left without paying his bill – a deceit that would cost him dear – and flew to Bangkok.

SHEILA AND DARIN DAMUDE

Sheila Damude, a 49-year-old school administrator from Victoria, British Columbia, had flown into Bangkok for a two-week stay with her son who was on a gap-year tour of the world. 22-year-old Darin had broken his leg while travelling with friends, and she wanted to give him some motherly attention. They had decided to visit the Thai 'Paradise Island' of Phuket.

On 15 March, mother and son arrived at Phuket Airport and were collecting their thoughts, in the usual arrival turmoil, when Scripps sidled up to them. 'I was on the same plane as you. Do you have a problem?' he enquired.

Within moments, Scripps gleaned the information that Sheila and her son wanted to get to Patong Beach, but they were not sure whether to catch a bus or a taxi, or even how expensive a taxi fare might be.

With his marauding instincts fully attuned, John, ever the experienced traveller went into travel-guide mode. He told them about Nilly's Marina Inn, where a double room would cost them about $US18 a night. The small hotel lay on the quiet southern end of Patong Beach, one of the most popular beaches on the island. He even suggested that they share a taxi with him, which would give them all a cheaper ride. Sheila and Darin exchanged glances and nodded their agreement. They were clearly impressed by this helpful young man and soon they were on the bumpy way along the dusty roads and down the steep hill to Patong Beach.

John signed himself in at Nilly's Marina Inn, as 'Simon Davis, a shopkeeper from London. When I stayed there I examined the hotel's guest register, and it seemed obvious that no one had noticed a revealing slip of the pen. He had inadvertently signed his name, 'J Davis'. The consummate traveller, he had stayed there before, always drawing admiring looks from the pretty female staff who called him 'Mr John'.

The Damudes took the lift to the second floor and were shown into a spacious deluxe suite overlooking the bay – a *Miami Vice* view with jet-skis and speedboats swooping onto white sands. Scripps took a nearby room, just across a corridor. It overlooked scrubland piled with rubbish at the back of the hotel.

Sheila and Darin had two king-size beds, a well-appointed mini-bar, international-direct-dialling telephone, colour television, air-conditioning and an en suite kitchen area. It was the very same room I later stayed in, and there was a separate bathroom, shower, and even a safe, in which they could store their valuables.

If the room was quite luxurious, especially at the low cost, I can testify that the view from their window was priceless. Situated across from the beach and a narrow road, was the crystal-clear water of the Andaman Sea. Looking out from their balcony, the Damudes could see two tall palm trees growing out of the sandy soil, where two of the local girls were breaking open fallen coconuts. They looked up and when they saw the handsome Darin, they broke into giggles. At that moment, the Damudes must have thought they had found Heaven but, as the next day approached, they would be pitched into Hell.

Mother and son would spend their last evening on earth exploring the shops, looking for silk garments: Sheila bought a sun hat, while Darin found a leather belt. Meanwhile, John Scripps had hired a powerful 450cc Honda motorcycle and, with a red bandana tied around his forehead, he ended up at the seafront Banana Bar. Throbbing with music, the place was full of good-time girls, who would sell their bodies for less than the price of a meal. He danced into the early hours and had sex with a girl on the beach before retiring for the night. Then, at around 6 a.m., the Tourist Police spotted his yellow and green motorcycle parked on double-yellow lines outside Nilly's Marina Inn. The two officers walked around it a couple of times, admiring it and deciding that it was not good policy to issue a parking ticket to a holidaymaker. Nevertheless, they made a note of the number plate, and they would issue a ticket if the offence were committed again.

Later that morning, Sheila and Darin came down for breakfast, which they ate outside in the sunshine. After the meal, they searched the rather dismal fish tank in the foyer for signs of life, and Sheila flicked through the revolving postcard display for something suitable to post to her husband back home. This was to prove to be the last time anyone saw them alive for they returned to their room to make plans for the day ahead and came out dead.

At about 11 a.m., local people wandering around outside the small hotel next door noted a large flood of red-coloured water flushing down an open drain that led from Nilly's Marina Inn down under the road, but no suspicions were aroused.

Because John Scripps was never charged with the murders of Sheila and Darin Damude, he refused to discuss the matter with me when I interviewed him at Changi Prison. Nevertheless, knowing his modus operandi, and using proven evidence, it is possible to reconstruct what happened when the Damudes returned to their suite.

Shortly after the Damudes left the foyer, Scripps was seen by the receptionist getting into the lift. He would have knocked on the Damudes' door and entered the room under some pretext and, within seconds, he would have stunned them both with a stun gun – such a weapon was found in his possession when he was later arrested in Singapore. With his victims immobilised, he took out his hammer and beat them to death – swabs from his hammer matched bloodstains on the room's carpet – after which he dismembered their bodies, using the butchery skills he had learned so aptly at Albany Prison and practised to perfection on Gerard Lowe. Then he stole his victims' travel documents, passports and credit cards and went on yet another shopping spree, leaving a 'Do Not Disturb' ticket hanging outside on the suite's door, leaving the dismembered bodies within, awaiting disposal.

The decomposing heads, torsos and several limbs, belonging to the Damudes, were found between 19 and 27 March, scattered around the hilly countryside close to Patong Beach, while a Thai woman, also out walking her dog in the area, found other gruesome remains, partially tipped into a disused tin mine shaft. She later told me that her dog had led her to the grisly find – two sets of forearms – and she'd immediately called the police. The areas where the body parts were dumped were not accessible by car – but near a track easily travelled by a motorcycle. The identities of the victims were later confirmed using dental records,

ARRESTED IN SINGAPORE

The Western world has become hardened to this Scripps type of cold-blooded multiple murder; they are all too familiar and, when the latest sensational homicide case features in the headlines, we have a feeling that we have read it all before. Dismembered corpses, anonymous victims, apparently motiveless crime and bizarre acts of violence have become common currency.

But this is not so in Singapore where violent crime and murder are unusual. In this draconically ordered city state, where even the pavements seem to have been scrubbed clean and where the glass of skyscrapers sparkles spotless in the sun, crime comes in more sanitised forms.

There is that famous saying, 'Don't Mess with Texas', but even more harsh punishment awaits those who dare drop litter or carelessly discard chewing gum, for jail time and punitive fines are on the cards in Singapore. Here, taxis are fitted with a warning bell, which rings automatically if the driver exceeds the speed limit. It is not that Singaporeans have not encountered murder before; they have their share of domestic homicide, averaging fewer than 50 a year in a population of 2.5 million. Murders committed in the heat of the moment always seem to be more understandable. But the 'execution' and dismemberment of a foreigner – a wealthy one at that – is taken as the highest priority, and it fell to the slightly-built, no-nonsense, plain-speaking Acting Superintendent Gerald Lim to lead the investigation into the then 'Reported as Missing' Gerard George Lowe.

At the time of Lowe's murder, Superintendent Lim was the senior investigating officer with the Special Investigation Section of the CID, and his work began on 13 March 1995, in Singapore Harbour, with the discovery of a pair of feet. They were poking out of a black bin-liner and tied up by the ankles with a pair of large, blue, Woolworth-brand underpants.

A couple of days later a boatman found, bobbing among the pleasure craft off Clifford Pier two thighs – white, hairy and bound with strips of orange fabric.

Then, on 16 March, a plump, male torso was retrieved from the water. The human jigsaw was coming together, for down at the mortuary it was established that all of the remains had once belonged to the same Caucasian male body. (The head and arms have, incidentally, never been recovered.)

The inscrutable Superintendent Lim had dealt with fatal fights between immigrant building workers (he had three convicted murderers on death row at the time Gerard Lowe was killed), and he had come across domestic murder, but this was something completely and horrifyingly different. He examined the green-tinged, rotting flesh and wondered at the person who could be responsible for such cold and calculating destruction of another human being. And this body was not just headless and armless – it was nameless, too.

As most visitors to Singapore were, and still are, registered as hotel guests, Lim's first stop was the centralised hotel registration computer. Within hours, a fax had been sent to every hotel in Singapore asking if any guests were missing, or who had left without paying their bill. The Riverview Hotel responded immediately. Two guests – Gerard Lowe and Simon Davis – had checked out of Room 1511 without paying. But there was something else, the manager explained. His duty reception staff recalled that the Englishman had been seen lugging a heavy suitcase through the foyer the night before he and his companion disappeared. It was also noted that when Mr Davis returned a few hours later he was empty-handed.

On 14 March, the police in Johannesburg, South Africa, had received a report from a distressed Mrs Vanessa Lowe, who'd said that her husband was missing. He had not called her from Singapore to say that all was well, which, she explained, was totally out of character. Her concerns soon reached Gerald Lim, and he invited her to fly to Singapore, to view the disarticulated body and a few items of now dry clothing.

When the distraught woman arrived, Superintendent Lim met her at Changi Airport and, as delicately as he could, he asked her to identify the corpse. She bravely pointed our various marks on her late husband's body, recognising the appendectomy scar on the abdomen, the freckles on his back and the bony lump just below the right knee. She also identified the underpants, used by Scripps to tie up his victim's thighs, and the orange strips, she said, were from Gerard's T-shirt.

Now an arrest warrant could be issued for Simon Davis.

* * *

For some inexplicable reason John Scripps returned to Singapore after his activities in Thailand – using a passport in the name of Simon Davis. After a short struggle at Immigration Control, he was arrested and taken into custody. It was 19 March. When officers opened his backpack they were amazed at what they found. There, along with an 'Enjoy Coca-Cola' beach towel, a Pink Floyd cassette, and bottle of Paul Mitchell shampoo and some Featherlite condoms, was what they came to describe as a 'murder kit'.

This comprised a 10,000-volt Z-Force III stun gun, a 1.5-kg

hammer, a can of Mace tear gas, two sets of handcuffs, some thumb cuffs, two serrated knives and two Swiss Army knives. And that was not all. Another of his bags was filled with clothes, suitable for a middle-aged woman, consisting of skirts, dresses and even a pair of pearl earrings. Hidden among them were passports in the names of two Canadian citizens, Sheila and Darin Damude, each of them containing crudely pasted-in photographs of Scripps. He was also found to be carrying US$40,000 in cash and travellers' cheques, together with credit cards and other belongings of the Damudes.

THE TRIAL

'My right hand was covered with blood. Everything happened so quickly.'

John Martin Scripps, at his trial

In the Singapore equivalent of committal proceedings, the preliminary enquiry saw written statements from as many as 77 witnesses for the prosecution supporting the murder charge, and 11 other charges ranging from forgery, vandalism and cheating, to possession of weapons and small quantities of controlled drugs. A representative of the Royal Canadian Mounted Police, Douglas Herda, arrived, wanting to question Scripps about the killing of Sheila and Darin in Phuket. The Singaporean authorities refused his request.

The trial of John Scripps started on 2 October 1995 in Singapore's new high-tech court. Security was heavy throughout the proceedings, with John sitting on a wooden bench between two armed, uniformed officers, behind a bulletproof screen. His ankles were shackled to a metal bar. He had entered no plea but 'claimed trial', which under Singapore law, means he was contesting the charges. Singapore does not have trial by jury, a judge, sitting alone, hears the evidence.

The first witness was James Quigley, who testified that he had taught the defendant butchery in Albany Prison, on the Isle of Wight. Wearing a smart grey suit, an immaculate white shirt and a Home Office tie, Mr Quigley, a large man with a red face, gave a full description on what he taught during his butchery course, adding that John Scripps was a 'very quick learner'. Judge T. S. Sinnathuray winced, made a few notes then looked at Scripps. The points had been made that the man accused of killing and dismembering Gerard George Lowe had been a habitual offender from an early age, and that he knew how to dismember carcasses.

Next into the witness box was Dr Chao Tzee Cheng. A government pathologist, he testified that the manner in which the dead man's body had been cut up indicated that only a doctor, a veterinarian or a butcher, could have dismembered it. 'I told police, "Look, you are dealing with a serial killer,"' he said in his evidence, while the judge made another short note in his book.

A stream of other witnesses followed, to include Vanessa Lowe, the manager, several staff at the River View Hotel, various shop assistants who had sold Scripps goods – for which he had paid with Lowe's gold credit card – along with the boatmen who explained how they found the body parts, and a taxi-driver recalled how he picked up Scripps one evening and drove him, with a heavy suitcase, down to Clifford Pier. 'I didn't take him back to the hotel,' said the witness in broken English.

For the prosecution, it was an open-and-shut case. They

alleged that Scripps, using a false name, had checked into the same hotel room as Lowe and killed him.

John had some explaining to do, and, in what amounted to a confession, he told the packed court he had met Lowe at Changi Airport on 8 March, and they had agreed to share a hotel room. He admitted killing the man in the room after he was awakened by a half-naked Lowe, who was smiling and touching his buttocks.

'I am not a homosexual,' explained Scripps, taking a sip of water, 'and at that time it appeared to me that Mr Lowe was a homosexual. I freaked out; I kicked out and started swearing at him. I had experience of such things in the past and I was very frightened.'

Scripps went on to elaborate that he used the hammer 'to hit Lowe several times on the head until he collapsed onto the carpeted floor. My right hand was covered with blood. Everything happened so quickly.'

After realising that Lowe was dead, Scripps testified, he sought the help of a British friend, whom he refused to name. The 'friend' disposed of the body without telling him how. He also denied cutting up the body.

The defence, led by Joseph Theseira, tried to show that their client had never intended to kill Gerard Lowe, and that the murder was an act of manslaughter, which carried a maximum penalty of life in prison. But, this defence was an uphill struggle from the outset, for the prosecution maintained that Scripps had committed premeditated murder with the intention of robbing the dead man – which, undeniably, he had.

It was perhaps rough justice for John Scripps who had hammered many of his victims over their heads, that on the fourth day of the trial, prosecutor Jennifer Marie would hammer him. She showed how Scripps had practised forging Lowe's signature, suggesting that the murder was premeditated. She offered, in evidence, items seized from John's luggage, including a notebook and tracing paper with practised signatures of Mr Lowe's name.

In a nit-picking exercise, the defence questioned two police detectives, trying to show how they conducted an inadequate search for blood traces next to the hotel room's bed where, Scripps claimed, Lowe fell and bled to death. Both officers said there were no traces of blood on the carpet, only very small, almost minute spots, in the bathroom. The prosecution countered that this evidence supported their contention that the killing was premeditated. Clearly on a losing wicket, defence co-counsel Edmond Pereira implied that if the police found no blood traces on the carpet, it could have been because they did not conduct sufficiently thorough tests, and not in the exact spot where Lowe fell.

During the court proceedings, on 24 October, Scripps said that after being arrested he had tried to commit suicide by cutting his wrists with a small, sharp piece of glass, to escape being hanged.

'I believed I was going to be hung,' the 35-year-old defendant said on his fifth day in the witness box. 'I kept thinking about Lowe and the Filipino lady that got hanged.' He was referring to the Filipino maid, Flor Comtemplacion, who was executed, on 17 March 1995, after she confessed to two murders.

Now, digging his own grave, Scripps agreed with the suggestion, by Judge Sinnathuray, that it would take about five minutes for a skilled butcher to dismember an animal. Then, the prosecutor jumped in.

'Could your skills be used to dismember a human?'

'The bones look similar,' Scripps replied.

'Are you an experienced human anatomist?' snapped Jennifer Marie.

'What's that?' replied Scripps.

'A medically trained professional with vast experience of the human body.'

'Nope!'

'Then, Mr Scripps, how do you know the bones look similar?'

Cutting to the chase, prosecutor Marie turned on the heat.

'Did you dismember Mr Lowe?'

Scripps looked down at his shackled ankles, and replied unconvincingly, 'No, I don't have the skills you mentioned.'

'But, this court has heard that you were trained to become a butcher, Mr Scripps. Prison Officer Quigley has testified that you learned how to butcher carcasses quickly and efficiently, did he not?

Now, waving a butchering certificate in her hand, the prosecutor said, 'Your name is on this certificate. Is it not?'

Scripps mumbled an answer. It was almost inaudible.

'Is this, or is it not your butchery certificate . . . you earned this in a British prison . . . '

'Yes.'

'Did you, the other day, admit that you could dismember an animal carcass within five minutes.'

'Yes'

'And, you have just told this court that the bones look similar?'

'Yes!'

On his sixth day on the stand, Scripps was asked by the prosecutor why he did not report killing Gerard Lowe to the police, if, indeed, it was in self-defence.

'Because this man died at my hands,' Scripps replied, 'and under Singapore law that is an automatic death sentence. That's what I understood that the time.'

'So, who is this mystery man who dismembered Mr Lowe?

'He is a British friend staying at a hotel in Sentosa. While he was doing it I fled.'

Scripps said that he had known this 'friend' for eight to ten years, and remembered that he had once worked at an abattoir. 'He's a very dangerous man,' he said meekly. 'I fear for the safety of my family.'

Prosecutor Marie peered over the top of her spectacles, this time at the judge, as if almost questioning him. 'You have known this 'mystery man' for some eight years, Mr Scripps, and you do not know his name?

Silence.

'In what hotel, in Sentosa, was he staying?'

Silence.

'Can you tell this court, Mr Scripps, the name of the abattoir where this 'mystery man' worked?

Silence.

'How and when did you meet him?'

Silence.

Judge Sinnathuray then cautioned Scripps that his reluctance to give even basic information on his 'friend' could harm his defence.

'Here you are facing a murder charge,' the judge reminded

him, 'which carries the death sentence in this country. I have to ask myself, at the end of the day, this question – "Did the accused, John Scripps, go to a hotel in Sentosa?"'

Sitting back in his seat, the judge sighed as Scripps still declined even to describe the hotel, a refusal that prompted the prosecutor to accuse the defendant of lying, and to suggest that the activities of his friend were all a 'complete fabrication'. Discrepancies between Scripps's earlier statements to the police of 29 April, and his testimony from the witness stand, were also highlighted.

'You made no mention of the attempted homosexual assaults while in prison in 1978, and the alleged assault by Mr Lowe, did you? I am suggesting that this 1994 incident never occurred,' said Marie. 'It's another fabrication of yours.'

With Scripps now firmly on the hook, the prosecutor started to reel him in. Pressed about his movements between 8 and 11 March, Scripps said that his memory was hopeless.

'You have got a memory?' he was asked.

'I haven't,' he replied nervously. 'I'm dyslexic. I get things mixed up.'

On 6 November, Jennifer Marie told the court in her closing arguments: 'The conduct of the accused after the killing suggests that he was cold, callous and calculating, a far cry from the confused, dazed, forgetful man walking in a dream world, the picture he gives of himself. He is a man very much in control over his faculties. When he embarked on the shopping spree using Lowe's credit card, buying a fancy pair of running shoes, a videocassette recorder, and a ticket to a symphony orchestra concert, he becomes a man who has no qualms about lying continuously, consistently, and even on the stand.' She added, with a rare touch of venom, 'This man's excuse that he killed Mr Lowe because of a homosexual advance is just one of a string of lies to mask a premeditated murder by a greedy serial killer who preyed on tourists. And Mrs Lowe has stated, on oath – a decent loving wife has come here to say that her husband had come here on a shopping holiday. He most certainly was not a homosexual. The accused has not only murdered and dismembered her husband; he now rubbishes his good name.'

In his closing statement for the defence, Edmond Pereira said, 'We urge this court to come to a finding that the accused is not guilty of murder, but is guilty of culpable homicide not amounting to murder. The killing occurred in a sudden fight in the heat of passion upon a sudden quarrel,' and he added, 'He is not a man prone to violence.'

Pereira also urged Judge Sinnathuray to ignore the information from Thailand. 'There is no evidence to suggest that the accused is responsible for the deaths of two Canadians,' he said, calling the Thai information 'nothing more than circumstantial and prejudicial'.

On 7 November 1995, Scripps, dressed in khaki, with a prison-style crew-cut and standing in the court's glass cage, was said to be laughing and joking with his guards, before the verdict was handed down.

'Karma is Karma. It's in God's hands now,' but the smile was wiped off his face and his attitude changed within minutes.

Judge T. S. Sinnathuray told the packed courtroom, 'I am satisfied beyond a reasonable doubt that Scripps had intentionally killed Mr Lowe. After that, he disarticulated the body into several bags, and dumped them in the water.' Having announced the guilty verdict, the judge sentenced Scripps to death by hanging. The condemned man was less glib as he was taken down the steps next to the judge's bench and away to a place of lawful execution.

When the trial concluded, defence lawyer Edmond Pereira told reporters, 'Scripps has a right to an appeal, which he can exercise within 14 days, and he shall be advised of the right.'

In an interview for the research for this book, Judge Sinnathuray said that he was convinced that Scripps had killed the Damudes, but added that he decided Scripps's guilt independently of the Thai evidence:

'On the evidence, I had no difficulty to find that it was Scripps who was concerned with the deaths of Sheila and Darin, and for the disposal of their body parts in different sites in Phuket. The disarticulation of Mr Lowe, Sheila and Darin, had all the hallmarks of having been done by the same person. The Thai evidence was materially relevant because it rebutted Scripps's defence that he killed Lowe unintentionally during a sudden fight.'

Upon hearing the news, at her home in Sandown, Isle of Wight, his mother, 50-year-old Jean Scripps, said, 'I brought John into this world. I am the only person who has the right to take him out. I cannot believe how my boy could have changed from a kind human being into the monster described in court.'

On 4 January 1996, John Martin Scripps virtually signed his own death warrant when he wrote to the prison authorities to withdraw his appeal scheduled to be heard on 8 January, but confirmed he would file for a clemency plea. This was the only sensible option open to him, and he had a brief six-to-eight-week window of opportunity to complete the paperwork.

EXECUTION

I was assigned to cover John Scripps's execution by the *Mail on Sunday*, and I was to report, for APTV, the gruesome event that would hit the 6 p.m. TV news around the world.

The death penalty was in use during the colonial period in Singapore, and was retained after the city state became an independent republic in August 1965. Today, death sentences may be imposed for various offences under the Penal Code – the Internal Security Act, 1960, the Misuse of Drugs Act, 1973 as amended in 1975, and the Arms Offences Act. Capital offences include murder, treason, hurting or imprisoning the President, offences relating to the unlawful possession of firearms and explosives, and perjury resulting in the execution of a person indicted on a capital charge. The 1975 amendment to the Misuse of Drugs Act made the death penalty mandatory for possession of over 15 grams of heroin, or fixed amounts of other drugs.

Capital offences are tried before the High Court. The defendant has the right of appeal against conviction to the Court of Criminal Appeal, and the law guarantees legal counsel. On the dismissal of an appeal, prisoners may seek permission to appeal to the Judicial Committee of the Privy Council in the United Kingdom, which, at that time, served as the final court of appeal for Singapore. If the Privy Council upheld a sentence, prisoners may have submitted a clemency petition to the President of Singapore.

On 14 February 1996, a spokesperson for the British High Commission in Singapore visited Scripps in prison. Afterwards, she told reporters, 'He won't be putting in an appeal. He's eager to get it over and done with. He's just waiting for the day,' she said.

This comment surprised Edmond Pereira who was moved to say, 'There are some instructions John has given to me, but I'm not at liberty at this stage to make any comment because the matter has not been finalised.' He added: 'But, even if a prisoner refused to petition for clemency, the matter still has to go before the President. However, if we don't request clemency, they won't exercise clemency.'

While he was held in solitary confinement at Changi Prison, Scripps spent most of his time watching television and reading. A priest visited him weekly, and, once a fortnight, a consular representative went to check on his welfare and to pass on messages from his family.

The Singapore *Straits Times* newspaper reported, on 10 March, that Scripps had declined to seek a pardon from President Ong Teng Cheong. 'It was his wish to let the law takes its course,' the story concluded.

★ ★ ★

'They won't hang me. I'm British,' John Scripps said to me four days before his execution.

It was announced that John Scripps was to die, at dawn, on Friday 19 April. He had turned down a request by Scotland Yard detectives to interview him about the 1994 murder of British backpacker, Timothy McDowell, in Mexico. He spent his last two days writing garbled love poems to his former Mexican wife, Maria, described as the one true love of his life, from his cell. He was confined in a windowless cubicle measuring 8 foot by 6 foot, illuminated 24 hours a day and kept under continuous surveillance by CCTV. There was a hole-in-the-ground lavatory and a straw roll-mat to sleep on.

His sister Janet and mother Jean said their farewells to him in his cell 12 hours before his execution. They had turned down an offer to be present at his death. Janet said, in an interview with me, 'How do you say goodbye to your own brother like that? We didn't actually say the word. I just couldn't.'

For his last meal, John asked for a pizza and a cup of hot chocolate. He then requested a scrap of paper and left a final, rambling misspelt note which read:

One day poor. One day reach. Money filds the pane of hunger but what will the emteness inside? I know that love is beyond me. So do I give myself to god. The god that has betrad me. You may take my life for what it is worth but grant thows I love pease and happiness. Can I be a person again. Only time will tell me. What really upset me was where you are told every day that you are not a member of the uman rase.

★ ★ ★

In accordance with the execution procedure, hangings are carried out in private on a large gallows that can accommodate up to seven prisoners at a time.

The recommended drop is based on the need to produce a force of 1,260 pounds on the neck and upper spine region of the condemned person as he, or she, plunges through the trap. This figure, divided by the prisoner's weight in pounds, gives the length of drop in feet. Therefore, to kill instantaneously, it is crucial to get these calculations correct.

It is also normal practice in Singapore to hang several prisoners simultaneously, although no specific details of the executions are released to the media. The 'official' version, which is issued after every execution as a matter of policy, was that:

> John Scripps was woken by guards at about 3.30 a.m., and escorted to a waiting room where he, and two other prisoners, two Singaporean drug traffickers, were prepared. He spoke to a priest and a prison chaplain before his time came when he walked bravely to his death.

The relatives of Scripps's neighbours on the gallows received similar letters.

However, the apparently smooth procedure was later thrown into disarray when the priest, who had been in attendance at the triple execution, unexpectedly resigned. As part of his clerical duties, he had witnessed most of the executions at Changi during the previous ten years, but he was so horrified by the death of John Scripps that he resigned immediately afterwards. And, far from walking bravely to his death, the priest told me and an APTV television news crew, Scripps had put up a bitter fight to the end.

The guards did indeed come for Scripps at 3.30 a.m. He was ordered to step out of his prison-issue shorts, to avoid soiling them with urine and excrement, and told to dress in his civilian clothes. John refused, so his prison garb was torn from him. He would leave this world as he had entered it – stark naked.

John should have been weighed on a set of bathroom scales

to calculate the length of drop; however, he had previously told me that he would give his jailers an execution to remember, for he hated the guards who daily reminded him that he was not a member of 'the 'uman rase'. Crucially, he refused to be weighed with all the dreadful consequences that might have for the efficiency and humaneness of his execution.

Too long a drop, and he could be decapitated; too short a drop and he could strangle to death. In the event, it took twelve guards twenty minutes to drag him to the holding cell next to the gallows. During this struggle, he sustained a broken nose, cheekbone, jaw, two black eyes and multiple bruising.

So, as no photographs of the old Changi gallows exist, how best can I describe this macabre machinery to the reader?

Many of us will have seen the crude video recording of the execution of Saddam Hussein. The condemned are led, bound and shackled up a flight of rickety wooden stairs to a platform, then to the noose allocated to their necks. It can be a lengthy procedure for some who struggle while others take it in their stride. Superimpose the Hussein gallows onto those at Changi and you have much the same apparatus.

As the appointed time drew near, John was heard to be sobbing. The other two doomed men were already pinioned, hooded, waiting silently on the trap when he was prepared. Again, he lashed out before being bound with leather straps. Now 'neutralised', naked and tightly buckled, he lost control of his body functions. Quickly, a rubber bung was forced between his teeth. Then came the rough hessian hood, followed by the noose, which was snapped tight under his left ear; a pull on a lever, a loud crash, and John Scripps plunged into eternity.

For 30 minutes, John's body swung imperceptivity in the pit before being taken down. The consequences of the failure to calculate a proper drop were only too obvious, for his head had almost been ripped from his body – something that John's sister later complained about to me and anyone else who would lend an ear, afterwards.

At 10.30 a.m., I watched as Scripps left prison for the last time, Wrapped in a white sheet and placed in a cardboard coffin, his body joined the other two corpses in an old, green tarpaulin-covered truck, and was taken to a funeral parlour in Sin Ming Drive. When Jean Scripps, with her daughter, viewed the body, she almost fainted. With the press pack beating on the funeral parlour door, they finally made good their escape.

John Scripps and the two Thai criminals were cremated that afternoon, at the republic's expense. And, in a final irony, John Scripps's ashes spent that night at the Riverview Hotel. The urn containing his ashes was placed in the charge of one of the representatives of the Scripps family, lots having been drawn to decide who should have this responsibility. On their arrival in England, and at a private service, attended only by relatives and close friends, the ashes were scattered at a secret location.

CONCLUSION

John Scripps had followed the tourist trail to Thailand and Phang-Na, popularly known as 'James Bond Island', which was one of the movie locations for *The Man With the Golden Gun*. While there, he had his photograph taken and printed on a souvenir plate.

'I can't believe Mr John killed them,' Nipa Eamsom-Ang, the receptionist at Nilly's Marina Inn, told me. 'He was not crazy. I liked him very much,' she added. 'He was always smiling, smiling, smiling.'

Locals say that she had become nervous about ghosts since Scripps was convicted, though she seemed nonplussed when I asked her whether the hotel business had suffered in the aftermath of the Damude murders.

Nearly everyone who knew Scripps agreed he seemed a 'really nice guy'. During his trial, he looked sensible, decent even, and chatted politely to his guards about the weather. Once, when the judge sneezed, he turned around and said quietly, 'Bless you,' to which the judge replied, 'Thank you.'

The Roman Catholic priest, whom John called 'Father Frank', said, 'I try to imagine how his face would have looked when he was chopping up the bodies,' concluding, 'It's impossible. I can only see him as he was with me – young, handsome, soft-spoken and gentle.'

This is an all-too-familiar perception. When people meet serial killers they often think they are shy, quiet, nice people who are not easily aroused to anger. The reality is, that of the over-controlled personality, which may well lead to occasional outbursts of rage in appropriate situations.

So, what was Scripps's motive? Was it the lure of easy money that drove him to kill? Strangely, in view of his actions, many observers think that this was unlikely. He robbed his victims, but there was more to it than that, as Brian Williams, liaison officer for the Royal Canadian Mounted Police in Bangkok, said. 'You can rob without killing, and you can kill without cutting up the body into bits. This man went to such an extreme and I can only think that he relished what he was doing.'

Brian Williams may well be correct in his common-sense appraisal but, ultimately, it comes down to a common enough motive and, this I believe, boils down to financial gain.

Scripps was a cold, calculating killer, who had planned his *MO* almost to perfection. His butchery skills merely added to the clinically efficient way he disposed of the bodies. That he 'relished' the dismemberment is open to debate. However, although he completely disposed of the body of Timothy McDowell by feeding it to alligators, his MO fell apart with the murders of Gerard Lowe and the Damudes – their remains were discovered, and this led to his arrest.

John Scripps was not insane in the legal sense. When he slaughtered Gerard Lowe in their hotel room in Singapore, he was deluding himself if he believed that the island republic's system of justice would not hand down a death sentence to an Englishman. As an experienced traveller in South East Asia, he must have known that some countries in that region have an unequivocal attitude to murder and drug smuggling – crimes that carry a mandatory death penalty.

For their part, the Singapore authorities are tough on criminals. The Deputy Superintendent of Police, Chin Fook Leon, said to me during an interview: 'We impose the maximum sentence of death without concern for sex, race, colour or creed. Break the Penal Code in Singapore,' he warned, 'and suffer the consequences.'

The deterrent value of the death sentence in Singapore is there for all to consider, if there is an intention to break the law.

It is even printed on red-and-white notices, prominently posted around the city and at all points of entry. Singaporeans argue that it is effectively the wanna-be criminal's own choice. Spit on a pavement and a month's imprisonment is mandatory. Drop so much as a chewing gum wrapper and 14 days behind bars is mandatory. Go against the law of the Republic and suffer the consequences; this uncompromising attitude is always applied, and who can blame them?

I was also in Singapore when five Thai men were executed. After illegally entering as labourers, they took it upon themselves to abuse their hosts by robbing construction sites between November 1991 and January 1993. In committing their crimes, they murdered a citizen of Myanmar and two Indian nationals.

Panya Marmontree (22), Prawit Yaoabutr (22), Manit Wangjaisuk (31), Panya Amphawa (29) and Pasong Bunsom (32) were sentenced to death on 16 January 1995. Their appeals against execution were dismissed on 10 July and they were duly hanged at Changi prison on Friday, 16 March 1996.

Thai Ambassador, His Excellency Adisak Panupong, told me when we attended the cremations: 'My countrymen were aware of the laws and punishments of Singapore and, in breaking them, they also knew what the consequences might be. The decision to commit their crimes was theirs to make.'

★ ★ ★

John Scripps had made visits to the Far East before he killed Gerard Lowe, therefore he knew and understood the local law very well. He was aware of the risks of committing serious crime in both Singapore and Thailand, and of the consequences of being arrested and found guilty of drug smuggling and committing murder. When he killed Timothy McDowell, in Cancún, he did so for financial profit. There can be no doubt about that. When he killed and butchered Gerard Lowe, he did so for financial gain and the Singapore authorities took the view that, by committing aggravated murder on their sovereign soil, he merely validated his own execution. It is consistent with this outlook that he demonstrated, by his unlawful behaviour, that murder was permissible. As far as the Singapore justice system was concerned, those were *his* standards, and he was treated accordingly.

Consideration of punishment, whether it meant life in prison or execution, was also determined by John's own actions, I am obliged to say. It was not his victim Gerald Lowe, the police, the judicial system, the Singapore Department of Prisons or the executioner, who initiated the sequence of events leading to his death at the end of a rope. It was down to John Scripps himself. And if he had escaped the noose in Singapore, what fate would have awaited him in Thailand? It would have been execution by machine-gun.

Following in Singapore's footsteps, legislation in Thailand was extended to include imposition of the death penalty for offences other than murder. The Royal Act on Habit-Forming Drugs (1979) introduced an optional death penalty for possession of more than 100 grams of heroin, while maintaining a mandatory death sentence for its production, import, or export. Although Thailand is reluctant to implement the death penalty in respect of convicted Europeans, who usually receive commutations by Royal Pardon, the numbers of people under sentence of death and the number of executions carried out on Europeans have been rising steadily.

It seems, therefore, that John was playing a lethal game of Russian Roulette, with his own life at stake. Not only did he risk the death sentence for international drug trafficking, he had committed two counts of aggravated homicide, which carries the mandatory death sentence in Thailand.

A final dimension to his recklessness was provided to me by Special Investigation Officers at HM Customs & Excise, who passed over to me an envelope of documents concerning their dealings with John Scripps. I spent several weeks in Singapore hunting down anything that could point me in the direction of a safety deposit box, and I did. With the assistance of Singapore Drugs Squad officers, such a stash of heroin and cash was recovered from a bank in Nathan Road. The amount of drugs far exceeded what would have been sufficient to send him to the gallows in any event.

★ ★ ★

As a tailpiece, although I was legitimately working in Singapore on behalf of a British national newspaper, eyes were upon me everywhere I went. Hours after visiting the offices of the *Straits Times* police came into my Riverview Hotel Room, threw me against a wall and cuffed me while they ransacked my belongings. They never said a word, to leave without an apology.

While filming with APTV *outside* the gates of Changi Prison after John's execution, and before his body was driven away, my cameraman and I were detained for some time and given the rough treatment. This, it seems, came about because a guard had noted several US visas in my British passport and had determined that I was an American citizen, thus, some kind of spy.

However, as some kind of belated recompense from the authorities for their inconsiderate behaviour, they sent me a parcel containing a 'Happy Birthday' mug depicting a hanging man. My birthday had fallen on the day (Singapore time) Scripps had been executed, so these inscrutable Singaporeans do have a black sense of humour after all!

NOTE: This chapter is based on an exclusive correspondence and an interview between Christopher Berry-Dee and John Martin Scripps at Changi Prison, Singapore, in the week prior to his execution on 19 April 1996, the assistance of the Scripps family, HM Customs & Excise (Special Investigations), the Singapore Police, the Royal Thai Police, the Royal Canadian Mounted Police, APTV, the BBC, the *Mail on Sunday*, and the support of my then agent, Derek Block.